North of Iskut

1 2 3 4 5 6 – 15 14 13 12 11 10

Caitlin Press Inc.
8100 Alderwood Road,
Halfmoon Bay, BC V0N 1Y1
www.caitlin-press.com

Edited by Meg Taylor and Ruth Gaskill.
Text designed by Vici Johnstone
Cover designed by Pamela Cambiazo.
All photos courtesy Tor Forsberg.
Cover Photograph: Paul Tubb.

Printed in Canada.

Caitlin Press Inc. acknowledges financial support from the Government of Canada through the Book Publishing Industry Development Program and the Canada Council for the Arts, and from the Province of British Columbia through the British Columbia Arts Council and the Book Publisher's Tax Credit.

Canada Council for the Arts Conseil des Arts du Canada

British Columbia Arts Council

Library and Archives Canada Cataloguing in Publication

Forsberg, Tor, 1948-

North of Iskut : grizzlies, bannock and adventure / Tor Forsberg.

ISBN 978-1-894759-42-7

1. Forsberg, Tor, 1948-. 2. Outdoor life--British Columbia, Northern. 3. Iskut Region (B.C.)—Biography. 4. British Columbia, Northern—Biography. 5. Artists—Canada—Biography. 6. Authors, Canadian (English)—21st century—Biography. I. Title.

FC3849.I85Z49 2010 971.1'85 C2010-900677-1

North of Iskut

Grizzlies, Bannock and Adventure

TOR FORSBERG

CAITLIN PRESS

This book is for my partner, Paul Tubb, who not only suggested I write a book about my life, but has also made it all possible. Thank you, Paul, for believing in me and for being consistently and patiently loving.

Contents

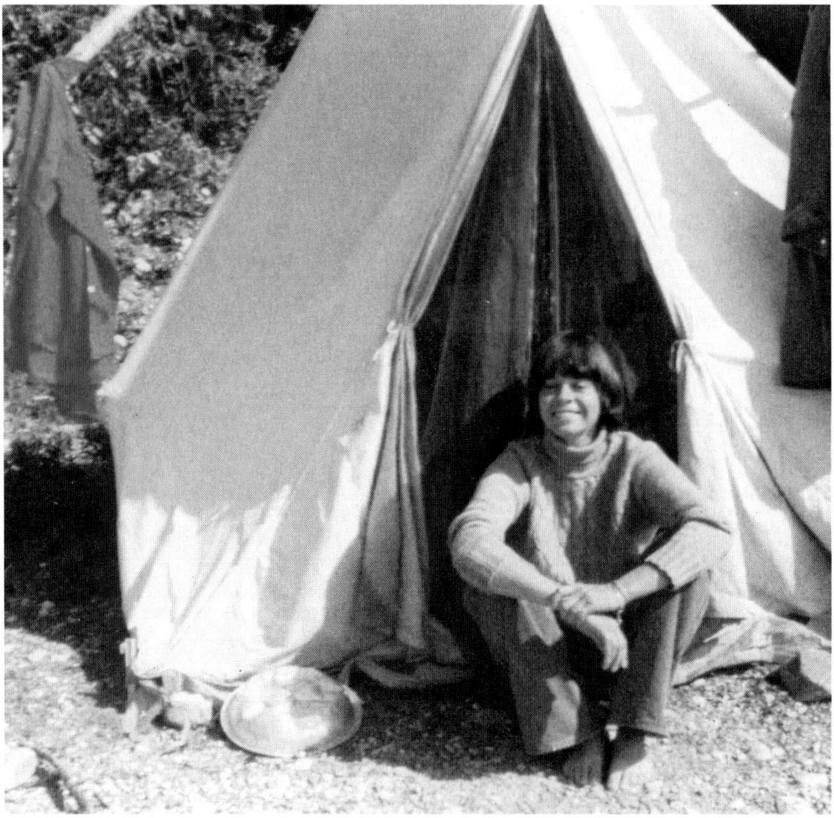

Preface

Why did it take nearly forty years for this story to be written? The answer is I was simply too involved in living my life and enjoying it to the max to write. And I was an artist, not a writer.

The Yukon was only one of the scenes of my childhood, but it was the place I considered my home after growing up with a father who felt compelled to move every couple of years. My family had lived in Hayter and Edmonton, Alberta; Stewart, BC; Uranium City, Saskatchewan, to name a few of the places we'd briefly called home before we settled in Watson Lake, Yukon, in 1960.

My British mother, an only child, had married my RCAF war hero father, Walter, in England and come to Canada as a war bride. She adapted quickly to a life she could not have imagined, as my father took her to remote places such as Lac La Ronge, Saskatchewan, where she would be left alone for days at a time with small children in housing that, at least on one occasion, had no running water or electricity.

My mother was, and is, a woman of great resiliency and courage. No matter where we lived and under what conditions, she made a home for us, a home in which my younger sister, Cindi, and I felt safe and loved and infinitely rich.

Watson Lake provided me with a childhood so ideal that I remember thinking how good it was even while I was living it. It was a safe and friendly little town. Kids had tremendous freedom in those days, going pretty much wherever we wished, walking or biking. Our only restriction was being home in time for dinner. We built forts, we swam in the lake, we canoed; we were outdoors winter or summer, for every hour of the day that was not taken up with school or family duties. There was no television; evenings were spent reading or playing games.

Families got together on a regular basis to play softball at the town field or to go to Lucky Lake for a wiener roast. There were parties, mostly gatherings where children were present as a matter of course—then there was more interaction between adults and children than there seems to be now. My parents' friends were always addressed by us as Aunt or Uncle, and courtesy was the rule, not the exception.

Having a pilot father was an extra bonus: I went on many flights with him in a de Havilland Beaver or a Piper Cub. We visited mining exploration camps and hunting lodges, and we fished in lakes so remote and wild they were unnamed, standing on the floats of the airplane to cast our lines into a silence as profound as a dream.

Even then I was a mostly solitary child, constantly doodling and drawing, making notes that filled scribbler after scribbler. Outside my door the land that enclosed the town and went on forever called me, luring me to enter that irresistible, mysterious world where I would walk or sit and listen, attempting to understand the language of the wild, or to simply be in it.

In 1965 when she was thirty-seven, my mother became pregnant. The pregnancy was a surprise but was not unwelcome, and the whole family happily anticipated the baby's arrival. We'd just moved from Watson Lake to Whitehorse, where my dad had found a good job; for the first time I knew of, there was talk of buying a house. I was in F.H. Collins Secondary School, the biggest I had ever attended. Lilias Farley, an artist and sculptor, was the art teacher there, and in her I finally found a mentor. I had always been deeply interested in drawing and painting, and we struck up a relationship that was to have a big influence on me and lead to my artistic abilities being formally recognized by prizes and awards. Art became something that could, and did, become a career. And I had a boyfriend, Brad Callison, a young man who was handsome and romantic. It was a happy time.

My father died at home one night of a massive coronary. He was thirty-nine years old. It was particularly shocking because as a commercial pilot, he'd had a medical exam every six months; but in those days of less sophisticated testing his heart condition had gone undetected. He was my hero, and his death is still one of the most traumatic and painful events of my life.

My grandmother came from England to help and brought an offer to move us all to England to live with her and my grandfather. Mom, although still in shock and with a newborn son, stood by her resolve to stay in Canada and somehow take care of all of us. There was very little money and no property.

After three years of working and being on her own with two teenaged daughters and a young son, my mother married Bob Stubenberg, who adopted my brother, John—nicknamed Buster, my father's wartime nickname as a member of the Dambusters squadron—and raised him as lovingly as any biological father. He owned the Sportsman Hotel in Watson Lake, and it was there that we lived.

Bob died in 1985; the loss was felt most keenly by my mother and my brother. Although my sister and I had left Watson Lake long before he died, he had always welcomed us on our visits and made us feel we still had a family home. I'd felt easier about leaving to pursue the building of my own life, knowing he was taking care of my mom and my little brother.

Now in her early eighties, Mom still lives in Watson Lake with her third husband, Lorne Armstrong, and continues to amaze and delight us with her humour and her unstoppable zest for life.

After my years in the Iskut area, I lived on Salt Spring Island, where I married again and where my daughter was born. It was during those years I began my goddess art business, taking time out to work for Canada World Youth on their exchange with Somalia and then again in Thailand. It was on Salt Spring, too, that I worked in the funeral business.

I returned briefly to the North when I became head of the Yukon Human Rights Commission. During this time I also completed a body of paintings funded by a Canada Council grant and another art project funded by a Yukon arts grant. I skied and canoed and did river trips. The Yukon was where my second husband and I divorced.

Then came a life on Pender Island and Vancouver Island, during which I continued to grow my art business, fell in love again, raised ostriches, sailed, travelled, became a beekeeper, drove exotic cars, went through menopause and again, simply lacked the time or desire to write.

I lived in Vancouver for a short time before returning North almost six years ago, to live once again in Watson Lake. Here I met a man from my childhood, and it is that man, Paul, who told me I was a writer. He gave me my first computer for Valentine's Day, and although it took a couple of years, during which I emailed and played FreeCell (a solitaire-based computer game), I did eventually begin to write.

I won a writing competition and began writing a column for the *Yukon News* in Whitehorse. Soon I was writing the occasional feature article and then another weekly column. I began work on this memoir, taking the advice, "Write what you know." What I did not know was how to go about getting a publisher. I had been told that one was not likely to find a publisher without first getting an agent, and getting an agent was nearly impossible. I found a literary agent on the internet and sent her the synopsis of my book. She replied immediately, telling me that her agency did not handle work such as mine, but she sent me the addresses of three publishers she knew of that did. I checked out the first one, Caitlin Press. The owner's name was Vici; I had been called "Vicki" when I was growing up, and that was enough for me. I sent her my first three chapters and the rest is history.

No one writes a book alone, and I have been incredibly lucky in having several people nurture and advise me on this path. It was just two years ago that I emailed the editor of the *Yukon News* in Whitehorse and asked if I could write a column from Watson Lake. Richard Mostyn not only agreed, but he also then spent a significant amount of his time encouraging me and teaching me how to write like a journalist. He continues to do this, and I continue to be grateful.

Vici Johnstone, owner of Caitlin Press, turned out to be pretty much as I'd hunched she would be. Her enthusiasm made me truly believe I had actually written a book. She felt like a friend and an ally right away. For someone who'd never had a book editor before, working with Meg Taylor has been a great experience. She has made me feel there is no detail too small and no question too silly for her immediate and generous attention. Ruth Gaskill, copy editor, polished the manuscript, and what a difference her talent made to the final offering!

My daughter, Zoe Miles, has always been a staunch supporter of my every endeavour. In this latest one she has acted as a reader of each chapter hot off the computer printer. A fearless but gentle critic, she has helped a great deal with the writing of this book.

Thank you all. Let's do it again soon!

Prologue

I knew I'd finished with bush life the morning I found myself sitting on a pannier in an icy spring rain chewing on a cold piece of bannock and feeling less than enthusiastic about the twenty-mile ride home beginning right after this breakfast. The camp had been broken down and packed, the horses were saddled and the beaver pelts we'd worked to trap and skin were rolled and tied on top of the packsaddles, everything carefully covered with tarps.

We'd been out beaver trapping for twelve days—tenting, sleeping on spruce boughs, eating boiled beaver hind legs with rice, and working ten hours a day. I was bone-tired and dirty. My hair felt and looked like steel wool and my nails were broken and rimmed with grime. One knee was swollen; it'd been aching since we arrived at camp, the result of my horse bashing my leg into a tree shortly after we'd set out on the long ride. The day before, on the trail, I'd been charged by a grizzly bear, my third such encounter in five years. When I thought about the hot bath I could have when I got home to my cabin I reminded myself of all the effort that bath entailed: warming the cabin, hauling the water, heating it bucket by bucket on the wood stove and pouring it into the galvanized tub that hung on the wall of the cabin. A long process, none of it made easier with a stiff knee. And because it took at least twenty-four hours for the big logs of the cabin to warm, the bath would not be a luxurious experience; the air would be too cool for lingering in water that would quickly be cold.

For five years now none of these difficulties of living in the bush had fazed me. Every moment since arriving in the Iskut area had been challenging, and I had gloried in those challenges, but this morning I knew in my gut—the infallible indicator, my ultimate compass—it was time to move on. A month later I was living in a studio apartment in the West End of Vancouver.

I wish now, nearly forty years later, that I could lay claim to a vast fund of bush lore, a deep knowing of the ways of the land, but I was too young at the time to do more than revel in the novelty of the experience. I didn't pay enough attention to what was being

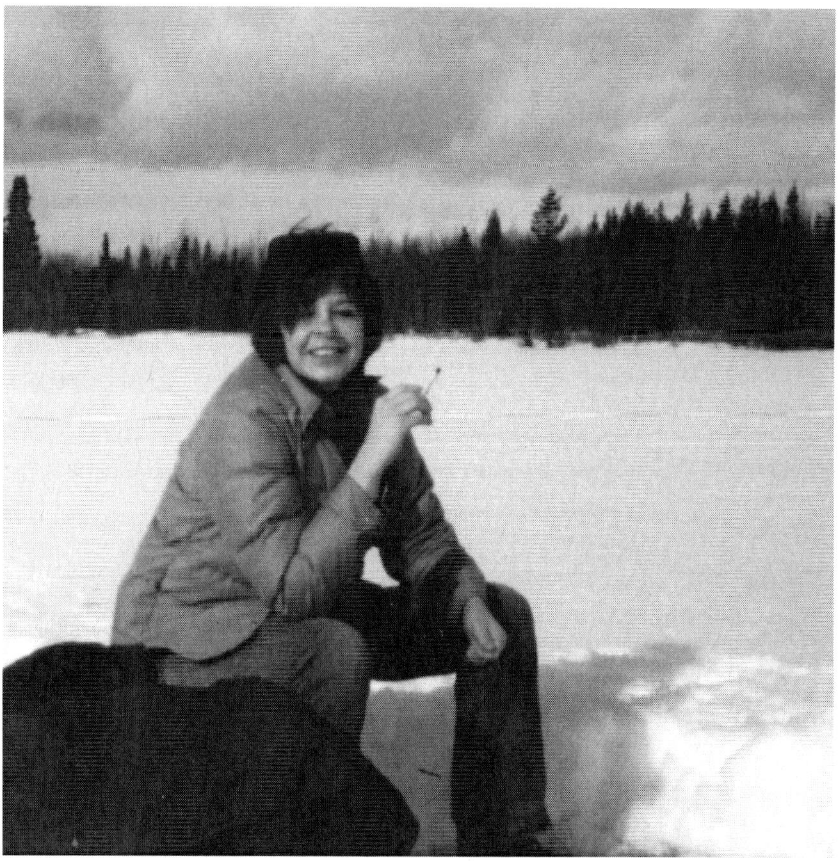

The land was a stern teacher. It taught me to be self-sufficient, it taught me survival and it taught me to live with myself.

offered to me on a daily basis by the people I encountered. Many of them took the time to teach me, never insisting that I learn, but allowing me to simply enjoy myself and skim from their teachings only what I needed to know.

In many ways I was a dilettante; I left the bush almost as much an amateur as I'd been when first I came to live in that wild and glorious country, which to this day occupies a special place in my heart and in my mind.

The land taught me too, and it was a sterner teacher. No matter what agenda a person brings to a life in the wilderness, no matter what state the heart, spirit and mind, the wild will teach, and change that person. I think among the gifts of those years was learning connectivity and self-sufficiency; not only did I learn to live without running water, electricity, a thermostat and the ease of getting stuff from a mall, I also learned to live with myself.

At that time, in that country, there were none of the ways to communicate we now take so much for granted: no telephones, no cell or satellite phones. Very few people had two-way radios; I had mine for only the last two years and then only in the summer months when they were provided by mining exploration companies as part of my expediting service. The roads were rough, not to be driven for frivolous reasons, which made visits, especially in the winter, rare and meaningful.

I learned to go weeks without the sound of another human voice. I learned real solitude, the kind that opened doors I never suspected existed, let alone would have discovered in the busy life of a town or a city. The lessons of that kind of solitude are with me yet and have been instrumental in forming the person I am today. I learned to live with myself and also with the land, listening and hearing the voices in the silence and sometimes, in moments of pure magic, feeling my connection to it all.

The feeling of connection is something I have carried with me—the knowingness of how we are all interrelated. The meaning of that occupies my heart and mind to this day, and I try to more deeply understand its significance: how our every action impacts everything and everyone around us, and beyond. It is a quest that I believe is more and more relevant as our planet and its inhabitants become forced to recognize that interdependency.

This is the story, many years and many changes later, of those exhilarating, never-to-be-forgotten years and the people who were my teachers, my friends, and who shared with me part of their lives.

Early Days in Iskut

Even now I don't know how or why I made the decisions I did. My life underwent enormous changes without any trauma (at least to me) every few years, and it all seemed effortless. It was as though I was obeying some inner impulse as strong as a bird's need to migrate or a salmon's drive to return to its place of origin. I was never one to lie awake at night agonizing about what to do—I just did it.

In hindsight I am sorry for the carelessness, the youthful selfishness that informed my decisions; some people were hurt, and confused, by my actions, and it didn't seem to matter to me. I simply didn't give such matters a great deal of thought. I went from a romantic marriage to a pilot and five years of life with him in Montreal to living with a man in Watson Lake who was older than my mother, a man with two marriages behind him and four grown sons.

And so it was to the Yukon I went in 1971 when I felt a pull to leave my five-year marriage. There was no real reason to leave, other than I felt I'd exhausted the possibilities of married life in the city and had become somewhat politically radicalized. Exposure to a host of ideas new to me had left me feeling dissatisfied with my life and curious to see what else was out there and what else was in me. I knew I still wanted to paint; I'd taken a detour from my plans to become an artist when I'd met and married Bob McIntyre.

Bob and I had met the summer after my graduation from high school in Whitehorse. I was back in Watson Lake, living with my parents and working at their hotel, saving money to go to art school in England. Bob was a glamorous figure to a Yukon girl. He was not only lovely to look at, but he was also from Montreal, a world away from Watson Lake, and I had always been drawn to anyone from Outside. This particular someone was handsome and bright, with beautiful manners. He was spending his summer co-piloting a B-17 that was doing aerial photography in the Yukon. Flying was his passion. It was wonderful to me to meet someone else who had a strong vision for the future. We fell in love.

Being in love was not going to stop me from chasing my dream of being an artist. I went to England that winter accompanied by my family, who were going to spend Christmas with my grandparents in Yorkshire. After they went home, I planned to study art at a school in London. This grand scheme began to change with Bob's arrival at my grandparents' place just before Christmas. My birthday is on New Year's Day, and he took me to Paris to celebrate. We got engaged there, buying the diamond engagement ring in London before taking the train back to the family in Yorkshire. Our plan was to marry quietly in London and leave immediately afterwards for Nigeria, where Bob had a flying job. Mom insisted we marry from my family home; when Mom insists on something, that's what happens. I never did make it to art school, though I stayed in England till the wedding in Watson Lake.

The political situation in Nigeria made the move too dangerous for us. We settled in Montreal, and it was a lively and interesting time to be living in that city. Bob's family from the start were tremendously warm and welcoming to me. They had a cottage in the Laurentian Mountains; I learned to ski. Bob flew planes for aerial photography; I became the first civilian woman aerial photographer. Bob was interested in photography; I worked as a fashion model, being photographed. His family was bilingual;

I studied French. We travelled a lot and we had a busy social life.

Bob got a job with a small airline and was sometimes away from home for a few days at a time. I began to make some friends on my own, friends who showed me different ways of being, of thinking, of seeing, and friends who admired my art and encouraged me to become more committed to it. This was the world I left the summer Bob was going to be working away from home for most of July and August. I could have gone with him but I didn't want to. I wanted the time for myself.

I went to my family home in Watson Lake to take a breather, to relax into familiar surroundings and consider what to do next. I quickly fell into the typical young northerner's summer of partying too much and working too hard, leaving no time to ponder. Although I managed to set up a studio in an old cabin beside the Watson Lake Hotel, the most significant work I did was painting signs for local businesses. The studio became more a place to hang out with friends and drink beer than a place to do serious painting.

I met Tee, the owner of a general store in town, and the intensity and the novelty of our relationship coloured most of my days for the next two years. It was a careful relationship in many ways. Although we had periods of intense togetherness, travelling to Mexico, Edmonton, Vancouver and Seattle and camping together for several weeks while working some claims we'd staked off the Alaska Highway near the Rancheria River, we were often apart. He travelled for business, and I was occupied with my own life. It was over a year before we moved in together. Even then, we often went days and weeks without being at home at the same time.

That summer I also got to know Lynch Callison, who was the father of Brad, one of my high school boyfriends. Lynch was a character, with a capital C. He'd run mail by dogsled, hunted moose to feed the crews that built the Alaska Highway, trapped, guided, rode the rodeo circuit in his younger days and was considered to be one of those charming bad boys that many women find irresistible. He was gallant and courteous, clearly a man who liked the opposite sex, and they liked him right back. Young women were called "Sis," women of a certain age were "Ma'am;" in addressing the latter, he would take his cowboy hat from his head. I believe they felt safe with him, as well as admired—an unusual and valued feeling for women in the seventies, when the reawakened issues of women's equality were throwing the relationship between men and women into confusion.

Lynch came through town on his way back to his ranch in northern BC, still charming in an old-fashioned, courtly cowboy sort of way. One could tell he'd been a handsome young man; he still acted like one. I met him in the bar where I was hanging out with the somewhat disreputable group I'd fallen in with for the summer and we talked, catching up on the news of mutual acquaintances. He was a canny old fellow and soon cottoned on to what I was currently doing with my life, finishing our chat with an invitation to come out and stay on his ranch and get my head straight, as he put it. I thanked him for the invitation, he left and I carried on to yet another fairly drunken evening in the bar.

He came by the store early the next morning and sat in his old truck honking the horn. I woke up, threw some clothes in a bag, told Tee where I was going and got into the truck.

It was a long and uncomfortable drive on a road that called itself the Stewart-Cassiar Highway, or Highway 37, despite having no reason whatsoever to be called more than a goat track. Less than an hour out of town, I was sick to my stomach, suffering a wicked headache and wondering what in the hell I was doing jolting around in a dirty truck with an old guy in a cowboy hat who I hardly knew and didn't remember ever wanting to know, heading to a place I knew nothing about other than it was in a remote wilderness. Lynch was not particularly sympathetic but he was kind enough to stop the truck while I staggered out to empty the contents of my stomach on the side of the road. The rest of the trip passed with me trying to sleep while Lynch talked and sang, ignoring my silence and closed eyes.

When we arrived at the ranch he carried my bag to a small cabin, started a fire in the little wood stove and left, saying he would see me in the lodge for breakfast. I crawled into a sleeping bag on a lumpy cot and didn't wake up till noon the next day. I awoke to the sound of birds and squirrels, to the sun pouring in through uncovered windows, one of which showed the branches of a pine tree and the other a clear blue sky. My twenty-five-year-old body was rested, and with the resilience of that age, I was hungry and eager to see where I was.

The lodge was a large low building about fifty yards from my little cabin, which was perched on the top of a low embankment with a broad creek tumbling below. Beyond were mountains; I learned later they were called the Spatsizi Range. There is something about mountains—their soaring heights, their remote rocky faces and snow-topped crowns—that lifts the spirit. I felt lighter as I walked a well-trodden path to the lodge, stopping to use the outhouse along the way and picking up the good smell of fresh coffee as I neared the back porch.

Inside was a small slim woman with iron-grey hair, sharp blue eyes and the most perfect skin I'd ever seen. She unsmilingly introduced herself as Verna Bailey, accompanying her few words with a strong handshake. She was Lynch's partner in the ranch and in the game-guide and outfitting business they were starting up. The ranch was named the LV Ranch. With a marvellous economy of movement that I would come to most associate with her, Verna poured me coffee, sat me at the long table and served me a wonderful hearty breakfast of eggs, sausage, fried potatoes and her homemade bread and jam. She was not chatty, being of a reticent and taciturn nature, but she could be wooed into talk, and I was the consummate wooer, wanting to know everything about her and the ranch and game guiding and outfitting.

Lynch looked pleased to see us getting along when he came in for his lunch, joining me at the table while Verna got his food for him. They'd known each other all their lives, having both grown up on ranches in the Peace River country. They were partners in a business sense only; Verna was married to an ex–RCMP officer named Walter, and Lynch was, at the time, single. I sensed

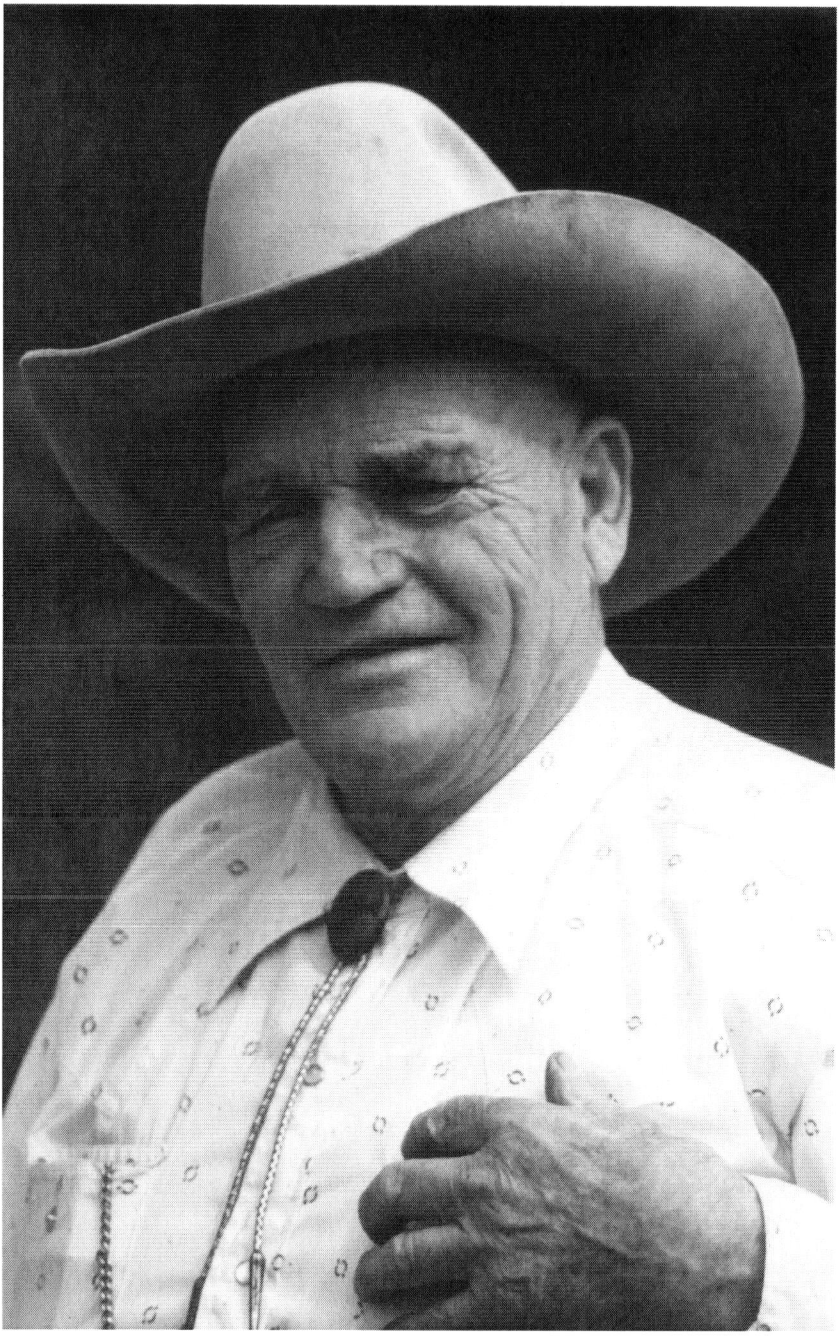

Lynch Callison was an old-fashioned cowboy and ladies' man extraordinaire.

a lot more going on between them. Lynch was courteous, as he always was with women, but also slightly flirtatious, which flustered Verna while not entirely displeasing her. Where was Walter? I wondered aloud. He was at their home in Fort St. John, I was told; he would be coming sometime this summer and I would meet him then.

While I helped Verna with the washing-up, my tireless questioning and her innate courtesy enabled me to learn she had been the Canadian pistol champion for so long they finally asked her to step down. She could hunt, trap, skin, cook and bake, and knew everything there was to know about horses. She also collected antique china. The more I found out about her the more inadequate and faintly foolish I felt about myself. I could feel myself resolving to be just like Verna.

When Lynch had eaten and gone for a mid-morning nap, she told me stuff about Lynch I hadn't known. He'd married young,

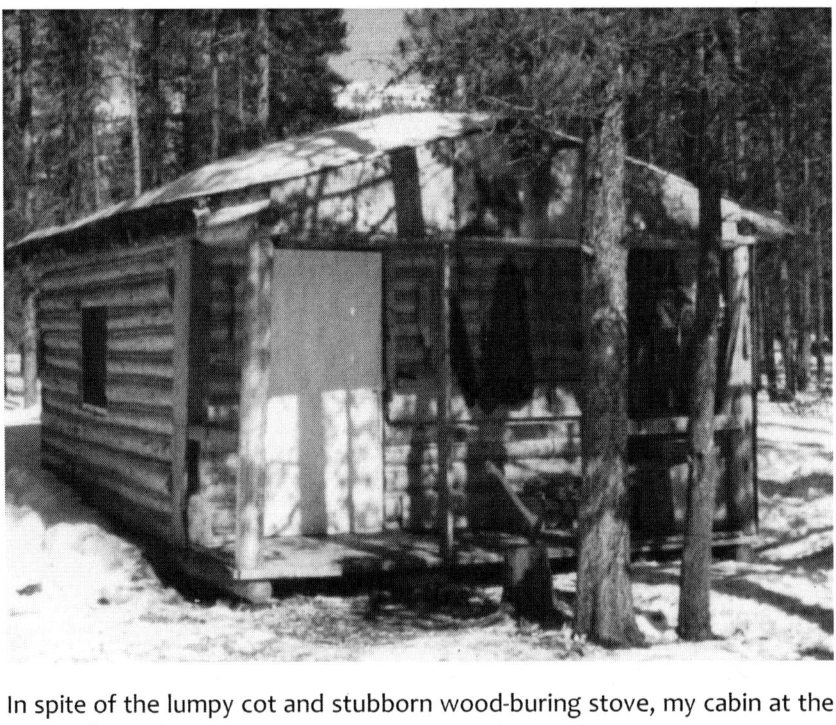

In spite of the lumpy cot and stubborn wood-buring stove, my cabin at the LV Ranch was home.

and he and his wife had three kids. Lynch was always away, leaving his young family alone, and he "fooled around." There were two children known of from his affairs; Verna referred to them as his "catch colts."

A house fire had killed all three kids. Lynch and his wife had three more: a girl, Cheryl, and two boys, Brad and Coyne. I knew the second lot of kids. I'd dated Brad, met his younger brother and visited with Cheryl once in Fort St. John, but the first family was news to me and explained a lot about the Callison kids and their uneasy relationship with their father.

Dishes done and floor swept, I went out to look around. It was a beautiful sunny day in early summer and the air was delicious, like food, nourishing and good. There was a garage/shop some distance from the lodge and another little cabin like mine along the same ridge, with Lynch's larger newer cabin further along. Every building was made of logs, even the outhouses, as were all the fences and corrals.

Walking out to the middle of the "highway" I could see a mountain so perfect it looked like a child's drawing. Tall and peaked, with snow on its crest and dark trees marching up its sides, it was a mountain with a presence immediately felt. Locals called it Icy Mountain, though looking at a map some time later I discovered its real name is Mount Edziza. Even later, I learned it was meant to be Edzertza, after a local Tahltan family. Seeing some activity in one of the corrals, I wandered over to find I was not the only guest at the LV Ranch.

Charley Bacon, from University of California, Berkeley, was there. Icy Mountain had a crater—it had been a volcano in its heyday—and Charley was doing a PhD thesis on volcanic rock. Lynch, Charley and Verna were choosing horses and gathering gear for the trek up the mountain. I badly wanted to go and lost no time in asking if I could accompany them, but Verna took me aside to tell me I was not in any shape for such a journey and promised me there would be others. Meanwhile she would welcome my company while Lynch took Charley to the rocks, and we would ride every day, getting me fit for an expedition.

She kept her word. For the next week I worked alongside her every day, fascinated by all she did, and every evening we saddled horses and rode for a couple of hours. A rank beginner, I had to learn everything from how to catch my horse and saddle it to the rubdown at the end of a ride and daily feeding. Catching a horse was fraught with difficulties; it didn't take these savvy bush beasts long to know they were dealing with an amateur, and I would swear they enjoyed our encounters. I came to believe horses can laugh because I heard them, snorting and giggling to one another as I chased them through the ubiquitous buckbrush, bridle in one hand and tobacco can of oats in the other.

The first ride we took, one evening after the dinner dishes were done, was up the mountain behind the ranch, a slope not as steep as Icy Mountain, but a good workout just the same. We rode through swamp and buckbrush and over rocks, with the lingering light of the evening bathing us all with soft gold. I was enthralled with it all: the sounds of the hoofs and the creaking of the saddles, the twittering of birds bidding farewell to the day, Verna's low voice weaving through and binding all the sounds into a song of the woods and the promise of summer. The smell of the brush as it swept the sides of the horses, the smell of the horses themselves, were odours new to me and I found them rich and satisfying.

The view from the top was magnificent. The scenery here was moving me in ways like nothing I had encountered anywhere. I actually felt my being expand in this vast empty wildness; I felt free, yet more engaged in the simple acts of living. Hauling water, chopping wood, caring for the horses, preparing food—all ordinary tasks—were laden with significance. There was pleasure, and pride, in my growing competence and with the feeling of physical strength in my body.

It seemed there was always someone stopping by for a visit, usually from the Native village of Iskut, about six miles south. Sometimes a truck driver, known to Verna or Lynch, came in for a chat and refreshment. Rarely was there a tourist—few braved the highway, though those intrepid enough to do it were invariably thrilled with the journey. Verna fed everyone, especially me, whom she seemed to regard as a thin orphan. There were three huge meals every day, each featuring a meat dish as well as a dessert, and anyone who happened to be on the premises was automatically served. Two coffee breaks a day were accompanied by cookies, cake, pies or biscuits with homemade jam. Although the lodge was, I believe, intended to be a business, along with the provision of horses and the service of guiding, I rarely saw a visitor paying for their food or coffee.

The amount of work Verna did daily was staggering; yet she never appeared to be hurried or stressed. No matter how early I got to the lodge she would be there first, pulling bread from the oven or peeling vegetables for the dinner stew, while evenings saw her mending harnesses or baking something. I did not once see her idle.

Lynch and Charley returned and there was a day of unpacking and horse care. The energy of the ranch changed; the peaceful busy days I had been enjoying with Verna were now simply busy days, as Lynch got ready to take another party into the bush. Feeling a bit superfluous, I spent more time on my own, reading in my cabin and going for rides on Flame, a big bright roan that had been designated my horse for the duration of my stay. I was careful not to go far, sticking to the well-worn trails or following Tsaybe Creek as it wound through the wide valley.

One fine day I decided to hike up the valley, taking a backpack with a lunch and a sketchbook. I was about to have my first face-to-face encounter with the wild.

"Griz Been Spotted Up the Valley, Sis!"

Lynch was sawing wood. He'd place logs, one at a time, between a couple of sawhorses and, using a swede saw, cut them into stove lengths. He looked up as I passed by and said, still sawing, "Griz been spotted up the valley, Sis. She's got a cub." I didn't stop to inquire what that might mean regarding my proposed little trek, just smiled at him and continued at a brisk pace. It was a lovely hike; the trail was well-defined and the brush not so thick that I couldn't see or hear the creek. Icy Mountain was visible, its glaciers gleaming in the sun.

I couldn't have been more than half an hour from the lodge when I came to a spot beside the water and stopped to have a drink. The creek widened here and as I looked up to gaze at the low bank on the other side I saw something very large and very dark standing in the willows at the top of the bank. It was accompanied by something lighter and smaller—something that spotted me and gave a little woof of surprise right about the time I recognized I was looking at a mother bear and her cub. A mother grizzly bear and her cub—the telltale hump on her back gave her away. The mother stood up, her head weaving as she tried to catch my scent. Every scary story I'd ever heard about grizzlies was

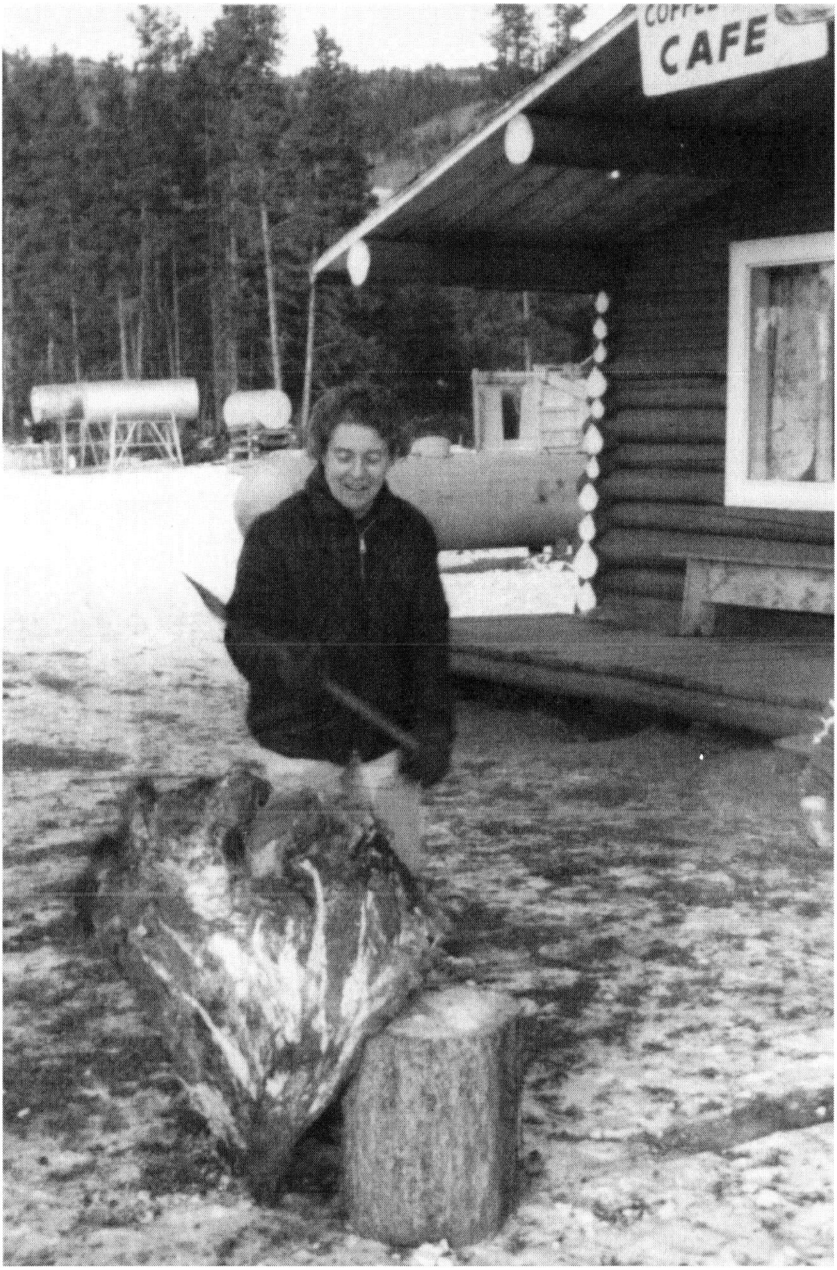

Verna Bailey was Lynch's partner in the LV Ranch. She was a Canadian pistol champion and she could hunt, trap, skin, cook and bake. When the dogs needed dinner Verna would get out her axe and attack a chunk of frozen moose meat. I soon decided I wanted to be just like her.

unreeling through my head as I stared at her, my feet refusing to move. She dropped down on all fours and immediately came towards me through the creek, so fast that the water splashed up higher than her back on both sides of her huge body.

I truly don't recall what happened next. All I knew was that I was up a tree, a very bushy spruce tree, so thin I could wrap both arms around its meagre trunk. I was high enough that I could feel it swaying a bit with my weight. The sounds below me were of ripping and crunching, interspersed with low grunts. I didn't look down; I could not make myself look down. It seemed hours before the sounds ceased and I dared peer below to see my backpack in shreds and scattered around the bottom of the tree. The bear appeared to be gone.

It seemed even longer before I dared to come down from the tree, stiff with terror and with every nerve alive and tuned to my surroundings—so alive and tuned that every sound from that moment until I got back to the ranch caused me to climb a tree. The crack of a branch, the caw of a raven, the wind in the leaves of the trees—each noise became a warning of danger. I knew I was crying but I was not sobbing; I didn't dare make any noise. My heart was pounding so hard it was hurting and I was certain its barely muffled thumping would bring the bear back. If the bear came back, I would simply die. My body could not hold any more of this feeling of terror, nor could my mind, which had retreated into a corner somewhere and was refusing to acknowledge what was happening, instead choosing music and lyrics from *The Sound of Music*—the song about the whiskers on kittens—to play over and over again as I stumbled down the trail.

Lynch and I rode down the trail a couple of days later and counted seven trees with their branches broken and all the little twigs that usually clustered thickly to their trunks shorn off.

Lynch claims I was gone for about an hour and a half, but it felt like an endless time before I staggered into the clearing where he was still sawing wood. My clothes were torn and bloodied from a multitude of small scratches. My head sported more twigs and needles than hair and my nose was running, the snot mingling with the tears pouring down my face. My hands would take nearly a week to heal, the nails torn and palms gashed from grabbing broken branches. Lynch stopped sawing, but he didn't put down the saw.

"See the bear, Sis?" he inquired.

Oddly, my experience with the bear did not lead me to question staying on at the ranch. It certainly reverberated for a few days, and for awhile I didn't sleep well, dreaming of grizzly bears in a variety of scenarios, none pleasant, and waking up soaked in the sweat and stink of profound fear. It changed how I saw the forest: any Disneyesque fantasies were utterly gone, never to return. I was assured it was a rare event and that indeed I was almost lucky to have had such an adventure; it would be my own story.

My own story it may well have been, but that didn't stop Lynch from telling it to whoever appeared at the lodge the following week, and making it hilarious at my expense. Probably a good idea; I quickly learned to laugh at it too, and any possibility of post-stress trauma was banished by the gales of laughter Lynch could invoke with the telling of Tor and the griz. However I didn't go far from the ranch alone for the next while, as I healed from the cuts and bruises sustained during my grisly grizzly encounter.

A sense of direction was something I had never been able to claim, and here in the wild it was of maximum importance as it was incredibly easy to get lost. Although I had a compass, in my five years of living in the bush I never did learn to use it. The horses and the dogs always had their bearings, and I quickly came to depend on my animal companions to get me safely back home.

There was always something to do around the ranch. I helped Lynch haul water from the creek to the lodge using a team of old roan mares and a stoneboat with added board sides. The stoneboat was a wooden platform with boards nailed under it to skid on and with sides high enough to keep the forty-five-gallon drums of water from falling off as it was hauled to the main building. I liked doing this chore, watching the mares as they responded to Lynch's hollered directions and tugs on the long reins, hearing the squeak of the harnesses and the muted jingle of the brass hardware. We hauled wood the same way, bringing the logs to the sawhorses and the chopping block. After witnessing my early efforts with an axe, Lynch and Verna put me to work stacking the wood outside the lodge and the cabins. Verna eventually showed me the proper way to use an axe, but only after Lynch had had some fun by telling me I should chop while kneeling, to prevent injury.

I tried to make bannock. Lynch's bannock was hearty, Verna's light as air; mine was weighty, without flavour, and left me feeling like the fairy-tale wolf who'd had rocks sewn into his belly. No one even pretended to find it palatable, including Patsy, the ranch dog famous for her indiscriminate appetite. One visiting fellow tried to comfort me by saying I'd made an artifact and that years from now archeologists would be digging up my bannock, maybe decid-

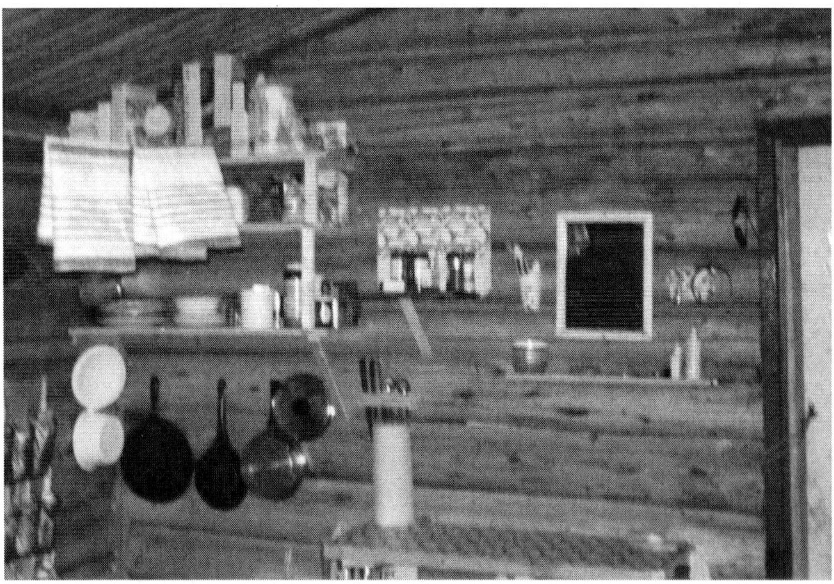

In spare moments I tried my hand at sprucing up the cabin. My carpentry skills were adequate, but not pretty.

ing it was a religious icon.

I tried my hand at simple carpentry, putting up shelves for my books. Pretty they were not, but they worked and made the cabin feel more like my home. I put a cloth on the table and attractive blankets on the two narrow cots, one of which served as guest seating or my couch. There was a colourful Navajo rug on the floor and the glorious scenery in the windows. In this small space everything had a place, and I soon learned to ensure everything was kept in that place. Not having a light switch meant I needed to know how to lay hands on things in the dark, like my flashlight and matches. Eventually I could have lived in that cabin stone-blind, so well did I know where things were.

It was still cool enough this early spring to require a fire in the evening before bed and again in the morning before coffee. Lynch had been coming to my cabin every evening to start the fire for me, but I wanted to become more independent of him and the lodge; I wanted to continue my tries at making bannock, and I wanted to make my own coffee in the morning. I had brought a stovetop espresso maker and I was missing having my cup of very strong, syrupy coffee to start my day.

The stove in my cabin was about two feet long and a foot and a half wide, half of it being the firebox and the other half a small oven. It was called a Teslin stove. Lynch chopped my first box of kindling, telling me I would have to do it myself when it was gone, which it was after my very first attempt to light the stove. I gathered a clothesbasket full of the small lichen-hung twigs that were thick on the little spruce trees, but the firebox ate them before my chunks of wood could catch fire. I slept cold that night and went to the lodge kitchen for my morning cup of java.

Later in the day, fetching something for Lynch from the garage, I came across a can of gas. Aha, I thought, this'll solve my heating problem. It did. A bit of gas tossed on small bits of dry wood caught fire beautifully, if a little scarily, and I was snug in the cabin at night, drinking hot chocolate that I'd made myself on my own stove in my own wee cabin. I built my morning and evening fires with gas instead of kindling for a few days before Lynch, hearing the bang with which my fires started, figured it was time he gave me an easier way. He brought me a pail of kerosene with wood chips floating in it—the perfect fire starter, minus the bang and the danger of losing more of my eyebrows and lashes.

We went to the village of Iskut once a week to collect the mail and buy a few groceries, mostly the rather limp produce that'd made its way by truck to this remote place. Mail day was busy, with everyone from miles around gathering to get parcels and letters and visit with one another. I was introduced to the Catholic sisters who taught at the little school in the village. They were kind, offering me the use of their bathtub on mail days. It was a luxury I appreciated—my sponge baths in the cabin were okay but washing my hair was a major production. I met Jean Black, the community nurse, and her brother and sister-in-law who owned a motel, gas pumps and a small store at Eddontenajon Lake, a cluster of buildings close to Iskut.

Every two weeks a movie was shown in the community hall in the village. This event was as well-attended as mail day. There was such a noise of children, chatter and scraping of chairs as people came and went the entire time that to actually see the movie was clearly not the object of the gathering. One had to surrender to the fun of it all or not go to movie night.

About a week after my bear adventure, Lynch had to go to Stewart to get supplies before taking some people on a trail ride. I begged to go with him; I wanted to see Stewart and the infamous Hyder, a town right across the border in Alaska that was known for its rowdy bars. I also had a list of necessities to shop for. Although it was summertime, Tee was not able to come for a visit and bring me some much-needed clothing, books, painting supplies and drugstore-type necessities. Summer was a busy time for his store in Watson Lake, with the orders from the mining exploration companies and the tourist traffic at its peak. I needed a trip to town. Lynch agreed easily—he always liked company and an audience, and it was a long hard drive.

Back then the Stikine River was not bridged. In the summer a barge served as a ferry, and in the winter a road across the frozen river served as an ice bridge. This meant that in the early spring and late fall, there was no way to get to the Alaska Highway north.

I was wild with excitement at the thought of being in a town, with restaurants, stores and lots of people; I was ready to leave at the crack of dawn, as Lynch demanded. We set off in his big old truck with its stock box, an enclosed space designed to transport horses. It was noisy and it was dirty, but it would take us to a garden of earthly delights.

Although it has been well over thirty years since my first trip to Stewart from Iskut, I still blush to recall that first night. The drive in was rough, the road every bit as bad as it was from the Alaska Highway to Iskut, but also like that stretch of the road, the scenery was outstanding, with each bend in the road revealing a new dramatic vista of rivers, lakes and mountains.

It was a long drive, over five hours, and by the time we reached Stewart, I was exhausted, starving and wanted nothing more than to check into a hotel, have a bath and go to bed. Lynch wanted to go for a beer before anything else and I agreed to accompany him, thinking I could also order a hamburger and fries while sitting in the bar.

I remember being introduced to Charlie and Jackie Fenner, a couple who in those days were busy acquiring most of the town of Stewart. Not that there was much—the Granduc and Premier mines had long been closed, and there was nothing happening in this tiny town nestled among towering mountains at the end of "the chuck," a long arm of the sea where the tides came and went on the flats.

The Fenners were raising their two girls and working hard at their business, which at that time was the only grocery store in town. They were young, attractive and full of energy. We got along instantly, and I forgot my tiredness and was soon happy to be sitting in the bar of the King Edward Hotel drinking with them. At some point in the evening we ate a meal, and then it was off to Hyder, Alaska, a distance of less than a mile.

Hyder consisted of bars, and not much else. There were three of them in business at that time but the Sealaska was where we inevitably ended up because it belonged to a friend of the Fenners', Gary Benedict. Anyone coming to Stewart was expected to pay a visit to this wee place at the end of the road and get "Hyderized"—a ritual that involves drinking a shot glass of pure alcohol going by various names like "everclear" and "snakebite." It is deadly, and swallowing it necessitates a chaser, usually of beer but often of something almost as drunk-making as the shot glass full of the Hyder potion.

It was a happening place packed full of people intent on having as good a time as possible, with loud music, energetic dancing and lots of shouted conversations. Fights were not uncommon and mostly comical, with the participants usually too inebriated to do much damage. I vaguely remember dancing, and I don't believe I did any fighting.

I awoke the next morning to find myself in Charlie and Jackie's downstairs guest room. Lynch had dropped off my backpack at some point, and the big black plastic garbage bag containing my laundry. Wobbling up the stairs, I found the kitchen where the scent of coffee gave me hope for a resumption of my happy life. Charlie had gone to work, but Jackie, looking as rumpled and hungover as I was sure I did, was making breakfast and quickly poured me a mug of coffee. I refused food, feeling it would be asking too much of my stomach to resume normal activity right away, but the coffee was welcome, as was the company of my hostess, who sat down with her own cup.

Rather than feeling embarrassed and needing to apologize and escape as quickly as possible, Jackie's ease and friendliness had me feeling welcome and at home. After a couple of cups of coffee, I was ready for the good and grounding breakfast she served me. While eating I asked about a laundromat, only to have Jackie insist I do my laundry right there, which I did, with the two of us continuing to chat as though we had known one another forever. She let me use her VW to do my shopping. It was the beginning of a friendship that has lasted, through all the changes in our lives, to this day.

I met a lot of people on that trip, many of whom played roles of varying significance in my life over the next five years, but few remained as central to my story as the Fenners. They were hospitable, generous with their home and their time. They were the core of the group I hung out with when I was in Stewart, exemplifying the energy of those long-ago days when we were all young and full of exuberance, fascination and hope. We worked hard and we played equally hard, and we maintained a loyalty to one another through thick and thin.

I think I slept most of the way back to Iskut despite the bumpy ride and Lynch's road songs, waking only as we passed the magnificent spectacle of Bear Glacier, the ice blue and eerie in the morning light. Once back in my little cabin, with my shopping all unpacked and stowed away, I fell into bed, my last thought being that I didn't need to go to a town again for a long, long time: I was towned out.

Life on the Ranch

Tee finally made it out to the ranch; he was able to get four days away from his business. I hadn't seen him for over a month and now we were to have so few days together. Before he'd even arrived, I was complaining about the short stay, but by the end of the second day, I couldn't wait for him to be gone.

He arrived bearing gifts, the sort of thoughtful gifts that only a man who'd lived in the bush himself would have thought to bring. There was a gas lamp! No more kerosene stench and feeble light! He brought a whole box of books to read in the light of my new lamp, several new pairs of jeans and two jean jackets, an insulated vest and a dozen pairs of thick socks. There was a pair of hiking boots that fit perfectly and a new backpack. He brought my favourite candies, bottles of wine and some perfume. The afternoon he arrived there was quite a crowd at the lodge and I could feel the envy of the women as I unpacked, at their insistence, the many packages and boxes while the men drank coffee on the porch. The envy wasn't so much for the piles of goodies as for the great good luck I enjoyed in having such a man as my partner.

Needless to say, our first night was sheer bliss, though after we'd properly and improperly had our private reunion we ended up having to sleep in separate beds. My narrow cot simply would not accommodate two bodies, no matter how willing they were to

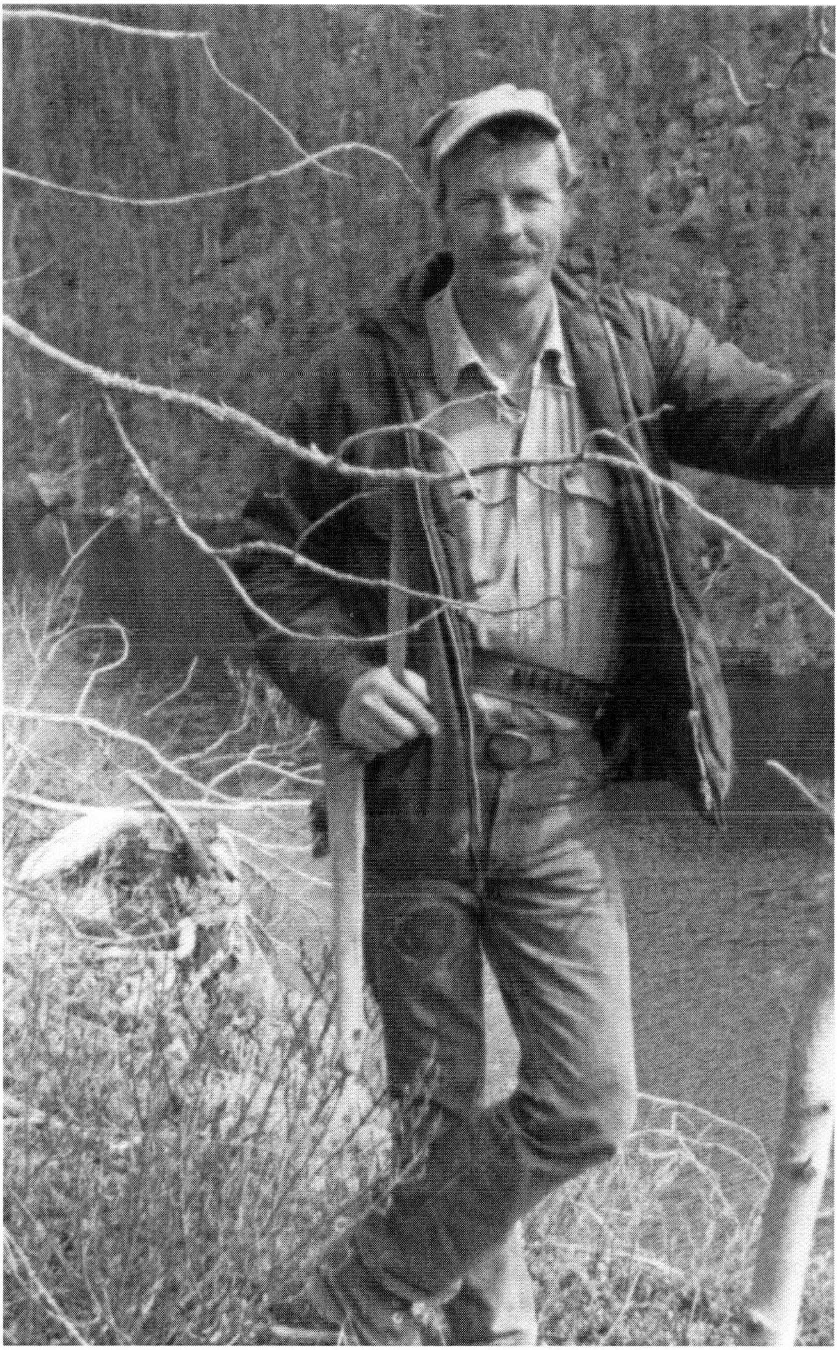

When Tee came to visit the LV Ranch he was a wild man in his element.

cuddle. The trouble began in the morning. Tee got up first and got the fire going and made the coffee. He brought it to me in bed—in the wrong cup. I always used the red mug; he served my coffee in the yellow one. Realizing my response was likely unreasonable, I smiled sweetly and thanked him, waiting till he'd gone to the outhouse to pour my morning brew into the red mug.

Seeing my clumsy attempt at shelving and knowing I would be in need of more space for all the new books he'd brought, he rebuilt and added to my shelves, increasing the space and making the whole structure less likely to fall on my head. He did this in his customary quick and capable manner, completing the whole project in the time I was at the lodge helping Verna with dinner. But he'd put all the books back in the wrong order. I thanked him and left them, itching to straighten them up but vowing to wait until he'd gone home before doing so. It was hard, seeing them all standing there in spots where they did not belong, books beside books they had nothing in common with other than being books, but being the mature person I was, I could let them be, for now.

We had one of Verna's wonderful moose roast dinners at the lodge, with lots of talk and laughter to go with the meat, the potatoes and the fresh-baked apple pie. I was happy to see Tee was clearly liked by Verna and Lynch and that he liked them back.

The second morning was a repeat of the first, with me scrambling out of bed as soon as Tee had gone so that I could pour my coffee into the red mug. I'd put up four hooks inside the door: the first was for my outdoor jacket, the second for my indoor sweater, the third for my nightgown and the fourth for a guest to use. Tee hung his jacket overtop of my nightgown. He moved my flashlight six inches to the left of where it was supposed to be and he put my book of matches in his pocket after lighting the fire. I was going mad. I knew it was crazy, which is why I didn't say anything other than to gently remind him to put the matches back. Despite these small annoyances, we had a wonderful time, riding horses, hiking, fishing—cramming as many of the pleasures the area offered in the short time available to us.

I was so happy to see him leave, but after restoring my cabin to its proper order I cried myself to sleep missing him. It would be six weeks before I saw him again.

Laundry was an ongoing issue. Verna had a wringer washing machine that she hooked up once a week to do the wash for the lodge, herself and Lynch, and although she had offered to do mine, I simply couldn't allow it: she already did too much for me. When I asked if I could use the machine she said she'd rather I didn't—it was old and tricky—but she did lend me a big square tin washtub and a washboard. I did laundry every two weeks, growing to loathe the whole process of the painstaking heating of water and the incessant, hard scrubbing needed to clean jeans. Thank God I had no sheets to wash; I slept in a sleeping bag, which I aired over the railing of my little porch every fine day. The only bed linen needing a regular wash was my pillowcase.

As the weather warmed, having the little stove going all day to heat enough water became a matter of acute discomfort. There had to be a better, easier way. Fooling around by the creek one hot afternoon, I noticed how the water rushed through the culvert that allowed the creek to go under the road. The creek was much wider than the culvert, so by the time the water had gathered itself to get through, it was running very speedily.

The next laundry day I took all my bits and pieces and poured some liquid laundry soap on them before looping them over a piece of rope. I then tied the rope to one side of the culvert, crawled over the top and attached the other end of the rope to the other side. The idea was the rush of water would act as an agitator and clean (and then rinse) my laundry. It seemed foolproof, and remarkably clever; I wondered why no one else had thought of easing their burden of chores by doing this very thing. Almost before I'd straightened up from tying the line it became evident why my brilliant idea was not going to work.

The water was moving at a rate no washing machine could hope to match: my line was ripped from its moorings in no time, the current carrying it and all my laundry down the creek. On the downstream side of the culvert, the banks of the creek became suddenly steep, dense with willows and slippery, with any access to the water extremely difficult and in many spots dangerous. Tsaybe Creek was water from the glaciers on the mountains and it was very, very cold.

So cold that, when I fell in trying to retrieve at least one piece of clothing that'd gotten hung up on a branch, it literally took my breath away. Not to mention that the swift current also took my feet out from under me and was tumbling me along at a vigorous pace. I realized there was suddenly a real chance I could drown. I couldn't yell for help because I had no breath to do so, having to use any I could get to keep my lungs filled, as the current would suck me under the roiling surface every few seconds. I could feel the cold numbing me, my fingers less and less able to grasp and hold any willows hanging over the water, and I couldn't feel my legs or feet at all.

Finally I got a good grip on some branches and began the laborious and seemingly impossible task of hauling my half-dead body out of the creek. The bank was less steep in this spot, though the wet soil made it horribly slippery. I don't know how I did it, and it seemed to take forever, but I managed to get myself entirely out of the water and lie on the rough, swampy grass greedily gulping air and spewing creek water almost simultaneously.

Eventually I was able to squelch my way home, the almost impenetrable bush scratching my face and hands and tearing at my clothing. I managed, by crawling beside the creek on the other side of the road, to avoid being seen as I slithered into my cabin, scarlet with seeping blood and embarrassment. I never did tell anyone what had happened, dismissing my scratched face as a fall from the horse. I habitually wore jeans and T-shirts, with a jean jacket for evenings, so no one commented on my suddenly limited wardrobe, though I cannot imagine Verna missed the fact that I wore the same clothes over and over and that my laundry days were more frequent.

It was a good lesson in several ways. I learned a healthy respect for the creek, which I hadn't really taken seriously before because the section of it that ran alongside the ranchland was broad and shallow, with flat banks. It looked sparkly, friendly and inviting, but now I knew its dual nature: after it went under the road and into the bush it became a cold, fast killer.

Laundry became a fact of life and not something to be dreaded, hurried or resented. I never did learn to love doing laundry but I learned to accept a day of packing water and heating water and scrubbing in water to have the pleasure of clean clothes and towels. Mostly, I realized that if I did not pay attention every moment in this new life I was having, I could die. The same could have been said of my life in the city, I suppose, but this felt different. I could have more control over what happened to me here if I would listen, watch and learn.

In the short time I was at the ranch, I had handled an axe, built fires, ridden horses, met a grizzly and fallen into a glacier-fed creek. It was time to be in the moment with full awareness rather than the head-in-the-clouds dreaminess I'd been enjoying. I understood then that what I was doing here was no longer merely a jaunt, an adventure to savour and describe when I returned to my real life. The land and the people were demanding a fuller engagement with me, and I was finding I wanted to respond. I wanted to learn more, to get deeper.

It took me a bit longer to understand I was undergoing a spiritual overhaul.

Among the treasures Tee had brought was an oddity: a braided bullwhip. At first I thought he might be expressing a desire to add a new dimension to our sex life and the whip was a not-so-subtle hint, but it seemed too businesslike for that. It'd come with a little can of oil, which I applied according to directions, working it into the leather to make the whip sleek and pliable.

Lynch had impressed me with his ability to use the whip, using it to pick up various items from the shelves in the shop in a demonstration of what could be done with it. I wanted to learn to pick things off with it too, and with that in mind I set some pop cans on a box and spent a little time each day attempting to remove the cans with the tip of the whip.

My days were becoming busier since my epiphany at the side of the creek. Lynch was teaching me how to shoot a rifle, a .22 to start with, and Verna was patiently showing me the rudiments of cookery. I was spending a couple of hours most evenings riding, either with Verna or on my own, and I was trying to keep up with my painting. I needed to finish enough canvases for a show in Vancouver in early October. There were still the wood and water chores to be done daily too. Most nights I found myself too tired to read by the light of my new gas lamp; usually I was asleep by ten.

I was tanned, and my hair was to my shoulders. Any fat I'd had anywhere was gone and I had smooth muscles in appropriate places. My hands were callused. I felt marvellous. I'd never paid much attention to my health, taking it for granted as a child does, but now I was aware of the confidence I could have in my body; it was strong and responsive and could do most anything I asked of it. One afternoon I was asking it to handle the whip with perfect dexterity. I'd set up the box with the cans on it in the yard in front of the lodge and was practising my wrist flick and steady arm, intent on my targets.

Hearing a vehicle coming down the road, I began to coil the whip before getting out of the way. Vehicles were rare enough on this highway for me to stop what I was doing to watch it go by. We all watched vehicles, and since everyone knew what everyone else drove, and usually knew where to and why, remarking on who'd gone by and in which direction was as good as reading a newspaper: "Al Adams is back. His truck went by this afternoon and I think I saw a snowmobile in the back. Bet he bought that one Charlie had for sale in Dease Lake." Or, "Did you know Theresa's been going out with that new guy at the BC Rail camp? Saw them in his truck down by Meziadin. Boy! Old Isaac is gonna be mad."

This vehicle was unfamiliar—a new Chevy Blazer. No one I knew of had anything like this. Suddenly it altered course, turning into the yard, and almost before the wheels had quit turning a tall bearded guy with glasses and wild hair leaped out of the truck, leaving the door open in his rush towards me through the cloud of dust. He grabbed my whip from my unresisting hands, saying, "I know how to use this—stand back!"

I did so, standing well to one side as the guy raised his arm over his head and gave a mighty swing of the whip. There was no time to react; the tip came back, neatly whipped his glasses from his face and smacked them onto the gravelled ground, breaking the frames in two and shattering the lenses.

"What happened?" the stranger asked, peering at me. "Where are my glasses?" He looked bewildered and helpless now, despite being a guy of considerable size.

I bent and picked up what was left of his specs, putting the pieces in his hand.

"They're smashed," I told him. "Lucky you didn't take your eye out. Who are you?"

"Jeannie's gonna kill me," was his response, as he held the remains of his glasses close to his eyes. "I was supposed to be back yesterday. You gotta drive me home—right now." He turned to his truck and got in the passenger side, taking my whip with him.

"Where do you live?" I asked, reaching across the seat to grab my whip back without getting into the vehicle. The guy was definitely weird and I wasn't about to go anywhere.

"Come on, come on. Jeannie's gonna be so pissed off at me. Hurry up."

I turned and walked towards the lodge, hearing him stumble

after me. Verna was watching us now from the porch, shading her eyes with one hand, the other holding a dishcloth.

"You okay?" she asked, looking past me to my new almost-acquaintance. "Coming in for coffee?"

"Do you have a radio? I have to call Jeannie." He went past her into the lodge.

"We don't," was Verna's terse reply as she measured his six-foot frame and bulky shape. I could see her figuring out how she was going to handle him if he got any odder. "Why don't you sit down and have a coffee and introduce yourself? I'm Verna Bailey and this is Tor Forsberg," she said. "And you are?"

The man seemed to snap out of his trepidation regarding the mysterious Jeannie and recall some of the niceties of society.

"I'm Leon Fleming. I bought Tatogga Lake Lodge. I have to get back there; I'm in trouble with my wife. Went to Watson Lake to pick up some freight and got a little sidetracked. Can one of you drive me? I got spare glasses there; I can drive you back." He gulped the coffee Verna had set on a table in front of him. "Thanks. Let's go." He was looking at me.

"I'll go. Okay, Verna?" I said, looking at her to see if she thought he was harmless.

She nodded. "I heard some people from the States had bought the place at Tatogga. Come right back so you don't miss dinner."

The drive to Tatogga was about twenty-five minutes, during which I got filled in on the how and why of the Flemings' presence here. Leon had had a farm in Washington state, living there quite happily until he began to get crop circles—those mysterious shapes that sometimes appear stamped into fields. Convinced the symbols were made by aliens, he moved his family to northern BC. No fields here, he thought.

Well, I told him, the Adams brothers have farms here and they grow hay.

Their land isn't flat enough for crop circles, Leon told me, aliens couldn't make them anywhere in this landscape; he and his family would be safe here.

The family consisted of his wife, Jeannie, and three kids. Deb was the oldest at fifteen, followed by Vonda who was twelve and then Brett, ten years old. Jeannie was not at all terrifying; quite the opposite. She was pretty, with blue eyes and black hair and dimples at each end of a wide and welcoming smile. There was no sign of any rage or even mild displeasure at Leon's belated appearance, his broken glasses or his new driver. She insisted I come in for a cold drink and a piece of pie, sending Leon off to find his spare glasses and send the kids in to meet me. The kids were blue-eyed blonds, well mannered and pleasant. I'd never been much interested in children, but these three were appealing; they were excited about their new home and pleased to meet someone else who lived in the area. The family was busy getting settled in and starting up the business, which consisted of cabins to rent, gas pumps and a small café. Everything was attractive and clean, and Jeannie's pie was wonderful.

By the time Leon drove me back to the LV Ranch, I was feeling I'd made new friends and was looking forward to getting to know them.

"Do Not Disturb My *Wa*"

Life on the ranch was getting busier every day. There were the regular daily chores to be done as well as the ongoing task of gathering wood for the winter, and now there was more socializing as the people who lived in the bush full-time emerged from their cabins and began their summer visiting. When guests arrived, people took them around to the other homesteads to meet their friends. The mining exploration companies were now in full swing setting up camps in the wilderness, with geologists, helicopter pilots and cooks—a whole new and interesting population with whom to spend time. There was a gathering almost every night of the week, and a card game was always being played somewhere. I learned to play cribbage and hearts, and found the latter game offered many opportunities to gang up on some hapless player.

During these games tempers sometimes ran high. I was very competitive, playing to win, and not always gracious in defeat. Greg, one of the helicopter pilots, was the same, and our earnest desire to triumph made us great targets for teasing, resulting in a little drama. Greg cut himself with his knife one night while trying to cut the deck of cards in half, and on another occasion I was responsible for the fire going out when I threw the entire deck and the tablecloth into the stove. Such reactions were rare, though thoroughly enjoyed by all the participants except Greg and me. It was an exciting time, and I lost sight entirely of my resolve to be solitary, to read, to explore my spirituality and learn more about who I was and who I could be.

Greg was an avid fisherman and would fly into rivers and lakes to fish when he had the time. Several times I accompanied him and we spent many a happy afternoon catching rainbow trout or grayling in some remote and untouched place, bringing them home for Verna to cook. One hot afternoon, we flew up to the crater of Icy Mountain where we rolled in the snow in our shorts and sandals and had a snowball fight, our shouts echoing from the walls of snow and ice. Life in the bush took on a whole new dimension when there were helicopters around: one could literally get a bird's-eye view of the country, and almost anywhere became accessible.

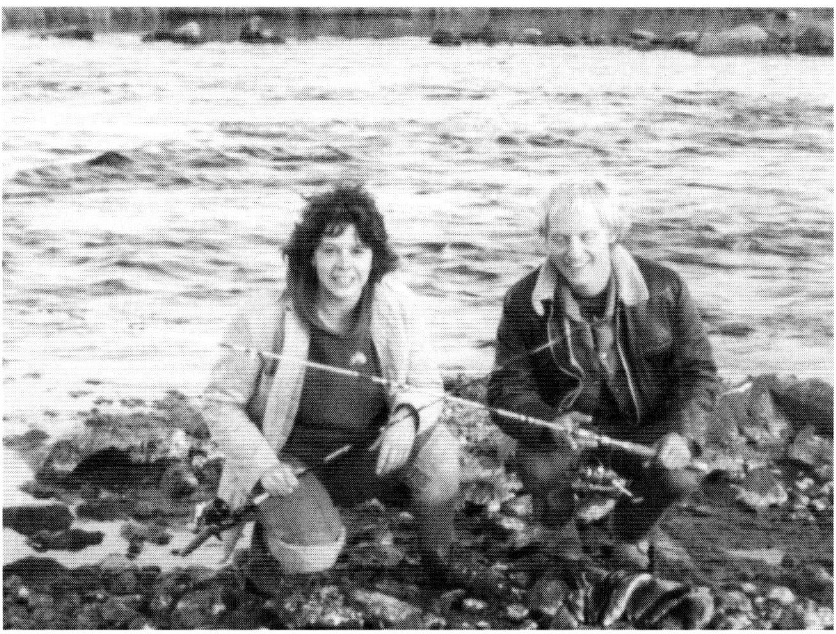

Greg was a helicopter pilot for a mining exploration company, and would often fly us to remote lakes and rivers to fish for grayling.

There was a cook named Karen Ralfs who was working in a camp where her husband, Ken, was a geologist. She was ebullient and fun-loving, a good cook and a good sport. It was her first time cooking in a camp and she loved it despite all the inconvenience, and despite the bears. We became friends during her few and brief visits. They lived in Vancouver and we stayed pals for many years, eventually losing track of one another as our lives took us in different directions. There were many others, many people whose lives intersected with mine that summer. We had some wonderful times together, hiking, fishing, canoeing or sitting around with beer and food and talking, talking, talking. We were all young, with our whole lives ahead of us, and we all had lots of ideas on how those lives were going to look.

Finally, one hungover morning, I recognized I was falling into the same pattern I'd been in while I was staying with my parents in Watson Lake. It was time to withdraw a little, spend more time reading and drawing in my cabin in the evenings and take some solo hikes during the day. It wasn't easy: my cabin had become a bit of a social centre and there was always someone dropping by with a plan, usually a good one, on what to do with a day or an evening.

I'd read about vision quests and resolved to have one. It would be a good way to shake loose of my social life. My new friends respected this endeavour; Verna shook her head with puzzlement and helped me pack.

Kinaskan Lake, a large lake on the highway north of Tatogga, was to be the scene of my quest. I would set up my camp at the extreme south end of the lake, near the creek that connected Kinaskan with the much smaller Tatogga Lake. There was a public campground situated halfway up the lake but it was seldom inhabited—Highway 37, narrow, rough and gravelled, was not much used by tourists in those days. I convinced Verna to drive me there with my gear, including a canoe, and not tell anyone where I was. Tell them I've gone to Watson Lake to see my family, I begged her; I want to be entirely alone for ten days. She reluctantly agreed.

My camp was spartan as befitted my quest: a comfortably sized tent, a thin foam mattress, my sleeping bag, tobacco, lots of drinking water and some herbal tea, books, sketchbook and a bottle of wine with some cheese and crackers with which to celebrate on the tenth day. Verna would come and get me on the eleventh day. When the camp was set up to Verna's satisfaction as well as my own, she left, still mightily puzzled but respectful of my passionately expressed desire to do this. The biggest block to her understanding was that I would be without food. Verna had been feeding me for two months, and having seen my appetite and enjoyment of meals, she could not imagine how or why I would choose not to eat for ten days. Truthfully, that was also my biggest worry, but I knew semi-starvation was part of the key to a successful vision quest.

It was early evening by the time she left, so I built up a nice fire in my carefully placed circle of stones and sat beside it, smoking a hand-rolled cigarette of Drum tobacco and feeling scared and apprehensive. What if a bear came into my camp? What if it rained the entire time? What if I got so weak from hunger that I became ill and died? What if nothing happened in the way of visions or new understandings? I crawled into my sleeping bag before dark to try to read and thus divert myself from startling and sweating with terror at every sound emanating from the surrounding bush. My last thought before I fell asleep was what an incredibly stupid idea this was. I would walk to the road and hitch a ride home tomorrow morning.

Atypically, I really had told no one but Verna what I was doing; there would be no embarrassing explanations of my return.

I woke to the sound of waves on the beach and birds singing. The sun was shining. Thoughts of leaving had vanished; my vision quest had begun.

Each day was spent in full consciousness of every moment

and as such was spent in a state of hyperawareness I've rarely experienced, before or since. By day four, however, I was feeling the effects of not eating. Chilled, I lay around the camp with a fire going despite the warm sun and drank cup after cup of hot water. All that night I dreamed of food, and my foamy didn't feel thick enough. It rained in the night and into the next day. I was in danger of boredom and again wanted to go home. My sweatshirt, heavy with damp, felt like an evil poultice. I lay awake most of the next night with a sense of ashes in my mouth and I had to remind myself to breathe. The next day wasn't much better but I was feeling too listless to make the effort to get back to the ranch. I was in a blue hole, a dim and dreary place, but also incredibly intense. My thoughts felt dark and clotted: was I losing my mind?

The seventh day I woke to find a little mouse sleeping in the crease of my arm. I was lying on my side with my hand under my head and there, inches from my nose, was its tiny brown body. Seconds later the mouse woke up. We looked at one another for a long moment and then the wee creature slid from my arm and went about its mouse business. Ah, the seventh day! I sprang from my sleeping bag full of light and energy. Standing by the lake, I held my arms up to the sun, the wind brushing my palms with dry kisses. Three laughing slender trees tossed their leaves in the air and trembled their pale bodies. A loon was on the lake, the quiet emphasized by its lunatic cries, and some low-flying ducks. Frogs too, mud-coloured with black markings, leaped through the grass at the edge of the lake. Needing to go somewhere other than my camp, I packed a bottle of water and headed for the bush.

My thoughts of the last few days gathered like liquid, flowing down my arms and to my hands. Then the liquid was outside my skin, like water. I shook my hands and felt all the small, sad, cruel and magic thoughts fly in opaque drops to the ground. There was no feeling of fear or alienation as I walked most of the day through the quiet green wilderness as noiselessly as any creature, feeling the woods full of small presences. I saw deer beds high on a lonely hill, and beside a creek fresh cuttings and a webbed print in the mud. I was part of everything I saw, heard and smelled. There was a little meadow, a natural clearing, full of flowers, and everywhere the soft silent reminders of the cautious beings living there. I lay in the centre of it, to gaze at the sky and feel my being fill with peace.

Back in camp before dark, I lit a fire and sat in a state of bliss, smoking a cigarette and drinking herbal tea. My sleep was light but restful, with a deep voice gently humming and talking all through the night. The next day I launched the canoe and spent most of the day on the water, experiencing the same feeling of connection with everything I saw, everything around me. There was no thinking, no reminders of people, places, things, situations—nothing to do with life as I had lived it till now; there was simply being.

On the tenth day I was paddling close to the shore opposite my camp when suddenly there was a human voice in the air.

"Hey! Hello! Hey!" It was awhile before I realized the voice was coming from an actual human, a man waving to me from the shore. There was another man with him; they were hikers from the look of their clothing and gear, and their beards.

"Can you paddle us to the other shore? We've been hiking and we're going to hitch a ride on the road." They began to put on their packs, obviously and not unnaturally expecting me to come over and take them on board. I hesitated, about a hundred feet from shore, sitting in the canoe without paddling while I slowly processed their presence and their request.

"No," I said finally, turning the prow of the craft towards the opposite shore and my camp.

"Come on!" the guy said. "We need to get to the road. It'll take another day to walk around the end of the lake and we're out of food. Why wouldn't you give us a ride?"

"It would disturb my *wa*," I replied, putting my paddle in the water and sliding smoothly away. I forgot about them as soon as my back was turned, slipping easily back into the state of being that my quest had become.

Late that night, my last night, I was sitting beside my fire heating some wine in a tin cup, slowly allowing the fact of my imminent return to the ranch to take root. I felt as though I had been away a long time and gone great distances.

"How's your *wa*?" said a voice from the darkness, abruptly bringing me back to the old reality. I looked up to see two very wet young men dragging two huge wet packs standing by my fire. I indicated they could come and share the fire, which they did with great eagerness and gratitude. I poured wine into their mugs, all without saying a word; I seemed to have lost language in my ten-day pilgrimage.

"We tried to build a raft to float across on," the chatty guy told me, squatting down to warm himself. "It worked, sort of, but not for the whole time. We barely made it here."

Warmed, they both looked at me, clearly curious, and oddly respectful. I thought I must have looked ethereal, somehow, after my fasting and my vanishing into another dimension. Later I realized I simply appeared eccentric at best, and possibly mad as a hatter with my uncombed hair, my sparse camp and my silence and seeming incomprehension of anything they said to me.

By the time the wine was finished, I'd returned, and we spent a pleasant evening exchanging brief histories and expressing our deep pleasure with the pristine wilderness we were enjoying in our various ways. These fellows were from Switzerland. They'd spent the last two weeks hiking in the Spatsizi Range and were incredulous at the size and depth of the wilderness. I listened, offering nothing of my own recent experience of being with the wild; it was too close, too personal to share. They slept beside my fire, and in the morning Verna arrived to take us all back to the lodge and feed us an enormous breakfast, no questions asked.

The quest, if told in detail, would be a book unto itself. Suffice to say it changed me, shifting my view of the natural world in some fundamental way and imbuing me with a longing that has never left me to experience the world in that particular way. It also affected how I was with people. I found myself being more aware of others, of their endless nuances and possibilities. I was even more curious about them, yet at the same time more distanced somehow. I was more peaceful in myself, more prepared to deal with my life and to create from it something that was real to me.

The Pull of the Land

Verna was gone, back to Fort St. John to her husband and their ranch. LV Ranch wasn't the same without her and I missed her taciturn presence and her wonderful cooking. Left on our own, Lynch and I took turns trying to make dinner at the lodge. Neither of us was very good at it, with Lynch leaning to moose stew all the time and me resorting to opening tins of soup. Our bread was white bread from the co-op store in Iskut, a sad and tasteless substitute for Verna's fresh crusty loaves, and there were no cookies or pies. Visitors were infrequent now with the mining camps closed up, the personnel having gone back to the cities and their lives there, and the local folks were readying for the winter. There was less traffic on the road.

Lynch lasted about a week before moving a woman from the village and her small son into the lodge. Susan's cooking wasn't a whole lot better than ours, but we were relieved to have someone else doing it, and she and her boy added more life to the ranch. They also diverted Lynch from his frequent visits to my cabin where he would sit and drink endless cups of tea, interrupting my painting. Since the quest, my painting had flowed, peculiarly slow, but sweet, like familiar sex. I was pleased with the results and wanted to be spending most of the day filling canvas after canvas.

Lynch was a sociable old fellow. I knew he sought me out

more for the comfort of another human being than for our commonalities, and I recognized we needed one another to survive in this isolated place. But I was glad to have Susan busy in the lodge, with Lynch drinking his tea there with her and her boy.

It was time to hunt meat for the winter. There were caribou on the low hills beside the ranch and Lynch was riding up every evening to pick out his steaks and roasts. One evening he banged on my door; he needed me to come with him to fetch down two caribou he'd shot. We would take the stoneboat and the team. I agreed to go. I was curious, and after all, I ate the caribou and moose and enjoyed it—it was only fair that I participate in some way in the harvesting. Although I grew up in the Yukon, my bush pilot father was not a hunter. This was rare; most people hunted their meat in those days because of the high cost of food in the North, with everything having to come by truck up the Alaska Highway. Any game meat eaten by our family had been a gift. I had learned to shoot and to handle a rifle, but I'd never shot anything other than targets and had not experienced any desire to kill anything, even for food. Hence, I was a bit apprehensive about seeing and handling freshly killed animals, feeling my dread build as we approached the place they lay.

They looked smaller than I'd imagined, and infinitely pathetic, their slender legs stilled, their dark eyes clouded. Determined to actively participate in what I knew was a vital part of living here, I helped load their still-warm bodies onto the stoneboat, my teeth and my gut clenched in an effort to control my sorrow. I chose to walk behind rather than ride on top of them, as Lynch suggested when we started down to the lodge. He stood to drive the team, clucking and encouraging the mares as they pulled the load over the rough ground. We were almost there when, to my horror, I saw one of the animals twitching. I screamed at Lynch, startling the horses and forcing him to brace himself on the upright posts as he sawed at the reins to stop them. When he understood what I was going on about, his surprise was obvious. Without letting go of the reins, he handed me an axe. Automatically I took it from him, understanding what he expected me to do but knowing I would be unable to do it. I dropped the axe and turned away, weeping. Lynch had to tie the team up, get the axe and deliver the killing blow himself while I stood there trying not to hear the sound and feeling sick to my stomach with grief.

He didn't ask me to help with the butchering; Susan and her son were more than willing and able. From my cabin where I lay in the dark, feeling ashamed and embarrassed, I could hear the three of them laughing as they worked into the night.

The experience made me more determined to learn and be a part of the hunting. When the first of the caribou meat was served, did I refuse it? The sadness and regret I'd felt when we brought them down the mountain was nowhere in evidence when the succulent slices were placed on my plate. I ate gladly; I ate with gratitude, which made it even more important to overcome my squeamishness. I began again to practise with a rifle and told Lynch I wanted to go with him when he went moose hunting. Ever patient, he agreed, saying nothing of the caribou incident.

A week later I got my shot. Lynch came to tell me there was a young bull moose across the creek with my name on him. It could hardly be more convenient, with no long ride or hike—the moose was visible from the lodge porch. Walking on the road, we crossed the creek, over the culvert and down the other side. I put the rifle to my shoulder, took a deep breath and shot the moose, which dropped immediately. Lynch told me it was a fine shot. I felt a thrill of excitement and accomplishment—I'd got meat for the winter! Almost running through the buckbrush, I was first at the scene. The creature died as I watched, the light literally leaving its eyes. I fell on my knees and vomited until I couldn't bring anything else up. Susan, arriving with a washtub and knives, quietly began to gut the animal. Lynch watched her for a moment and then came over to me, saying, "Get up now, Sis; there's work to be done." There was a note in his voice that brooked no argument. I staggered to my feet, opening my buck knife, and began to help Susan.

It was a long and gruelling business, and the longer I did it, the more cheerful I felt. Soon all three of us were talking and laughing. I understood the laughing—here was food, and we were grateful.

⮝

It was time for me to leave the LV Ranch. I was to have my first show in Vancouver, and afterwards I'd planned to stay on there to attend some classes at the Vancouver School of Art. Tee had business in Vancouver, so we would rent an apartment. He'd also planned to go to Mexico and Guatemala for a couple of months that winter to explore Mayan and Aztec ruins. He wanted me to go with him, and when we'd first discussed it, back in Watson Lake, I'd been eager to go. I'd been happy to think of living in Vancouver—my few visits till now had shown it to be a beautiful, exciting city with a lot to offer a budding artist. Now, looking around my little cabin, I didn't want to go anywhere. There was a life here different than anything I'd ever imagined for myself and I was only just beginning to experience it.

Tee arrived, and for the next couple of days the subject of my return to the ranch was foremost. I could not leave without some assurance of coming back. Tee finally came up with a plan: with help from Lynch, we would stake some land and make an application for a homestead. Lynch would cut logs for us and in the spring we could come and build a cabin. It seemed perfect; why was there still a niggling doubt, a sensation of not-quite-right? I disregarded this quiver in favour of being pleased and excited about the idea of actually building a log cabin to live in.

The site was as beautiful as could be, about three miles from 40 Mile Flats, where Lynch's place was. There were lots of tall trees and a magnificent view of Mount Edziza, which would be framed by our picture window.

Our trip south was delayed while we went to the Kinaskan Lake area to choose the huge pine trees that would become our home. By the time we left I was more prepared to make a departure, though something still nagged at me. There was no time to track this feeling. We were driving south, with the back of the station wagon crammed full of my canvases, and I was suddenly aware that I had nothing to wear but old jeans and T-shirts. There was some serious shopping to be done as soon as we arrived.

The shopping, the meetings with the curator for the exhibit, the finding of a suitable apartment, the enrolling for classes at the school, the making of travel arrangements, the getting together with my summer friends as well as some of Tee's business associates—all these activities swept me up for the next couple of months. Iskut and the LV Ranch, and my friends there, were never far from my thoughts, however, and often I would find myself feeling suddenly alien, and bereft, knowing deep inside that I was not in the right place.

The feeling was never allowed room; I'd squash it down, telling myself not to be a fool. My show had been a success, getting noticed in appropriate places and resulting in more shows. I was having a wonderful time with a man I adored in a place that was stimulating and offered endless opportunities for pleasure and amusement. We had lots of interesting people to spend time with and a very nice apartment to live in. We had money enough to do most anything we wished to do, including skiing at Whistler and going to Seattle for weekends of music and dining.

The trip to Mexico started in November and lasted till March. Tee rented us a house in Puerto Madero, Chiapas, a place for me to paint while he went off on jaunts to various ruins in Guatemala across the border. I'd accompanied him for the first few weeks but my interest waned after a few jungle-covered sites, and I wanted to paint. The little house was perfect. A toothless old woman came in every day to pass a broom around and fill the cistern. She was usually accompanied by children—until the day I started a canvas of a woman with a halo, wearing a leotard and straddling a cross, after which she came unaccompanied, threw a cloth over that painting and crossed herself. Despite that particular piece, she seemed fond of me and made certain I remembered to eat, bringing fruit and fish for my icebox. When I became very ill with the inevitable tourist response to Mexico, she was as tender and caring as a mother.

We were the only tourists then living in the little village that was to become another major tourist destination in the coming years. At this time it was a weekend getaway place for the folks in Tapachula. Our house on the beach was courtesy of Luis Pedrero, who ran a Dodge dealership in Tapachula and had befriended us when he learned of Tee's interest in ancient archeology. He rented us the house (the old woman came with it) for $40 a month. There was no running water, just a cistern in the kitchen and one in the bathroom, and the electricity in the village was, for some reason I never ascertained, available only for the hour before the tropical night fell like a curtain of dark.

When Luis learned of my liking for horseback riding, he arranged a horse for me, which was kept in a shed behind the house. I am not likely to forget some of the magic mornings I had with that horse. I named him Marcus. He was bright brown, quick and eager, well-trained but not "broke." I would ride only early in the morning, when it was cool, and Marcus and I would go for miles on the beach, with the sun coming up and the fishermen anchoring their boats on the reef. After brushing Marcus and feeding and watering him, I would go for a swim. I swam again in the evening after putting Marcus in his shed.

There were times I saw shark fins breaking the surface of the sea between the shore and the reef. As this was before the movie *Jaws* was made, I merely stood in the water waiting for them to move off before going swimming.

When the fishermen came in they anchored their boats out on the reef. I never knew why they did this, but the habit made for a picturesque scene when the women and children came down to the sea and swam out to meet the men who were floating their catch in to the beach using inner tubes and barrels.

The restaurants were for Mexicans, not tourists, and as such were very plain places with tables and chairs often simply set in the sand of the beach, with chickens roosting on the backs of the chairs. The food was simple and delicious and of course so inexpensive that we rarely ate a meal from our own kitchen. My Spanish didn't improve as quickly as I'd hoped, living in a wee place where few of the residents spoke English, because Luis would come with his friends every weekend to visit and practise their English.

Before returning to Canada, Tee and I spent a month travelling around Mexico and Guatemala, sometimes renting vehicles, sometimes riding buses, just exploring and enjoying the wonderful country and its friendly people. In the midst of the novelty of my surroundings and the novelty of my still-new relationship, I found myself thinking of Iskut, the LV Ranch and the hush of the land—I had not gone so far I couldn't feel the pull of the land. This feeling was new to me. I had so far always been entirely in the moment, rarely thinking of what was behind me and only sometimes wondering what lay ahead. The idea that I could make decisions about my future, that I could plan, was almost foreign to someone in the habit of "going with the flow."

Back in Vancouver I attended only a few classes before recognizing what I could no longer ignore: I really wanted—needed—to go back to Iskut. Tee had to get back to his business in Watson Lake. The manager he'd hired for the store was ready to move on and Tee had to take over again. He also had some mining interests that needed his attention. I knew he wanted me to stay in Watson Lake with him, but by the time we were there I could scarcely sit still, so restless was I to get back out to the bush.

There was still some snow on the ground when I headed down the Stewart-Cassiar Highway. My relationship was being left in less than ideal circumstances; there were a lot of issues needing some attention and discussion, but all I could think about was going home.

Beaverin' and the Second Grizzly

It was all just as I had left it, including my cabin, as though everything had stopped, frozen, until my return. Settling back into my little space, placing familiar objects in their accustomed places, I knew this was where I was supposed to be.

Verna wasn't there, and there was some doubt as to whether she would be coming up that summer, I understood, and Susan and her boy had moved back to the village. Lynch was happy to see me. He'd been on his own for a couple of weeks by the time I drove into the yard after hours of dirty, sometimes scary, driving. There'd been no improvement in the road; enormous potholes made the journey treacherous, and although the road was mostly bare, the melting snow had made the surface slick in places and muddy everywhere.

The inevitable bachelor stew was on the wood stove with a pan of Lynch's deliciously greasy bannock to break into chunks and dip in the gravy; I ladled myself a big bowl of it, sitting at the table with a sigh of pure contentment. The much-anticipated stew didn't taste like one of Lynch's—it wasn't bad, exactly, just different. Thinking my memories had assumed a rosy glow over the winter, I ate it anyway, listening to Lynch catch me up on all the goings-on of the area.

He needed to go out beaverin', he told me. I gathered that Verna's departure meant the cash flow was drying up: he needed some money. A young fellow from Fort St. John, a friend of the family, was on his way north to go out in the bush with him. I was mustering up a really good argument to persuade him to let me go too, when he beat me to the draw.

"Could use another hand, Sis, if you want to come along."

I was ecstatic—I was going into the bush! Of course I wouldn't trap, I told him; I considered it cruel, but I would wrangle horses and cook. With this Lynch seemed content.

Later, going out the back door on the way to my cabin, I noticed a carcass hanging on the porch. I didn't recognize the animal, though clearly it'd been eaten—there were missing bits that indicated the more palatable pieces had been carved off. Feeling slightly apprehensive, I went back into the lodge to inquire what the stew had contained.

"Lynx," my old friend told me, raising an eyebrow. "Not bad, huh?"

I exited quickly, feeling my stomach roil. I'd eaten cat, for God's sake! I had eaten a predator. Nothing would take the taste from my mouth or deaden the thought of the meal except a good stiff drink.

The fire warmed the cabin while I sat outside, bundled in a blanket, drinking whisky and warm water and staring at the night sky sprinkled with stars. My mind was buzzing with excitement. There was no thought of painting for my next show, or Tee or anything but the immense wilderness surrounding me and the opportunity I had been given to explore it more deeply.

Why didn't I miss Tee? We were a relatively new couple, still with a lot to learn about one another. There was certainly enjoyment of each other—the sex was awesome, and there was never a shortage of things to discuss. He was very supportive of my painting, and he didn't seem to object to my desire to be so removed from where he needed to be at this time. He was planning on living at

Iskut with me at some point, hence the arrangement with Lynch to get logs for our cabin. Those logs were right now lying at the site we'd chosen, waiting to be peeled. This was to be my task when everything had thawed and the sap would make the job easier.

At times I felt a bit like an indulged child; there was often an aura of amusement emanating from Tee when I was being dreadfully earnest or really excited. I'd felt some resentment about it, but not enough to take issue—after all there was an age difference of over twenty years between us. A large part of my original attraction to Tee was his well-known familiarity with the bush. He'd trapped, built cabins, prospected and worked a claim in the Nahanni area, which was one of the wildest in a wild country. He was a man who knew how to survive in the bush, a kind of Marlboro Man of the North. Indeed, that was how I'd once described him to friends back east when I was trying to explain leaving my marriage. Why he was attracted to me was sometimes a puzzle; at twenty-three when we met I was naive, despite a veneer of recently acquired sophistication from my five years of marriage, of living in Montreal and doing some travelling in Europe and the Caribbean. I'd gone virtually from living at home with my family to being married to living at home again with my family; in hindsight, I wasn't all that interesting. I'm guessing what I was to Tee was a novelty—a novelty that became more important to him than he'd anticipated. What he became to me was yet to be understood.

At this moment all I could think about was what to pack for the coming adventure.

▲

We were on our way! Dwayne had arrived the night before, a skinny young kid of about fifteen who was every bit as excited as I was about the trek, but was trying to conceal it and be very cool. Compared with me, he was useful: he was a ranch kid and could handle horses, and he'd done some trapping. Setting out were the three of us, our three riding horses, four pack horses and Patsy the dog.

The packing of the horses was a mystery to me. I had, against all expectations, slept in, and Lynch had all the red-painted wooden panniers packed when I got up and was tying the diamond hitch over tarps and various other items on top of the panniers. The knot was beautifully conceived—the resulting diamond shape in the rope at the top of the load held everything snugly in place.

I saddled Flame, remembering to check the cinch again before mounting. It'd taken a slipped saddle and a nasty fall the summer before to teach me that Lynch knew what he was doing when it came to saddling up. My belongings were all tied to my saddle: one sleeping bag and a small canvas carryall containing my few toiletries, spare jeans and T-shirts, a rain jacket, a flask of rum and seventy pieces of bubble gum. It was cold; I was glad of my quilted jacket and a scarf around my neck. The breath from the horses hung frosted in the air.

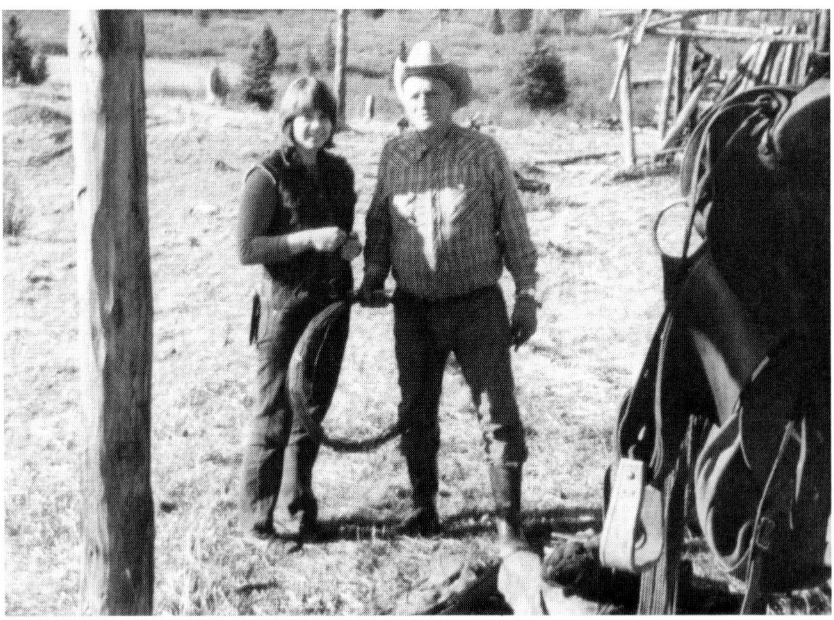

I was a novice in all aspects of trapping even when it came to saddling up, but Lynch was a master and always willing to share his expertise.

The first part of the ride was along the highway; I kept wishing somebody would drive by and be struck with wonder at the sight of us. We were "all strung out," Lynch said. Contrary to my understanding of the phrase, in bush language this was a good thing—it meant everything and everyone was in order, and the horses were not fighting for a place in the line, which, I was to learn, was a frequent occurrence at the beginning of such journeys.

Soon we were off the road and following a route only Lynch could see. The sun was shining and we were able to take off our jackets and tie them to our saddles. Conversation was difficult. We were riding single file, with Lynch leading, me right behind him and Dwayne at the end, making sure the pack horses were moving well and not irritated with their packs. The bush was just getting green with new leaves; there was a smell of mingled green and snow. The only sound other than birds was the creak of the packs and saddles and the occasional chuffing of a horse.

We stopped on a bluff to make a little fire for tea. The horses

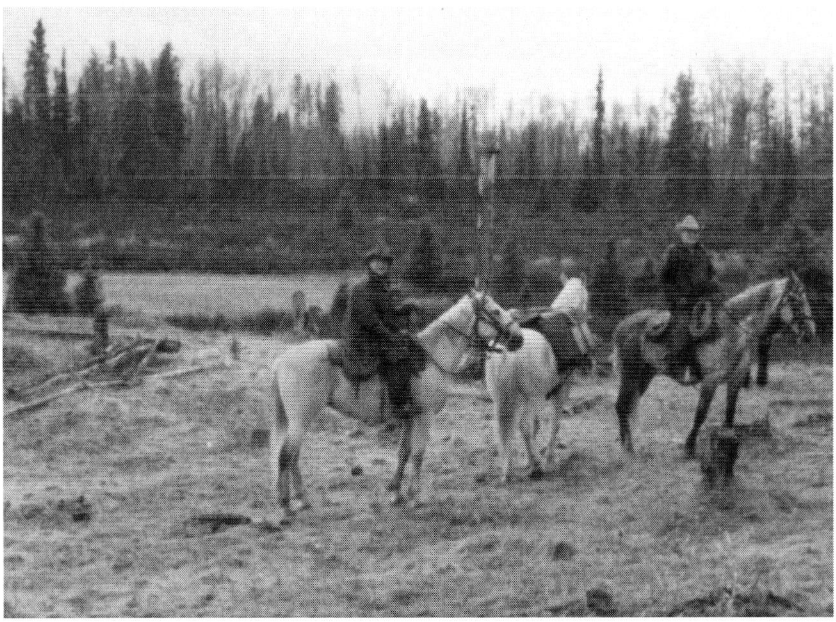

We travelled with three riding horses and four pack horses to carry the gear.

stood quietly, nibbling at the ground as we lounged around the flames drinking tea and chewing on some of Lynch's bannock. Below us the wilderness spread out as far as we could see, unmarked by any sign of man. The mountains, their snow-topped peaks gleaming in the sun, stood as sentinels all around, with streams of melting ice forming myriad waterfalls down their sides. There was an indescribable sort of hush over everything. I felt very small, and very intrusive, somehow. Where was the feeling of connectedness I'd experienced during my vision quest? I had been so certain I would find it again and slip into it like a comfortable coat.

Lynch and Dwayne had rifles in scabbards hanging from their saddles and there were traps in the panniers: was it our intentions that made me feel our alien status here? Although I was in some way disappointed at the difference in what I was feeling at being in the wilderness this time, I recognized the obvious differences in the two journeys, giving over to what was clearly going to be a whole new experience. I thoroughly enjoyed the ride as we went deeper and deeper into the bush.

Lynch was only about twenty feet in front of me when suddenly his horse sank into the ground. I stopped at the edge of what looked to be a bit of marsh with a shallow creek running through it, watching in amazement as Lynch sort of frog-stroked his way back to shore on the surface of the water while Buck thrashed his way to the opposite side, where he stood with his sides heaving, dripping muck.

"Figured the ground was still frozen," Lynch explained as he slapped mud and water from his clothes. "If we can't find another spot to cross, we're gonna have to rope 'em across."

The pack horses had begun to bunch up and move restlessly, their ears up and heads jerking as they looked at Buck across the creek. Lynch sent Dwayne off on foot to find a way through the heavy bush to where Buck stood patiently waiting. For awhile we got split up while Lynch took my horse and tried to find a way across; I stayed with the pack horses. It was creepy, this place where suddenly you didn't know solid ground from muck. We ended up with Dwayne throwing a rope across and Lynch tying it to a pack horse who then reluctantly crossed, up past his belly in the icy water, with Dwayne pulling on the rope. Thus we crossed not just this bog, but also so many others I lost count. I alternated between being worried and being excited with the drama of it all. I didn't notice or care that I was shaking with wet and cold as I kept saying, "Isn't this great?" with each painstaking crossing.

By the time we reached the beaver camp, about eleven o'clock at night, we were exhausted. Although I was still babbling with the sheer energy of it all, I was as glad as anyone to have arrived and be off the horse. My knee was swollen: Flame had hit me against a tree at some point and while I hadn't paid much attention at the time, the injury was now painful. Walking was difficult after so many hours astride, but the horses had to be tended to before anything could be done about the discomfort of the people.

The horses were stripped of their gear and, after being given a tobacco can of oats, they were turned loose to graze. They were

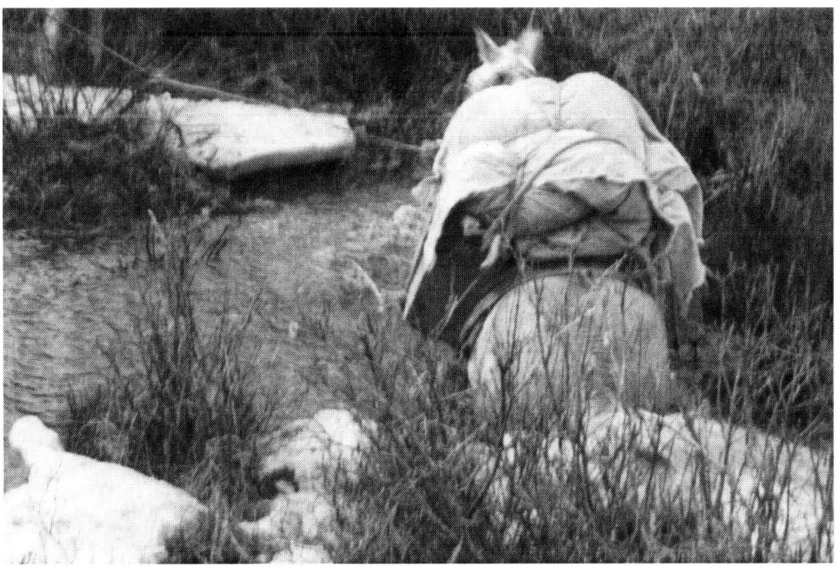

The pack horses were not always willing followers—sometimes a little encouragement was needed.

hobbled, and bells on heavy canvas straps were put around their necks. Lynch told me one of my jobs would be to round them up tomorrow morning; the bells meant they'd be easy to find, he said, and the hobbles meant they would not be able to go too far. We then built a fire and ate cans of stew and more bannock, all washed down with tea. After our meal we wanted to simply loll around the fire but there was still a lot to be done.

The camp was called Spruce Island Camp and had been built in the early 1900s. Most of the buildings had rotted and fallen in but there was one cabin, the largest, that was still marginally livable. Lynch sent me in to clean it up while he and Dwayne unpacked the traps. A low ceiling and the coming night made the inside difficult to see properly, but there was a feeling of recent inhabitants—everything looked as though someone was living there and had just stepped out for a moment. The furniture consisted of two narrow box beds built right into the wall, and a table and chair. A cupboard built into a corner revealed a lining made of

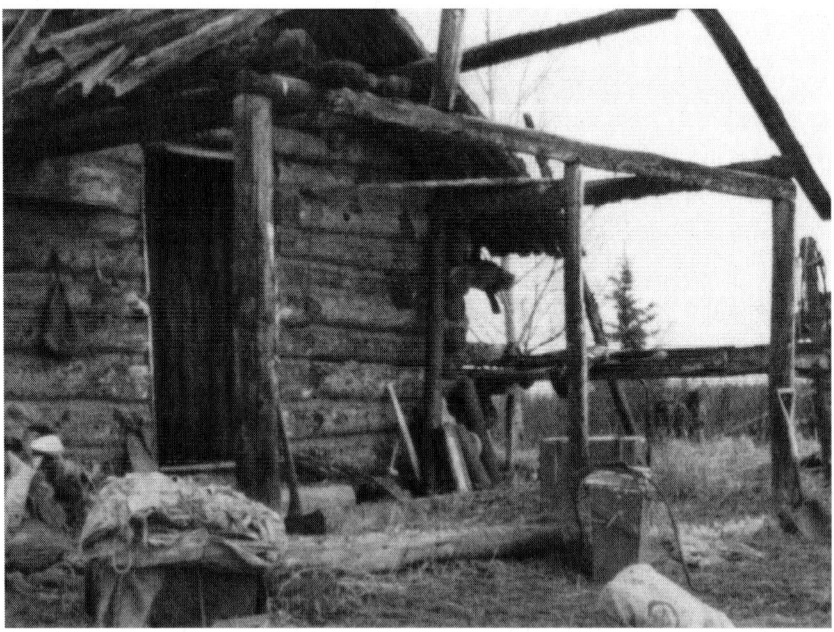

The cabin at Spruce Island Camp was built in the early 1900s, and was not exactly a luxury hotel.

flattened tin cans and contained a cloth bag of something mealy, which looked like some dried meat. Every bit of wood was hand-hewn, including the rough floor planks. There were dishes on the table and a pile of what looked like letter paper, with a pencil lying beside it. Feeling like a trespasser, I picked up the papers to find most of them were drawings of women's genitalia—clumsily done, but unmistakable. There was one stained piece of paper with writing on it, and just before I read it, I noticed there was a trap door in the floor of the cabin. The message made my hair stand on end: *I'm sick. Whoever finds me I want to be berryd at Telegraph Creek and tel Maggy.*

Stumbling from the cabin, I ran to where the guys were sorting gear. I waved the paper at Lynch and babbled about a door in the floor and a dead body. He read the paper with a suitably solemn air, though he couldn't hide the quirk at the corner of his mouth. Dwayne looked almost as scared as I was feeling, and he elected to stay behind when Lynch went with me to check out the

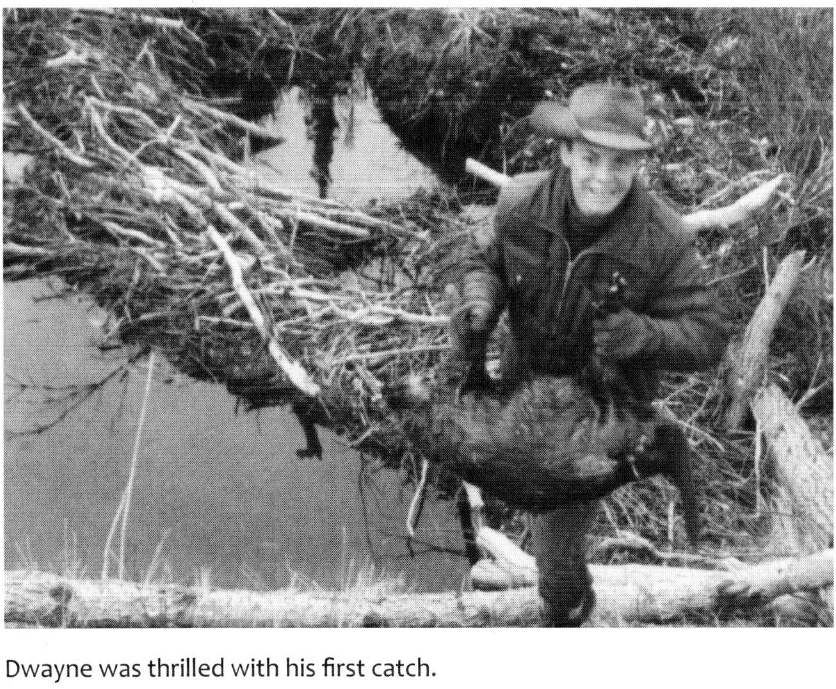

Dwayne was thrilled with his first catch.

trap door. I didn't go in the almost dark interior as Lynch lifted the trap door, the leather hinges creaking, and peered down.

"It's a crawl space," he told me. "Ain't a damn thing down there. Must be ol' Dick's handwriting; he spent a winter trapping here a few years ago, but I've seen him since, hale and hearty." I handed him my flashlight and stood behind him as he shone it down into the dirt and debris. There was nothing there, just as he said.

By the time we got to bed it was well past midnight. Lynch chose the bed full of straw and Dwayne got the floor with two foamies to cushion him. I got the featherbed, which I know was

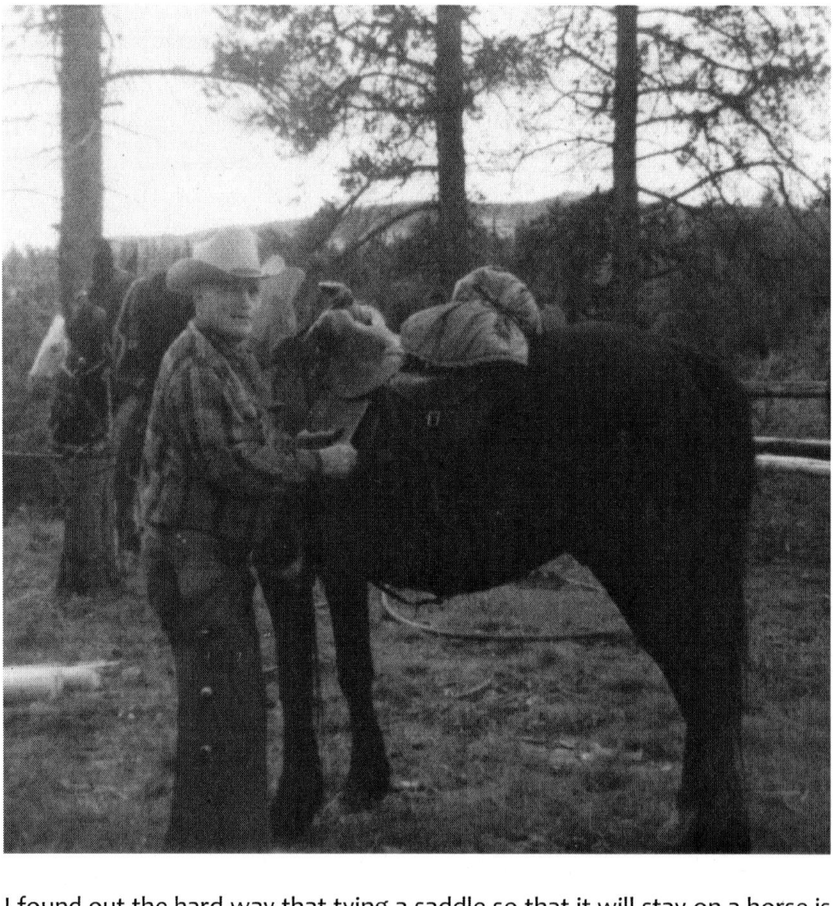

I found out the hard way that tying a saddle so that it will stay on a horse is not as easy as it looks. I learned to pay attention to Lynch's lessons.

really a mouse apartment house, but by the time I got into it I wouldn't have cared if it'd been stuffed with a live bear.

▲

We were up early the next morning, Dwayne and I awakened by the sound of Lynch banging metal as he cobbled together a stove out of half a gas drum on a washtub. Lynch sent us off to fetch the horses while he made bacon and bannock.

I could hear the bells; they were quite far off, and the going was rough through the buckbrush and swamp as we followed the sound. It was difficult to imagine how they could have gone so far hobbled, but I was to learn they were remarkably adept at getting around regardless of their shackles. The horses were not anxious to get to work and made the catching of them a difficult and frustrating task. By the time we had them back at camp, Dwayne and I had become friends from our shared efforts and our mutual dislike of these old bush-wise horses.

Lynch had eaten and was stretched out sleeping beside the fire with his cowboy hat over his face. He woke to tell us that if we were going to get any trapping done we'd have to learn to catch the horses a whole lot quicker than we had this morning. And we didn't need to have brought them all in—only three were needed today. Dwayne, embarrassed, ate his food quickly and set to work saddling up two horses and packing another one with the traps while Lynch continued to doze. They left me with Patsy, and a .30-30 rifle. The silence closed in, the sounds of their departure swallowed by the underbrush.

I had the camp cleaned up half an hour after they rode out and was looking forward to the rest of the day on my own, reading a book maybe, or going for a walk—once I had thoroughly checked out the area. I took the precaution of finding a climbable tree and doing a practice climb. My fear of bears ran deep and surfaced the moment I was in the bush.

The outhouse was dilapidated but useable; the roof had half-fallen in, there was bright orange mold on the seat and no door. The view from the seat was beautiful. A walk around the camp told me why it was named Spruce Island—it was entirely surrounded by bog, and there were no discernible trails, at least not to my untrained eye.

The weather changed: it began snowing and blowing, with more snow than blow. Clearly it was to be an indoor day. Deciding to surprise the fellows with a good dinner when they returned, I unpacked the panniers. There was tea, sugar, flour, a can of bacon, some lard, baking powder and a large bag of rice. I sorted through everything again, a feeling of panic building as I realized that the meagre store of provisions in front of me was all the food Lynch had brought!

I spent the afternoon lying on my bed with the fire roaring, chewing bubble gum and trying to read. It was the kind of day I could have spent anywhere at any time. Surely there was going to be more than this? Late in the afternoon I went to use the outhouse, taking with me a sock I'd decided to try to mend.

I'd worn contact lenses since they became available; they were a boon for someone with eyesight as poor as mine, and I took to wearing them with no difficulty. However I didn't wear them when I was just hanging out at home, and I had not put them in for this day of hanging around the camp, choosing my glasses instead. In the outhouse, I had taken my glasses off and placed them next to me as I sat on the worn seat and squinted at my sewing effort. I was peering at the needle and wool, holding them about two inches from my nose, when I noticed there was a large dark shape crossing outside the non-door of the biffy. One of the horses, I thought to myself—the horses had been hobbling in and out of the area all day, perhaps in hope of oats.

It was a gradual dawning of understanding: it couldn't be a horse because it wasn't hopping like a hobbled horse and there was no sound of a bell. Feeling only mildly curious, I put my glasses on. Immediately I wished I hadn't. The great dark thing perambulating past was a grizzly bear! The bear gave no indication of awareness of my presence, but continued to simply sniff around.

The roof! I thought. I'll climb up on the roof. It's got to be safer than sitting here like an offering of dessert in a bakery window. I slowly, slowly got myself standing on the seat, a position that gave me good access to what remained of the roof. I began to pull myself up. Many things happened simultaneously in the next few seconds.

The bear looked at me as I struggled to get up on the layer of small poles that constituted the roof of the outhouse.

The roof fell in, with what seemed like a thunderous noise.

Lynch and Dwayne rode into the clearing.

The bear took off at a gallop.

It took the guys several minutes to extricate me from the jumble of poles and boards, and it didn't help that the two of them were laughing so hard they could scarcely breathe. I had gone into a frigid state of fear, my body so numb the guys had to pull me from the wreckage, and my head was filled with the sound of dull roaring. The laughter snapped me out of what was feeling like a place of no return, and the searing anger that took its place was healing for me and sobering for my companions. Leaving me to stomp and yell out my rage and fear, they went about the business of unpacking the horses and readying them to be turned loose. By the time they had built up the fire and were cooking dinner, I was ready to sit with them.

Lynch wanted to know why I hadn't fired a warning shot at the bear. I mumbled about the rifle being in the cabin; it had not occurred to me to take it with me. Lynch took his rifle everywhere, even laying it alongside his sleeping bag at night. Naturally they told and retold one another the tale all that evening, laughing harder with each telling. I was silent, chewing on my bubble gum and refusing to eat the squirrels they'd cooked for dinner. My gum was going to be rationed now. Clearly we would be living off the land, and trying not to look at the tiny carcasses roasting over the fire, I decided that meant I would not be eating much.

McGinty and McGinnis

My night was not a peaceful one: the bear dreams came back, accompanied by more music and lyrics from *The Sound of Music* and a cold, foul sweat. There was no going back to the ranch. Without asking him, I knew Lynch would not take me back, and Dwayne didn't know the way. Even if I had been able to navigate my own return, the thought of being alone in the bush was insupportable. I was beaverin', and I'd have to come to terms with the wild and actively participate in the hunt. Lynch brought me along on the understanding I would be useful.

Watching the guys prepare to check the traps in the morning, I remembered the time Tee and I had come across a rabbit in one of Lynch's traps. It was a sickening sight, the wild eyes and the desperate, futile leaping and thrashing to escape. I felt my own heart hammering with terror. I wanted Tee to let it go, but he pointed out that its hind leg was likely broken—letting it go would not be a mercy. He killed it, using a heavy stick; I'll never forget the wet crunch as it hit and the jellied little body afterwards.

Before going to the LV Ranch I'd never thought about trapping. I knew people who did it, naturally enough, growing up in the Yukon, but I'd never asked them about it. Now it was a fact of my present life and I knew I had to come to some sort of terms with it. My stance seemed like a kind of hypocrisy—after all, I happily ate game, including rabbit. Besides, I couldn't stay in camp by myself now after seeing the bear. The rifle was no comfort; I would likely do no more than irritate the bear with a wild misplaced shot should it come calling again.

Dwayne rode out to catch Flame for me while Lynch waited, muttering about greenhorns and kids. It was wonderful to be riding again. After picking our way through the muskeg surrounding the "island," we were still surrounded by the particular devastation created by the beaver: miles of stumps, with rotting trunks pointing downhill. The air was so fresh, so fragile—like newly born air. We startled a moose and her calf just outside the camp. My horse jumped and nearly unseated me, causing the pack horse I was leading to throw a little fit, which in turn caused Lynch to look over his shoulder and glare at me.

I spent the next few hours trying to be quiet and useful. At my first sight of the traps, however, I simply had to talk. They were

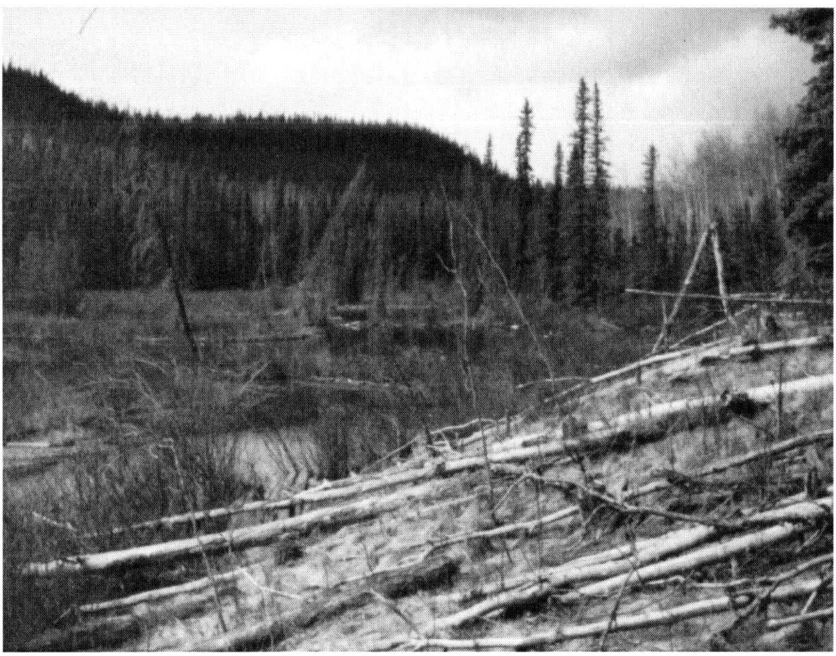

A beaver can alter an area dramatically, but what's left behind creates ideal moose habitat.

square and didn't look anything like the traps I'd seen around the ranch—the kind that had captured the rabbit.

"They're Conibears," Lynch explained, his love for imparting knowledge overcoming his irritation with me. "They're a kill trap." He pulled one side of the square shape down and clicked something. "The beaver touches this frame anywhere at all and . . . ," he said, touching it with a stick, "Whap! His neck is broken."

I mulled this over—a trap that didn't cause suffering, a trap that instantly and humanely killed the animal. Surely I could sort of get behind this and therefore become more a part of this endeavour? I decided I could, and I spent the rest of the time thoroughly fascinated as the traps were checked and the carcasses loaded onto the pack horse.

"Spring trapping beaver," Lynch told me, "you only want to

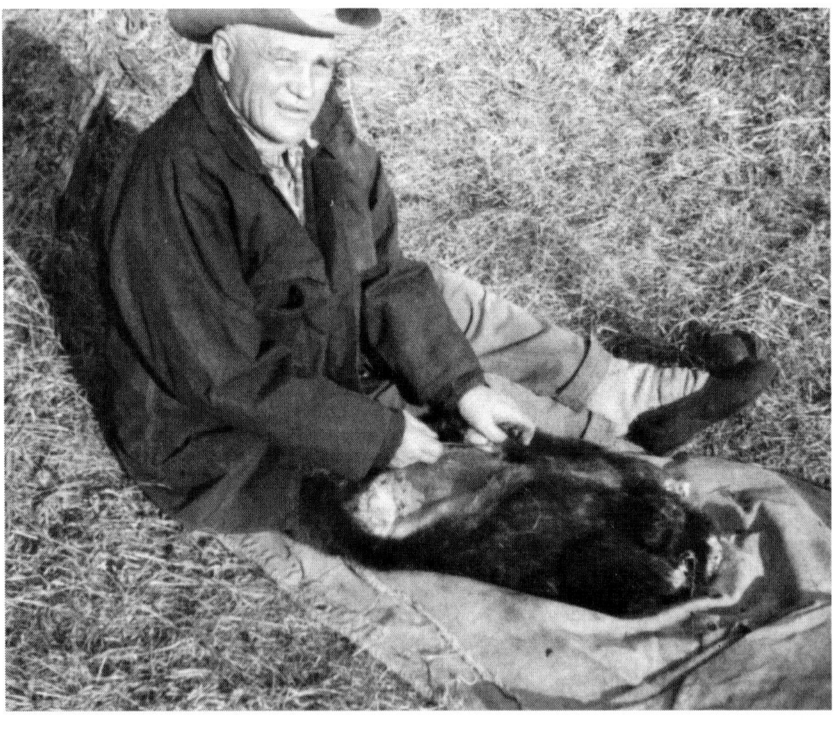

Lynch showing us how to skin a beaver the hard way—on a tarp on the ground.

get the males; the females are pregnant, so you gotta know where to set." He showed me the trails to the water. "You don't set on any trails close to the beaver house cuz that's where the ladies are. You set a good distance away, or on the dam." To attract a beaver to a drowning trap on the dam, Lynch peeled a few twigs and scattered them around the set. "Beaver thinks another beaver is poaching on his area," he explained.

The drowning trap was just that: a leghold trap on a cable sunk in the water. The beaver would get his front or back leg caught and then dive into the water. A hook on the cable ensured he could not surface again. I was not so happy about this trap, needless to say, but I could hardly start to nitpick now, so I stood on the dam paying rapt attention. Rapt attention-paying was a surefire way to get on Lynch's good side, and I was deeply interested in being on that side in these circumstances. And it was interesting—somewhat gruesome in parts, but definitely a novel experience.

It was also hard work. None of the sets were in a situation that made it easy to check them, and the carcasses were heavy and had to be hauled to where the pack horse stood patiently waiting to be burdened. We got back to camp in mid-afternoon. The guys drank tea while I unsaddled the horses and put all the gear under a tarp: it was raining. I fed the horses and "hobbled 'em up and belled 'em out," as Lynch referred to the task. Then Lynch showed Dwayne how to skin a beaver. I watched, vowing to give it a try tomorrow. Now I knew what all the pieces of old plywood were for, I thought, watching as Lynch tacked a round pelt to the wood with little nails.

That night we ate beaver meat—hind legs, boiled in a big cast iron pot with rice. I was hungry enough to try it and found it tasted like the dark meat of turkey, though the noodle-like veins running through the meat were like nothing I'd yet encountered and tasted like overcooked spaghetti. I ate just enough so that Lynch saw me eating, and then dulled my hunger with bubble gum. Dwayne and I did the evening cleanup while Lynch slept by the fire, belly up, burbling and snoring. We woke him up in time to go to bed, where

I spent at least a minute worrying that he might burble and snore again and keep me awake. That was my last coherent thought at the end of day two of beaverin'.

▲

And thus the days passed, with me getting stronger and more adept at setting the trap and skinning the beaver. I even ate my share of the meat—after the bubble gum ran out.

I named two of the beavers I skinned McGinty and McGinnis. They lay on the tarp with their rubbery tails arranged, looking small and pathetic. Little paws curled and yellow-toothed mouths open. Soon there was the sound of my knife in the flesh and the suck and burble of their guts. I was skinning the emblem of Canada.

One night the guys climbed onto the roof with some sheets of plastic: there was a leak over Lynch's bed. When the water had dripped over Dwayne's, Lynch merely suggested he move.

We didn't talk much anymore—everyone knew what had to be done and we just went about doing it. Catching the horses in the morning became much easier when Lynch told us about taking the tobacco can with some oats in it and shaking the can. The noise of oats brings them in. Of course he didn't tell us that right away; we had to spend three mornings thrashing around in the wet buck-brush before he imparted that information. When Dwayne said something about how nice it would have been to be told that earlier, Lynch just looked at him and said, "Thought you was a horse wrangler, son." A remark that made Dwayne duck his head and turn red.

Dwayne and I became pals. He was a good kid, a nice kid, with gentle ways for all his eagerness to hunt, trap and kill. He had a lovely dark voice that he had yet to grow into. Even when he cursed it sounded slow and pleasant. He shot a duck for Patsy one day and was insulted when she refused to eat it after he'd gone to all the trouble of cleaning and plucking it for her. We ate it instead; it tasted vaguely of fish, but anything that was not beaver meat was appreciated.

The bear had been around, feeding from the carcasses that we were careful to put a goodly distance from camp. We hadn't actually seen the bear again, but there were plenty of calling cards to indicate its presence. At night we lit the old coal lamp in the cabin, the pale light making the interior feel cozy and companionable, and we would sit upright in our beds to chat a little.

The guys were waxing eloquent about the joys of this kind of life one night during our bedtime chat when I put in that it was fun for now, but I wouldn't want to have to do it forever. Silence. Lynch blew out the light and was soon asleep, making a noise like hands clapping, only it was his lips that were slapping together. We knew this because Dwayne lit the lamp again so that he could finish sharpening my buck knife for me (he was always busy with something), and that's when we noticed Lynch's lips working. We immediately got the giggles, like a couple of kids. We tried and tried to be quiet, which only made us laugh harder. Lynch woke up, cursing, and blew the lamp out again. His voice was like a raven's croaking and we laughed harder when he mumbled about "damn fool kids." I fell asleep laughing.

The next morning I elected to stay in camp. I was going to somehow have a bath of some kind. I was just too grubby, my nails rimmed with dirt and God knows what, and my hair in clumps on an itchy scalp. As soon as the guys were out of sight, I chose a tree to climb in case the bear came. I nailed little pieces of wood, footholds, as high as I could reach, and I tossed a bag with water and some bannock in it over a branch. This bear thing is ruining any alone time I have, I remember thinking. A few days earlier the guys had walked a quarter of a mile to set some traps while I'd stayed on a ridge with the horses, in a lather of fear the whole time. This day was to be a test: I was going to enjoy this solitary time and even go for a little walk. I was determined to learn to walk through the bush without a rifle and without constant fear.

The bath took most of the time. I had to haul water and keep the fire going to heat it, before discovering the old washtub had a leak in it. I still felt about a hundred percent cleaner than I had before. Rather than go for a walk then, I made dinner so that when my partners rode into camp all tired, there would be a hot meal ready. They appreciated it. Afterwards we sat around the fire with our tea. It was not raining. I was out of cigarettes. Lynch suggested a walk; this in itself was unusual, so Dwayne and I were quick to agree, tired and beat though we were.

He led us to a ridge and indicated we would sit there, which we did all in a row like birds on a wire. We were overlooking a beaver area with a couple of large lodges and a series of dams. We could see some beaver swimming about, and I now recognized that the freshly peeled willows on the lodges represented "fresh sign" of beaver presence. It was still cold; there was a bit of ice on the edge of the water. I had the binoculars to my eyes watching a big beaver swimming with a branch in his mouth when Lynch hissed at me and pointed. There was our bear! At least I assumed it was our host bear, and he was enormous, especially when I got him in the binoculars. I felt the hair on the back of my neck rise. While we watched, the swimming beaver slapped his tail and dove. The bear ambled over to one of the lodges and took the top off, for all the world as though he were opening a boiled egg. That pile of mud and sticks was still frozen; the strength needed to remove the top had to have been incredible. He found something in there, Lynch said. Likely a pregnant female. I didn't want to watch, so he and Dwayne took turns with the glasses while I watched the sun set over the distant mountains.

As we crawled into our beds that night, I checked to see that Lynch had his rifle in its habitual place beside his bed.

Home Again

We got home after an eighteen-mile ride in cold rain. When we were within a mile of the ranch, the horses woke up from their heads-down mode of plodding on the trail and became very lively and hard to manage.

Lynch called a halt and got off his horse to check the packs, making sure that there would be no "spreading camp." Remounting, he hollered "Let's go!" and loosened the reins on his horse, giving it permission to go faster. They all broke into a gallop. It was fabulous! An exhilarating way to end this journey, pulling into the yard to find Lynch's young son, Coyne, with his girlfriend, Donna, and Olive, a friend of Verna's. I have to confess I loved that people were there to witness our return. I felt like a true bushwoman—an impression spoiled when I got off Flame and fell to the ground, my legs rubbery and sore. And my butt hurt; I had to carry a cushion back and forth from my cabin to the lodge for days.

Oh, but it was good to eat a real meal! And to talk to people other than Lynch and Dwayne. There was mail for me: books, letters and a package of art supplies, reminding me I hadn't painted for over a week. Tee was supposed to have arrived at the ranch the day before we were due back, and I found myself hugely disappointed that he was not there. Not present to see me windburned, wearing my Mexican serape and riding like a cowgirl. His letter said he'd arrive the day after, and I went to bed missing him fiercely, though I hadn't spared him a thought the whole time I was out in the bush.

I slept late and got to the lodge the next morning to find Lynch and Dwayne had gone off to look for horses and hunt wolf—without me! I was quite hurt that they'd so quickly and easily left me out, after the way we'd become working partners while trapping. Olive soothed me with homemade cinnamon rolls, coffee and a cigarette. Just when I was feeling the world was really a kind place after all, Tee walked in.

He stayed for over a week and I got only mildly annoyed at the logistics of his presence, probably largely because I was too tired. Mostly, we worked. The building site had to be hand-cleared of buckbrush, and it was nasty stuff to get out and away. We left all the large spruce and pine trees standing. After clearing, which took four days of ten hours each, we started the massive job of peeling the bark off the big pine logs that were destined to become our cabin. That too was back-breaking work, stooping over the log and using an axe or a two-handled tool designed especially for peeling. Luckily the sap was plentiful and the bark came off easily. It was not only physically challenging, it was also tedious and messy, with the sap staining our skin and clothes and getting in our hair. The sun shone hard every day, and we were so hot we had to work with nothing on but our underpants and boots. We were eaten by mosquitoes. After three straight days of this, I was more than glad to agree to go back to Watson Lake with Tee. In fact I was so sore and aching that the whole idea of living here was losing its appeal.

Lynch and Dwayne had gone to Fort St. John—Dwayne to go home to his family ranch and Lynch to buy horses. I'd ordered two, thinking it was time I had my own horses to live on my own place. I'd given Lynch $700, which he told me would not only buy me two good horses but also cover the cost of his bringing them back. He and the new horses were due back at the ranch in a couple of weeks; I would spend that time with Tee, a good long time of being together without working like slaves.

I wanted hot and cold running water and light switches and thermostats. I wanted to wear something other than jeans. I wanted to groan and moan from making love instead of peeling logs.

▲

When we got to town after the usual long and dusty drive we went immediately to my parents' place at the lake for a barbecue with the family. I wanted to swim but had forgotten to bring a suit. Mom told me there was one in the cabin I could use and I quickly took up her offer, coming out onto the dock in a black one-piece, feeling fit and rather sexy. My mom, at the sight of me, started to laugh and laugh.

"You look like Charles Atlas," she told me, gasping for breath. I went back inside to look at myself in the mirror and could see what she meant: I was sleekly muscled from below my ears to my ankles. Although not exactly looking like a weightlifter, I did look a lot stronger than I ever had before. I found I liked looking as though I used my body for something other than just walking around in. This was significant. Historically, remarks from my mother about my appearance (and every other aspect of my life) were generally critical, though often disguised as humour, and had a negative effect on me, making me angry with her and at the same time feeling my self-esteem drop, which made me angry with myself for being vulnerable. Now I was finding myself impervious to such comments, being more certain, and thus confident, about what I thought was attractive or important or interesting. It was a heady feeling.

The first night back in Watson Lake was a drunken one. Lots of people came over to visit and we ended up doing the usual thing of going out for Chinese food and then dancing at the Sign Post. At some point in the evening, I bought a VW Bug from someone in the bar. It was what I used to think of as a fun evening, but, along with all the other changes I was experiencing, it seemed the idea of what constituted fun for me now was yet another change. Too much liquor for too little return, I caught myself thinking. Same people, same place and same results: Jane would become maudlin, John would get angry, Kevin would take his clothes off, someone would want to go to the hot springs and then there would be an after-party, which would go on till no one could drink any more. The next morning I would feel physically ill and spiritually impoverished. It'd become predictable, and I wasn't finding that a comfort—I was finding it tedious. It wasn't the people so much as the circumstances and how I acted in them. I found I was bored with myself. At some point in that revelatory evening I tried to tell Tee what I was feeling, and he seemed to understand, encouraging me to do whatever I felt I needed to do to be happy.

I don't know what I drank, but the next morning I had a tic in my right eye and my ears felt oddly woolly. I stayed in town long enough to get the insurance and licence for the car, which I named Esther Bunny for its white paint and rosy interior. Then I booked myself a flight to Vancouver.

At first it was lovely to wear city clothes, to spend time with people who were interested in my paintings and knew about art in general. People who got excited about books and ideas, people who didn't drink solely to get inebriated. The apartment was in the West End, close to the wonderful sea wall walk; I walked there every morning, with the sound of the waves and the smell of the sea like a tonic before beginning my day. There were appointments to make and keep with dentist, optometrist and doctor. I bought art supplies and some carving tools.

Lynch, the horses and the cabin plans were what I found myself talking about— more than my work, or the next show, or the music and poetry we were hearing almost nightly at different venues in this very exciting city. I couldn't talk about the trapping or the hunting, though fishing was okay. My city friends had a lot to say about trapping and hunting and none of it was nice. I was particularly impressed by one fellow's argument concerning bait used in traps. He felt it was a violation of trust. That one remark swung me back into thinking I had to find a way to live in the bush without killing anything.

Vegetarianism was becoming popular as a lifestyle choice; a lot of people I knew were choosing it as a way of being in the world in a gentler fashion. Ever susceptible, I decided to be one as well. I bought books: books of recipes, poetry, anthropology, leftist politics, feminism and some good novels.

When friends returned from travelling or were planning a trip, I remembered how much I loved going to new places when I was living in Montreal. My husband and I had been twice to Europe, as well as North Africa and the Caribbean. I remembered sunlit foreign streets, the air heavy with strange scents, and the sound of languages new to my ear. There was such a lot yet to see of the world, to sense through the eyes and ears, nose and tongue, to feel with the hands and the soles of the feet. Maybe I too should be planning to go somewhere exotic; China and India were two of the places that had long interested me. I went to a travel agency and got brochures, but I didn't read them.

Every night there was a gathering in some pub or coffee shop where the debates and discussions went on till closing time, often continuing in someone's apartment until the wee hours of the morning. The city was beautiful, and like cities everywhere, offered a variety of things to do and places to go. There were hikes, sailing trips and best of all—conversation. I was a sponge; it was all marvellous to me and I wanted to learn about everything. Twenty-five years old and divorced: all I knew for sure was how little I had to think with.

Then, just a week later, I found myself buying things for the as yet unbuilt cabin, when I'd started out to buy stuff for the apartment, which was feeling small, and limited, somehow. The craving for the wilderness was building in my blood; I could actually physically feel my body yearning, as it did at the beginning of a love affair. At night I found myself dreaming of my cabin, living a solitary life surrounded by silence.

Now I knew one more thing for sure: I wanted to go back to Iskut. I wanted to take the new experiences and information that were beginning to buzz in my head and sort it out. It was time to go home, and home was not where Tee was, nor was it Watson Lake and my family—it was the wilderness. Nothing ever really felt permanent to me at that age, and this didn't either; I just knew I had to be there until I didn't. Solitude was what I needed now. It was time to learn for myself instead of being spoon-fed.

When I got back to Watson Lake, I was there just long enough to pack stuff into the VW; I left for Iskut early the next morning. It was a long, dusty and tiring drive but I revelled in it, stopping several times to stretch and deep-breathe, feeling myself loosen up, physically and mentally. Once across the Stikine River, my heart started to pound with excitement. I was nearly home.

Lynch was still away on his horse-buying trip. Although he'd been due back days ago, no one was worried; he was known for returning late more often than not. Verna was back, and with her was her husband, Walter, who was a grim old fellow, and clearly not a fan of Lynch's. Verna was different around him, even quieter than usual and definitely submissive to Walter, which was disturbing to me. I put it down to being a generational thing, and was sorry for it as I missed the easy camaraderie she and I had found. Walter seemed to always be around; he didn't do anything, just made his presence felt.

I spent hours of every day at our clearing just off the highway, peeling logs. Tee was to come in a week, and the logs would be done by then and we could start skidding them into the building site.

One afternoon Verna and I found ourselves alone in the lodge with tea and cake; Walter had gone to the village to pick up the mail. Usually when he had to make an infrequent trip away from the ranch, he insisted Verna accompany him, but this time she'd had to stay behind to take bread from the oven—a task no one seemed to feel could be left to me, though I had offered. Taking advantage of this rare opportunity, I asked Verna why she and

Walter didn't have children.

"Walter didn't want to have any," she told me, head down, looking at her hands holding her tea cup. "I had a sister who wasn't normal; she was retarded, and he didn't want to have a child like that."

"But Verna," I said, "you had eight siblings and they were all fine; what were the chances of having a kid with those problems? Did you ever talk to a doctor?" I was aghast that a decision with such implications for both of them had been made so arbitrarily by Walter.

"No," she said, still not looking at me and obviously pained by the memory. "He just didn't want to take the chance."

He also got to make her feel like less of a woman, I thought to myself, feeling I now understood her subservience to him, an attitude nowhere in evidence in any of her dealings with any other men. My story about Verna was she was in love with Lynch, with the classic bad boy whom she'd known all her life. Entering into the guiding business with him was a way of maintaining a relationship with him, a way that Walter, who was greedy, would not object to, much as he disliked it.

It was the day after this revelation that Lynch came home. He pulled into the yard with a stock box full of horses and a darkened eye and a split lip. Walter made remarks about his tardiness and the evidences of hard partying while Lynch swallowed some coffee and ignored him. I was practically dancing with eagerness to meet my horses. Over coffee Lynch told me I had a buckskin and a bay, both young and both "green broke," a term that meant nothing at all to me, if it even registered.

The unloading of the horses began; there were six of them and my buckskin was the first off. He was big, a bit skittish when I led him to the corral, but not fearfully so. I stayed there with him after I'd turned him loose, to watch and admire him while the other horses were unloaded and led to the corral. My bay was the last horse off the truck and I returned in time to witness Lynch half-carrying down the ramp a thin little horse with a half-naked tail and a sparse mane. Stunned, I took the rope from Lynch and held up the drooping head of a horse that honestly looked as though it would be dead any second.

"Give him a week on the fresh grass and he'll be great," Lynch told me heartily, but nervously. He could see I was less than pleased, and indeed, I was feeling as though I had been cheated—all the other horses looked fine, but this sad creature was mine. Without answering, I led the horse to the corral. I was sad for the horse and furious with Lynch and helpless with both these feelings. I skipped supper in the lodge, heating a tin of soup on my stove instead and seething with anger about getting ripped off in my first horse deal. Verna came over later in the evening, to find me sitting on the porch of my cabin smoking cigarette after cigarette and trying to decide what to do.

"It's hard to believe," she said, sitting beside me, "but that horse will probably be all right. Lynch does know horses. I know it isn't what you expected, but wait and see before saying anything, will you?" I agreed, for her sake, not because I really thought the horse would miraculously morph into a thing of health and beauty.

The next day the new horses were taken down the valley and turned loose with the herd to graze on the new spring grass. This part of the country was a free-range area, meaning everyone's horses could be turned loose, no fences necessary. Stallions, however, were not allowed to run loose because of their natural propensity to herd and the likelihood they would fight over the herd, as well as lead it far away. The horses were usually led by mares and didn't get into herds so much as little groups. People fed their horses pellets or oats from time to time to remind them of the place that was home. My two vanished into the bush with the rest of them, and in a couple of days I almost forgot their existence as I peeled bark from an endless number of logs.

Tee got held up in Watson Lake with business stuff, and it didn't matter because I hadn't finished the log peeling yet anyway and was beginning to lose all enthusiasm for the whole cabin building plan. The summertime crews for the various seasonal activities were arriving and there was more to do than spend the day covered with sap, though I did make a point of doing some work everyday and sometimes was able to "Tom Sawyer" some unsuspecting city guy into helping out for a couple of hours.

Greg, my helicopter pilot pal, was back, and he and I went fishing every chance we got, often using the helicopter to get us to wonderful out-of-the-way places guaranteed to yield a catch that would feed the multitudes. The nightly games of crib were started, as were the social get-togethers. The latter were now often at the

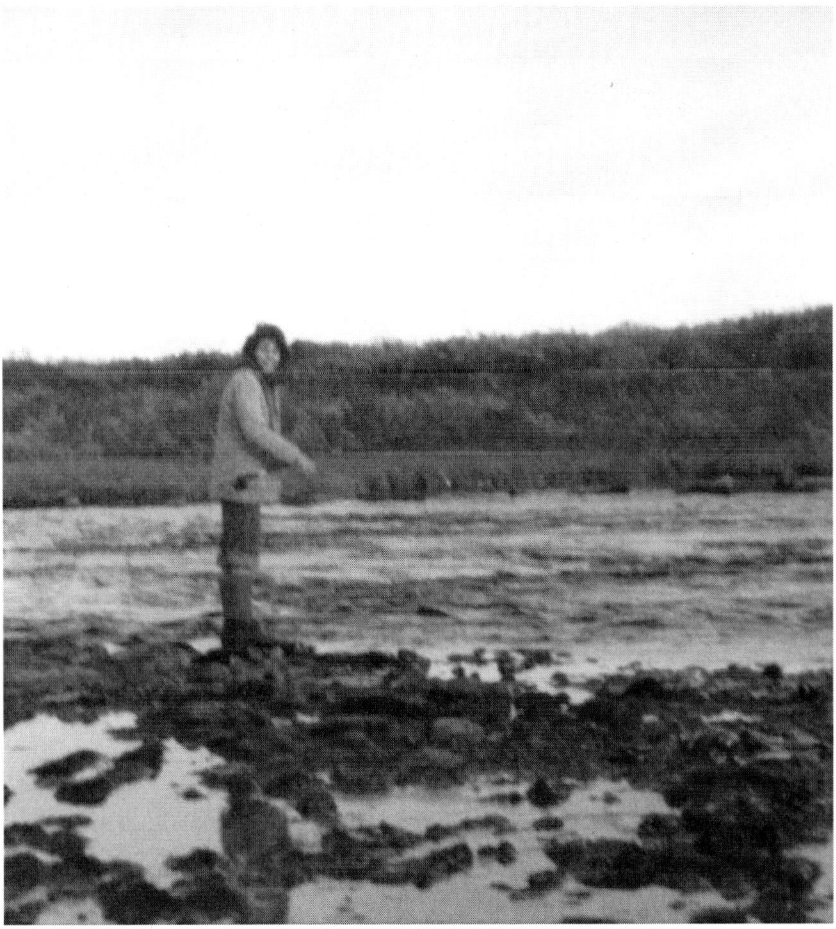

Fishing was a recreation that I enjoyed year-round.

Tatogga Lake Lodge. The Fleming family was welcoming and good company. Walter's heavy presence at the LV lodge was discouraging, even though Verna's cooking and her astonishing degree of knowledge about a variety of things ensured there would always be some visitors. This summer I was socializing a bit less, spending more time alone in my cabin reading, the hissing of the lamp and the turning of the pages the only sounds, along with the occasional yapping of coyotes accentuating the silence.

A Cabin in the Woods

After much deliberation and a lot of hilarity, my horses were named. It was my naughty mother who dubbed them Poon and Tang, Tang being the buckskin and Poon the bay. I'd also acquired a riding horse named Tiny, purchased from some people in Watson Lake whose daughter had owned and ridden her till marrying and leaving for a new life in Australia.

Tiny wasn't exactly small, though she was shorter than the other two. She was a lovely bright copper colour, a sorrel, and she was a fully realized personality. Verna took her out for a ride and reported she was well trained. She'd also been trained to harness. Obviously she had been a beloved pet, and she insisted on certain treats as her right, making her needs known and demanding they be met. Loose, she followed me around like a dog for the first few days and we had a wonderful time getting to know one another. One day some of the other horses drifted into the yard in search of a snack of oats, and when they left, she went with them, to learn the ways of the free range. I missed her.

Poon was looking better, as Lynch had promised, but he was a long way from looking as though he would ever be capable of carrying a person or a pack, and it irked me that he might never be useful. He certainly was not going to be handsome, no matter how much his tail grew in or his body filled out.

I'd kept Tang in one of the corrals at the LV in order to spend some time getting to know him. On the day I took him to our building site, I recognized he was not easy to handle despite the oats and the petting. It was a chore getting a halter on him, with him acting as though he'd never seen such a thing in his whole three years of life, and certainly never worn one. He was a good-sized horse too, and we'd had quite a tussle before I left him tied to one of the corral railings while I went to the lodge to have tea. It was about a mile from the LV to our place and I walked Tang there, with him yanking periodically on the rope and generally not behaving very well. By the time I put him in the bush corral of unpeeled logs that Tee and I had made, we were both hot and sweaty and not liking each other much.

I gave him a feed of oats and left him there to graze on the grass in the corral while I walked back to pick up my car. The plan, unbeknownst to anyone but me, was to borrow a harness from Lynch and begin to skid logs in to the building site—a surprise for

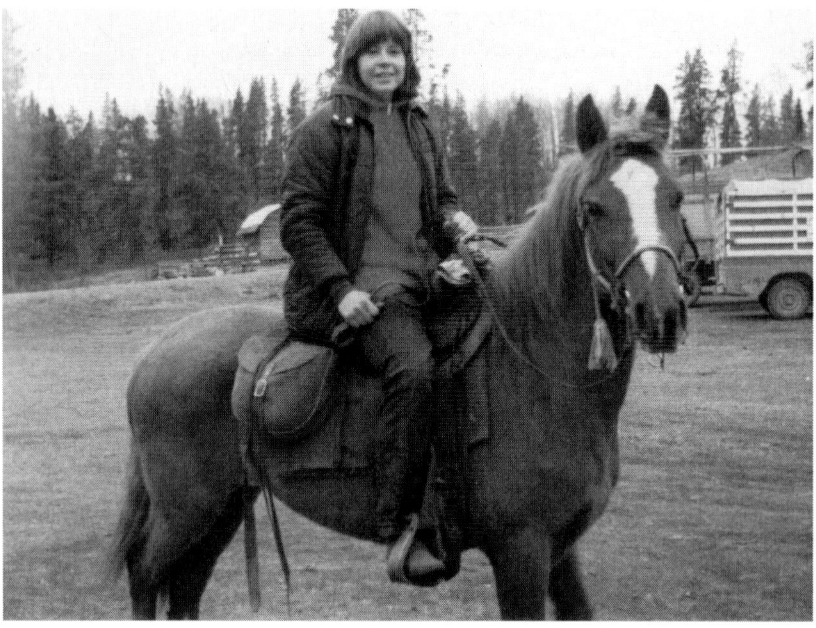

My best all round horse was Tiny the Tease. She was a well-broke riding horse and trained to harness.

Tee when he arrived. The peeling was completed, and I thought it'd be great if I could make a good start on getting the logs in position to start the cabin. The harness was clearly too big for Tiny, but I thought it ought to fit Tang just fine, and I was fairly sure Lynch would be okay with my borrowing it.

Tang was not okay with wearing it. Admittedly, I was awkward in getting it on him; I'd only watched Lynch do it and hadn't ever harnessed a horse or anything else before now. I remembered what both Lynch and Verna had told me over and over again about showing the horse who was the boss, and I tried to convince Tang it was me. We were soon hot and sweaty again, but the harness was on and I led him to where the logs were lying, gleaming clean and white, with the bark in heaps around them.

I had to tie him to a log while I figured out how to loop the chain around another one for him to pull, and he stood there trembling while I worked. He was not at all happy about any part of this endeavour, and not once did I think it was maybe because every single aspect of it was completely unknown to him. I thought he was just being difficult and lazy after too many days of being out on the range with his buddies.

Untying him, I shook the reins along his back and made the clucking noise I'd heard Lynch use to encourage the mares when they pulled. The horse had taken a few steps before he realized something was following him besides me, and when he did, he went berserk. The reins were pulled from my hands as I fell, leaving deep burns in both palms. When I got to my feet I could see Tang running down the road with the big log jerking along behind him. He was clearly in a state of panic, and I suddenly realized how foolish I'd been and how now my poor horse was paying for my ignorance.

Luckily he ran back to the LV. When I arrived, having run the entire distance, he was already de-harnessed and in the corral, with Verna rubbing him down and talking to him. The horse was shaking like a leaf, sweat dripping from him, and there was blood on both his hind legs from where the log had bumped him.

As I ran up to the gate Verna shot me a look that was not pleasant. "Put it back," she said, indicating the tangled heap of harness outside the gate, and returned to ministering to the distraught animal. I hauled the mess of harness to the shed and spent the next half-hour crying as I sorted and cleaned it.

Verna was sitting at the table in the lodge with a cup of tea in her hands when I came in, still crying with shame and guilt. I hesitated at the door, not sure of a welcome and feeling about as bad about myself as it is possible to feel.

"Get a cup, and sit down," Verna said, not looking at me as I obeyed, my heart knocking with dread. Was she going to ask me to leave? What could I possibly do to make amends, and how could I ask Tang to ever trust me? I sat, wiping my eyes and nose on my sleeves and not having a notion of where or how to begin.

Verna did. She began by telling me in no uncertain terms that what I had done was not only stupid, but also dangerous. Worse, she said, you put your horse through an experience no animal should have to endure. When you take on the responsibility for an animal, she went on, still not looking at me, it is a serious matter because you are the one in charge. Your job is more than feeding and watering; you have to know what to ask of them and how to do it and to be certain you have helped them to understand what you want. And you must always, she finished, finally looking at my damp red face, make sure that they are as safe as you can make it for them, and for yourself.

I could see that having had her say, she was feeling a bit sorry for me, and I used that glimmer of softness I'd caught to start babbling about how awfully sorry I was and how nothing like this would ever happen again and how dreadful I felt for Tang and was he going to be all right? She patted my hand and assured me he would be fine. She could see my remorse was genuine and that I had learned a valuable lesson, and being Verna, she was not going to keep rubbing my nose in the mess I'd made.

"Okay," she said briskly, getting to her feet. "Come and peel some potatoes and carrots for me." It was over; we were to carry on, both of us secure in the knowledge I had been rebuked and had understood the seriousness, the ramifications, of my ill-conceived endeavour. Grateful, I followed her into the kitchen, thinking I would peel a ton of potatoes and a ton of carrots for her if that was what she needed to forgive me and keep me on. Such is the power of a person who is straight and true and fair, all of which Verna could be relied upon to be.

It was altogether a sobering experience; I had learned from it, and was grateful the lesson had not been a more costly one to Tang or to me.

Tee and I had to make a trip to Terrace and the library there to learn how to make dovetail corners; no one local knew how to do it and I was set on having them. The big cabin at Spruce Island Camp had dovetail corners; I liked the look of them and how there was no waste of logs. Had I known how much work was going to be involved in making them, I would have been glad to settle

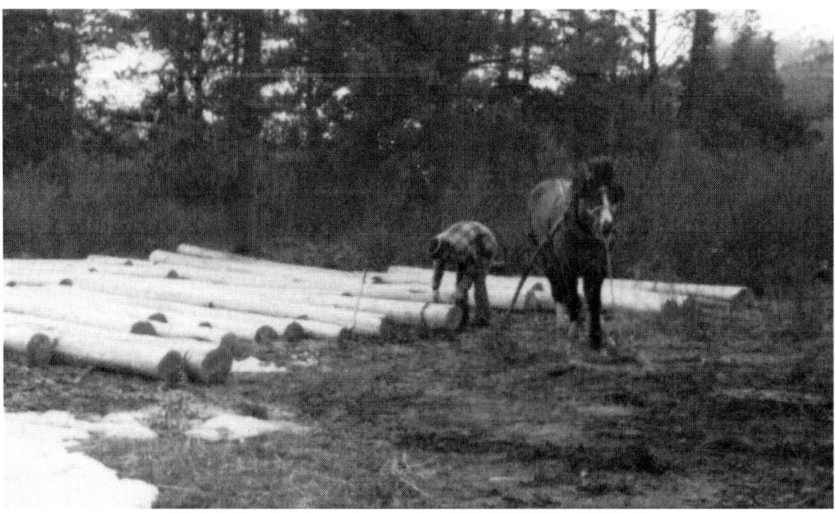

Skidding peeled logs into the building site. With one of Lynch's trained mares the job went quite smoothly.

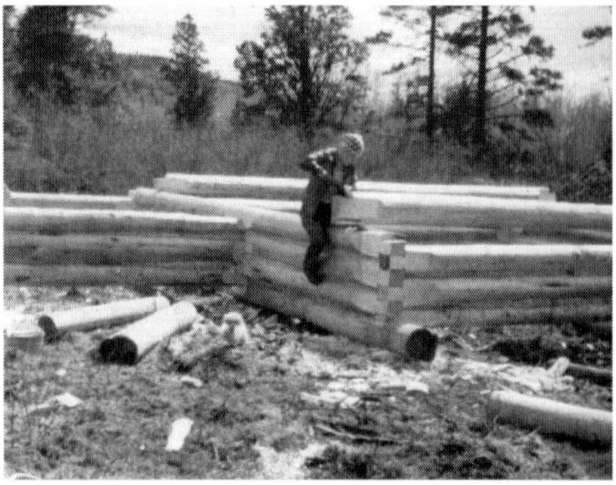

Each log was hand chiselled.

for saddle-notch corners. Every corner took painstaking chisselling and filing to make it fit properly.

The work commenced on the cabin and it went up quickly, with one of Lynch's harness-broken mares used to roll the logs into place. The cabin was twenty by twenty-four feet, with an added pantry that was twelve by twelve. There was a loft-style bedroom, the walls made of planking. The roof was the one part of the construction I had nothing to do with; I am comfortable with altitudes but not heights. We hired some guys from the village to help with the roof.

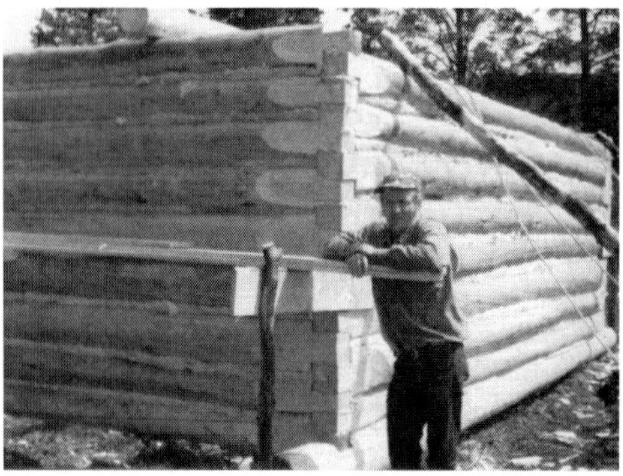

We opted for dovetail corners. If only we had known the painstaking work we were setting ourselves up for.

Picking up my mail in the village one morning, I was told by one of the Tahltan elders that I had not chosen a good place in which to build the cabin. He would not say exactly why it was not a good place, so I dismissed the remark as coming from an old guy just wanting to have an opinion. No one was going to rain on my parade these busy, blissful days of making a dream come true. Tee, who'd come out and helped as much as he was able to during the building, returned to his business in Watson Lake and I moved into the cabin.

It was gorgeous! The massive logs were almost pure cream; the pink insulation we'd cut in strips and used for chinking was hidden by quarter-round poles, peeled and nailed along the cracks between logs. The plywood floor was painted yellow, and there was a deep-red shag rug on the floor of the living room. Verna had sold us a black birch bedroom set that was up in the loft, and Tee had built a sort of low bed in the living room that would serve as a couch and a spare bed for company. A dark-orange easy chair, a wicker loveseat and a table with four chairs completed the modest furnishings. A hand-hewn stepladder was the access to the loft. The mudroom ceiling was still pink insulation covered with clear plastic, but there were deep shelves built in to the walls to hold a winter's supply of canned and dried food as well as other sundries. Hooks for hats and coats were in place, and there was a corner for the horse tack. There was a new wood stove for heating and new gas lamps for reading—it was all perfect. Best of all, there was no need for blinds or drapes; the big windows let in the light, the views of the trees and the splendid and uplifting sight of Mount Edziza in the distance. Everyone for miles around came to admire my new home. They brought thoughtful housewarming gifts, beer and food; the cabin was warmed with the sound of music and friendly voices.

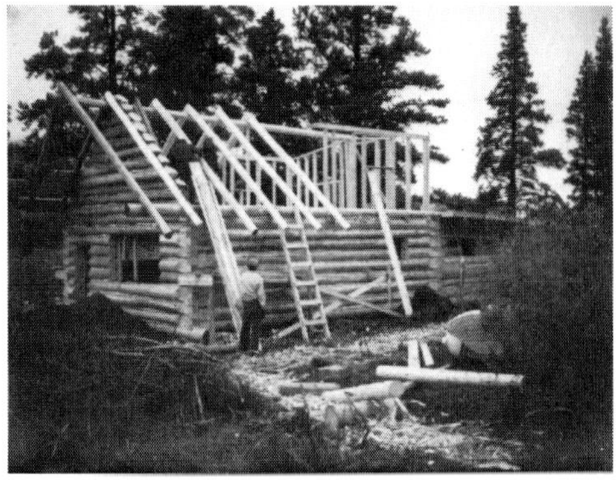

Putting on the roof.

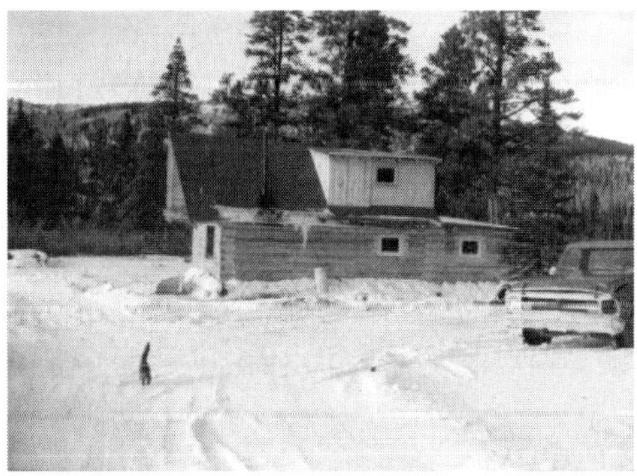

Home sweet home.

Then everyone was gone, and I was alone in my beautiful cabin in the wilderness.

This was my time, the time I'd wanted, and now here it was. I could paint and read and think, when I wanted and as long as I wanted.

In the way of dreams that become reality, what immediately

followed was not what I had anticipated. Like most young people, I hadn't really thought much beyond what I have described: build the cabin, move in, paint, read and so on. Life is bigger than that and has a tendency to fill up in unforeseen ways.

It took me less than a week to get bored with myself. I took to walking down to the LV every day to hang around Verna and chat with visitors to the lodge. I drove to Tatogga Lake Lodge to visit with Jeannie and the kids and to have a shower. I went to the village to see the sisters and to pick up my mail and do some grocery shopping. Soon I wasn't in the cabin much at all during the day; if I wasn't visiting, I was riding or walking in the bush. The biggest difference from the last summer was that I didn't go out so much in the evening, or have people over. Evening was the time I spent on my own with my sketchpads and books.

Tee was going to come and help me bring in a winter wood supply. The horses were out getting fat on grass. Living in the cabin in the summer didn't require much work or attention. The weather was sunny, too nice to stay indoors. I needed something to do, like going fishing, without waiting for Greg and his helicopter to take me to a spot. There were numerous lakes in the area and every one of them had fish.

A canoe would have been a more sensible watercraft to buy than the boat I ordered from the Sears catalogue I'd been idly browsing one day in Jeannie's kitchen. The boat was blue and yellow and made of rubber, or a rubber/plastic combination; described as a four-man craft, it could scarcely hold two adults. Two plastic paddles for the built-in oarlocks were included in the purchase, and a foot pump for the inflation of my new mode of transportation. I unpacked and inflated it beside Tsaybe Creek at the LV, where the bank formed a little beach and the creek was broad and shallow; I figured it would be a good place for my inaugural cruise.

Pushing the unwieldy thing out, I clambered in, rolling onto the floor and clutching the oars under one arm. Before I could organize the oars into the oarlocks, the current grabbed the boat and sucked it into the middle of the creek. I was scarcely able to get myself sitting upright before we were going through the culvert, the long bolts sticking down threatening the frail material of my craft. Fortunately the water was squeezed through the culvert deep and fast enough that the boat stayed in the middle before being dropped out the other end where we took on a fair bit of very cold water.

I was holding onto the empty oarlocks while suffering déjà vu of a terrifying intensity. This was the very creek that had nearly drowned me last year; how could I have been so careless, so forgetful of the current and the cold of the water? Surely this time I would pay with my life for my stupidity. The thought was barely formed before there was a great bang, and I was flipped into the water. A protruding branch had punctured one side of my boat, and the sudden inequality of air had caused it to turn over as neatly and speedily as a dolphin.

My second close encounter with the waters of Tsaybe Creek was a more merciful one. The boat stayed partially afloat and was held close to the bank by becoming entangled in a mess of branches from a tree that had fallen across the creek since my last unplanned venture down its frigid path. I was every bit as scared and scratched from this encounter as I had been from the first, but I was able to get myself and my tattered boat across the highway without being seen. Shivering, and bleeding from a dozen small scratches, I stuffed the boat (the oars miraculously still in the craft) and the pump back into the box and loaded the whole soaking mess into my car. I was able to get home without meeting anyone and having to explain my dishevelled state.

A few days later, I took the boat to Leon Fleming to get him to repair it for me, which he did without questions. Leon was too caught up in his own dramas, which were legion, to ever ask anyone about theirs, a quality of his that I cherished and depended on. There were to be several occasions over the years where he would, unknowingly, save me from humiliation and embarrassment. I would gladly have done the same for him but Leon was never able to hide his mistakes or his adventures-gone-wrong, and I don't believe he ever even tried. It seemed he was convinced that the omnipotence of his Jeannie made any such efforts a waste of time. He was probably right.

This was one of my few misadventures that did not end up being fodder for gossip and great entertainment. If Verna had witnessed this event, this further evidence of my ineptness (I always suspected she had—Verna didn't miss much), she never said anything of it to me or anyone else. A good friend and a noble human being, that was Verna Bailey.

It was Verna who gave me the half-grown pups, recognizing I needed something more in the cabin than paints and books. They were not from the same litter; the male was brown and black and white, the female black with bright brown markings. I named them Benson and Hedges after my brand of cigarettes, and they

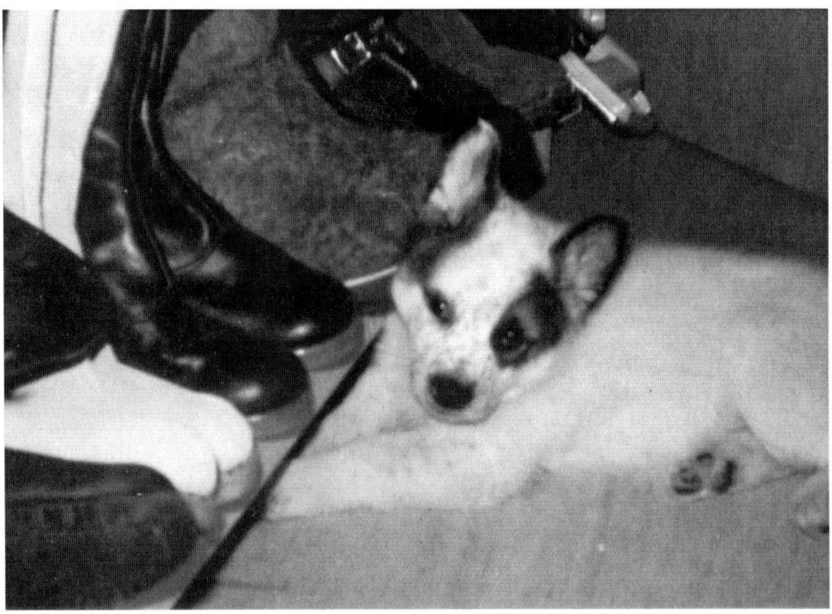

Benson as a puppy.

soon occupied an enormous amount of time and attention as I embarked on the tasks of housebreaking, feeding and training them. They accompanied me whenever I left the property and were soon well-trained and socialized dogs that provided me with perfect companionship. They also proved to be my saviours insofar as they always knew the way back from our long bush hikes, a talent I came to utterly rely on and which freed me to go wherever I chose, secure in the knowledge they would lead me back to the cabin

Our lengthy wanderings often made me too tired to do more than feed the dogs when I got back to the cabin, and I would fall asleep on the bed/couch in the living room, hearing the sound of the wind in the branches of the trees outside the walls and feeling the peace and harmony of my surroundings.

Tee finally arrived and was able to stay only ten days. He brought me a full-sized tin bathtub to hang on the wall of what would one day be a real bathroom. It was nice not to have to go to the Flemings' or the sisters' for showers and baths, to have another piece of independence, though those with hot and cold running water were consistently generous.

Benson had an encounter with a porcupine. After Tee removed the quills, the poor beast's face swelled, causing him to rub his head in the dirt to ease the itch and pain. The skin soon became even more inflamed, and nothing I could do seemed to give him any relief. Finally I took him to Jean Black, the public health nurse in the village. She was wonderfully compassionate and gave me penicillin and ointment for him. He recovered quickly after that, but I didn't, worrying and fussing over him and not wanting him out of my sight.

It was only a few days later that I had to go and see Jean again. I'd gotten a sliver under my fingernail, and it'd turned nasty, swelling tight with infection. It was so sore and tender that I couldn't bear for her to touch it, let alone attempt to remove the piece of wood that was clearly visible under the nail.

"You'll have to go and see Alec Jack's old lady," Jean finally told me. "She will know what to do."

It wasn't hard to find the old woman in her little cabin on the edge of the reserve. She didn't speak any English, but she looked at my finger and gestured for me to sit down. The cabin was dark and crowded with furniture and bush gear, with dried and drying bunches of plants hanging from the rafters. Although it was a warm summer day, the stove had a fire going in it, with a kettle steaming on top. I was offered tea and accepted, the hot brew tasting sharp, medicinal, but not unpleasant. The old woman had white hair hanging down around a wrinkled brown face. Her eyes were deeply set, calm and wise; I felt safe, and certain she would do something to help me.

Taking down one of the bunches of dried plants, she crumbled some of the leaves into a pot of boiling water. While it boiled she went into a grub box and took out a loaf of white bread. Thinking she was about to offer me some, I shook my head. She ignored me, taking a slice from the loaf and placing it on a clean rag. By the time I finished my mug of tea, the potion of the stove was deemed ready, and the old woman (I never learned her name—she was always referred to as Alec Jack's old lady) poured some onto the bread and quickly wrapped the rag around my afflicted finger. The heat was almost unbearable, but she held my wrist firmly on the table, only letting go when I indicated I would hold still. She then poured me another mug of tea. We sat in a companionable silence as I drank my tea and the bread cooled.

When she removed the rag with the bread, she showed me the sliver lying on the wet doughy mess. My finger was bright pink and normally sized, all the infection pulled out along with the sliver. I could bend it and touch it as though nothing had happened. The old lady smiled, refused any offer of payment and ushered me out into the sunshine where Tee was waiting in his truck. He was not nearly so surprised as I was by what had transpired; as it turned out he had experienced many times the healing arts of some of the old people. I, however, was very impressed, and grateful that Jean, an educated woman trained as a nurse, had the broadness of mind to accept and use the knowledge of the old healers. I also wished now that I had paid more attention to the plant she'd used; that sort of thing would be useful to know.

The horses were in when we got home, and there was Poon, looking quite fit and healthy, just as Lynch had predicted. He was still homely and a bit on the small side, but he looked good. Tee, for all his bush expertise, was not a horseman, but he was willing when I suggested he ride Poon while I rode Tiny. Tang was still skittish, and he was a big horse, so Poon seemed the best bet. I told Tee what Lynch had told me regarding the training the horse had had.

"He's green broke," I said, quoting Lynch, but not really understanding what the term meant.

Neither did Tee, but he at least had an inkling that it probably described a horse that had not been ridden much. Tee was a big man and Poon was a small horse, but when the man got on the horse the contest was uneven, to say the least. Helpless, I watched as Poon bucked and twisted and leaped, head down and nostrils fiery with determination.

The man was not so committed to the effort and was soon tossed into the feeding bin we'd built only the other day. It broke a little; one side gave way when Tee's body rolled into it, but otherwise little damage was sustained by man, beast or surroundings. Once again I had a horse standing trembling and fearful while I attempted to soothe him with soft words and gentle strokes as I took the tack from his wet body. I gave him some oats to calm him down, and then he was free to rejoin the other horses that'd been standing in a loose group a little distance away, watching the proceedings with some interest.

Tee was glad to forgo the ride, telling me to go ahead while he cut some more wood. I got my fishing gear and rode off on Tiny to catch some rainbow trout for dinner.

Friends in the Wilderness

My man had gone again, after a good visit during which I managed to mostly curtail my need for extreme orderliness. Several times during the visit I thought, "I have to learn to live with my love or lose it." It seemed the craving for solitude was still unrelenting, leading me to wonder what would happen when Tee moved out to the cabin permanently, as was the understanding. Hopefully by then I would have had enough of living on my own and be more welcoming, more committed to the relationship. It wasn't as though I found him uncomfortable or boring; he was the best of company, being smart and funny, tender and loving. I loved him. I just didn't want him around all the time—yet.

There was a little old cabin about a mile south of me, on the way to 40 Mile Flats where the LV Ranch was. Suddenly this place was occupied, and one of the residents was to become my best friend. Lorraine Charette moved to the bush reluctantly. She came with her husband, Claude, a taciturn pipe-smoking man whose dream it was to live in the wilderness. Lorri, as I came to call her, had never had a similar dream and was indeed a committed townie, but in the interests of her marriage, she came and settled into the one-room cabin with all her household knick-knacks and her pretty clothes. She hated it; she really, really hated it. Claude promised to build her a real house one day and she was hanging by the fingernails, figuratively speaking, waiting for it.

Lorri found it even harder to enjoy things when, soon after their arrival, Claude's father (we all called him Daddy—I never knew his real name) and his lady friend moved in with them, and indeed, it was hard to have four adults living in that incredibly small space. The men were gone most of the time, working, hunting and fishing, and Jackie, the lady friend, was lonely.

She was quite a bit older than we were, not very attractive and walked with a limp. Lorri and I, with the callousness of youth, were not subtle in our efforts to avoid her company. I felt deeply ashamed of myself and my poor behaviour towards Jackie when I learned, some time later, that her limp was the result of a car accident that not only had left her facially scarred and lame in one leg, but had also killed her husband and their three children.

Lorri and I became instant friends. We were two women who in ordinary circumstances were unlikely to have ever met, given how utterly different we were. She was short and blond, blue-eyed and vivacious. Even in this remote place where the chances of a casual visitor were almost nil, her hair was always done, her makeup perfect and her clothes colour-coordinated. She loved to socialize, to dance and sing. Her home was important to her; it was always spotlessly clean, no mean feat in this place of no electricity or running water. Lorri was a wonderful cook, introducing me to some of the traditional French-Canadian dishes and encouraging me in my own culinary efforts. She was not much for reading, often teasing me for having my head "stuck in a book." I resisted her every effort to smarten me up with hairdos and prettier clothes.

Unalike as we were, we soon became inseparable, with me learning to bake bread and put on eyeshadow and Lorri learning to ride a horse and drive a car. We were always laughing; there seemed to be something to keep us entertained no matter what the season or the conditions in our lives. One of my favourite recollections about the two of us was the day I talked Lorri into going riding with me.

I think we'd borrowed one of Lynch's horses for her, and I was riding Tiny as we ambled down the road one spring day. There'd been a heavy rain, puddles everywhere, and the air was delicious and the sun shining. We were having a good time despite Lorri's initial nervousness. Suddenly her horse spooked and took off running, Lorri screaming and clinging to the saddle, reins flying.

I ran Tiny up alongside her horse, and Lorri looked at me, eyes wild. "What should I do?" she yelled. Spotting a big puddle up ahead, I said, "Jump!"

Obedient, she flung herself off the horse's back exactly in time to land on her hands and knees in the muddy water. I grabbed the reins of her horse, stopped him and trotted back to where she was sitting. The parts of her that were not soaked were splashed, and she looked madder than the proverbial wet hen.

"I see blonds don't have more fun; they just get dirty faster," I managed to say before collapsing with laughter.

Lorri was not amused. In fact she was so furious that I was a little afraid of letting her get near me and kept the horses out of her reach as she hollered and threatened. She ended up walking home, cooling off as she did so, and thankfully not letting my joke sever our budding friendship.

Always on the lookout for something with which to occupy herself, Lorri decided to take a taxidermy course—by correspondence. Her first subject was, I believe, a marten when the experiment began, but there was no way of identifying it when Lorri was finished. It looked elongated and twisted, with a face like something from a Stephen King movie. When I first saw it, I didn't know what was funnier: the thing itself or Lorri's pride in her accomplishment. I laughed till I was on the floor, and although she did not share my amusement, she was too good a sport to not eventually join in. Lorri's love of laughter would always win. She eventually became very good at taxidermy, and hunters in the area sometimes had her do their hides for them.

As the years were to prove, nothing interfered with our

friendship. In the beginning we needed one another—there was no one else available for miles and miles, forcing us to learn to accommodate our differences and ending with us celebrating them. There have been few people in my life since then who have had Lorri's sense of fun, her readiness to find pleasure in everything. It was not an easy life for her. Living there wasn't her choice, but as the years have gone by Iskut has come to be Lorri's home in every sense of the word. It was me, who loved it all, who ended up leaving, while Lorri stayed to build a successful business and to happily occupy the gorgeous house Claude eventually built for her.

I visit as often as I can, feeling my face light up when Lorri comes out of the house to give me one of her big tight hugs, her booming voice shouting a welcome. She has remained a constant in my wandering life, someone to check in with every now and then, to renew the bond we formed so long ago.

The summer went on, busy with riding, hiking, fishing and visiting. Lorri and I had many adventures as we explored the area. She wisely refused my offers to accompany me in my rubber boat; Claude had an aluminum boat with a motor, and it was that that took us on our fishing expeditions.

Fishing was always rewarding. One could not come home empty-handed, and what we didn't cook up for dinner was smoked or canned for the winter. Lorri canned moose meat as well, putting garlic and a bit of butter in each jar. It was so delicious I often ate it cold right from the jar—when I was alone, that is.

About an hour's drive south of Iskut was an old burn. Over the years this old forest fire site had become an ideal environment for blueberries. The crop was reliably generous and every year saw people from the village and the surrounding homesteads harvesting the crop. The pickers tended to be mostly women, leading one local wag to dub the berry pickers "the bush league."

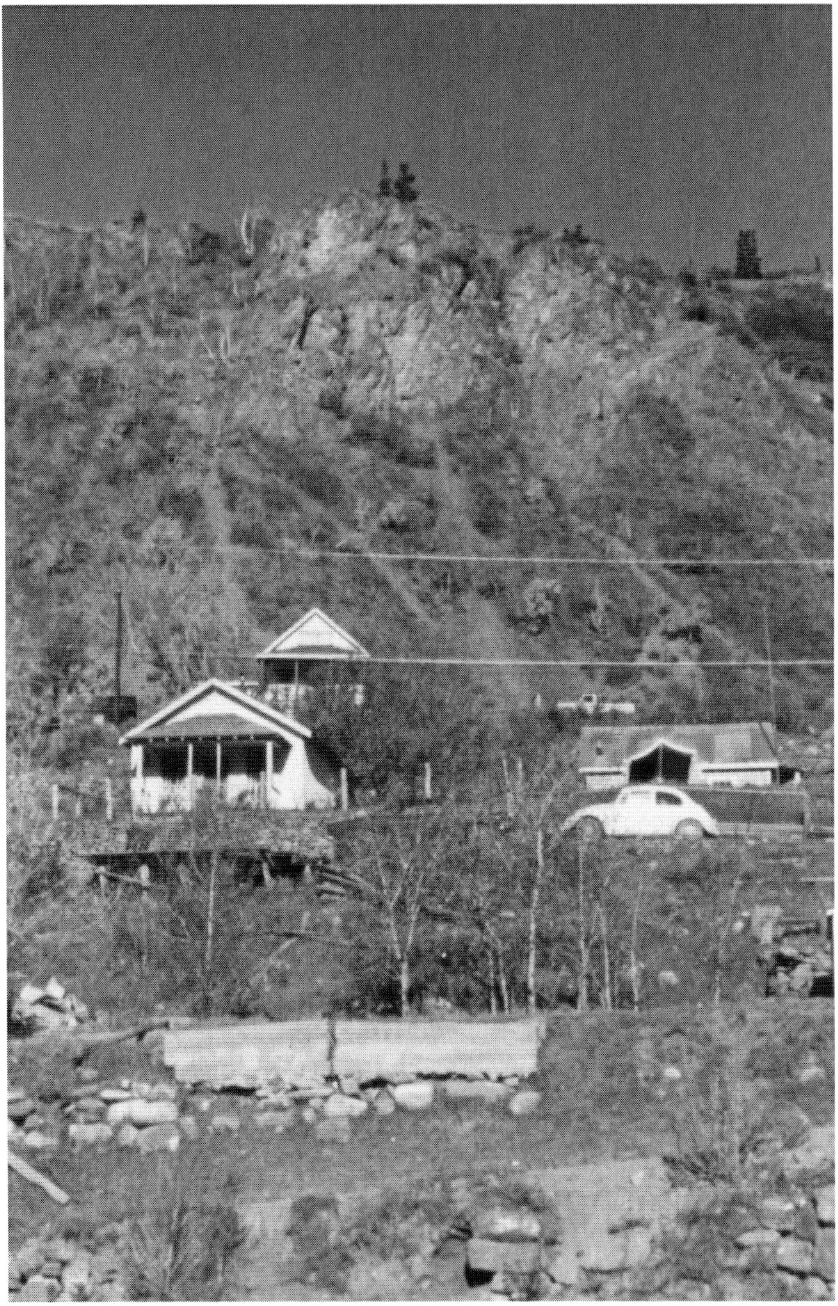

The road to Telegragh Creek was terrifying, but my little VW Beetle (right) got me there safe and sound. Regardless, when the time came to drive home I sold it and accepted a helicopter ride instead.

Jeannie invited me to accompany her and the kids to pick some of this bounty for our freezers, and I was happy to go. It was tremendous fun. There was an abundance of berries, growing so thickly clustered that it was possible to stand in one spot and fill a bucket. Bears were in evidence as they too were looking for stores for winter, but the amount of berries available meant there was no competition, and I don't remember one incident of an inter-species clash over this wonderful harvest.

The Tahltan First Nation people in Telegraph Creek enjoyed the steelhead salmon that came each fall to spawn. They had traditional fishing camps along the Stikine River where the fish were netted, gutted and smoked in the smokehouses that dotted the sites. The smoked fish from their camps was prized all over the country, and many people thought it worth the drive to get it. They had to love it a lot as the road in to Telegraph from Dease Lake was horrendous. It was impossible to take motorhomes into Telegraph because of overhanging rock in many places, and not only was the road gravel and very narrow, it also had no guard-rails in the many spots looking over an edge and into an abyss. Naturally the local people were entirely at ease on this nightmare path, but I was white-knuckled when I drove my VW to the village to join Tee, who had gone in the week before on business with his friend Bob from Stewart.

I was a wreck by the time I found the cabin where Tee and Bob were staying. It clung to the steep hill on the bank of the river, as did most of the houses in Telegraph Creek. The cabin belonged to Agnes Ball, one of the local legends. I don't remember the job Bob and Tee were doing there, only that they were there for a couple of weeks. I stayed for four days, sketching the old buildings, happily eating salmon every day, being constantly delighted with the drama and beauty of the surroundings, and all the while, lurking in the back of my mind was the knowledge I would have to go back over that roller coaster road some time soon. I gave some serious thought to not leaving at all—staying in Telegraph Creek and never having to face the trip again.

The dogs had been left with Verna on the understanding I would not be gone more than four days, as she and Walter were heading south for the winter. On the dreaded fourth day, Scott Wrigglesworth of BC Hydro offered to buy my VW. After talking to Tee about buying an old pickup truck that Bob was selling, how much more useful it would be, I sold my little Bug. The best part of the sale was the inclusion of a ride home in a helicopter; I could enjoy the rugged beauty of the country without having to creep through it on a goat path carved into the sides of the mountains.

Home again, I found Hedges had been killed by a truck on the highway. So little traffic on that road, and yet my dog had been hit. Verna told me it was quick; she'd died instantly and Lynch had buried her for me behind the shop. I cried as I stood over her grave. She'd been a brave and curious little dog and a good companion. Hedges's death and Verna's departure marked the end of the summer.

At night now in my cabin I heard the wolves howling—a sound that in the beginning taught me what "my blood ran cold" really meant, as I huddled under my blankets, thinking about the lack of a lock on my door. Although Benson was always made restless by the wolves' songs, the sound, haunting and wild, soon came to be beautiful to me. The leaves turned golden, falling like the coins of a pirate's treasure to fill the corral and blanket the paths. The sides of the mountains looked like rich Persian carpets of red and yellow, interspersed with the deep blue-green of the evergreen trees, and their white tops grew larger, creeping downwards as the snow fell. The nights were cold, the stove crackled with burning wood. Lorri taught me to make hearty, warming soups. The horses came in more frequently to eat oats and pellets, their gleaming summer coats growing shaggier with each visit as they readied for winter. The woodpile was neatly stacked, the pantry shelves filled with dried, canned and preserved foodstuffs, and the blue truck, named Danube, had been winterized.

I was ready and looking forward to winter, and to holing up in my snug cabin, reading and painting. I'd acquired an eight-track cassette player, and Tee had shown me how to hook it up to my truck battery; now there would be music, too, to fill the winter nights.

Another dog arrived; Tee brought me a teacup toy poodle, of all things. She was the size of a pop can when he brought her out to Iskut, and of a colour called apricot. Her name was Barika, which is Hungarian for "little lamb." She was registered, a pure-blooded show dog, and what he'd been thinking when he bought her, I could not imagine. She was from a kennel in Burns Lake, where Tee had been to buy some sort of equipment from the owners when he saw her and thought she'd be just what I needed to assuage my grief over the loss of Hedges. I had never been interested in wee dogs, nor had I cared much for the notion of purebred, and at first I was taken aback by this gift. It seemed to me she was going to need a lot of special care and attention and be more trouble than pleasure. Barika was none of those things—she was pure delight, brave as a barrel of bears and game for anything. I am sure she never thought of herself as small, and she certainly was not in the least timid or fearful. She was soon integrated into my bush life. Everyone who met her was charmed by her tininess and her feistiness. She also liked to sing, joining in with Lorri, who used to sing professionally in her town life, to sing favourite country-western numbers. When I rode Tiny, Barika came with me in a leather bag hanging from the pommel of the saddle, her eager little face watching the passing scenery. She had been with me for about a week when I noticed we had another resident.

Going into the pantry/mudroom one morning in search of a tin of tomatoes, I was hugely startled by something rearing up behind the row of tins—something with a lot of pointy teeth and making an angry noise. Jumping back, I saw what at first I thought was a marten, standing on its hind legs and fiercely lecturing me about the rudeness of grabbing for a can without some warning beforehand. It was a weasel, almost white now for winter, and obviously intending to spend the season in my cabin. I could see the spot he'd chosen as his bathroom; through the clear plastic that covered the pink insulation in the ceiling were some telltale

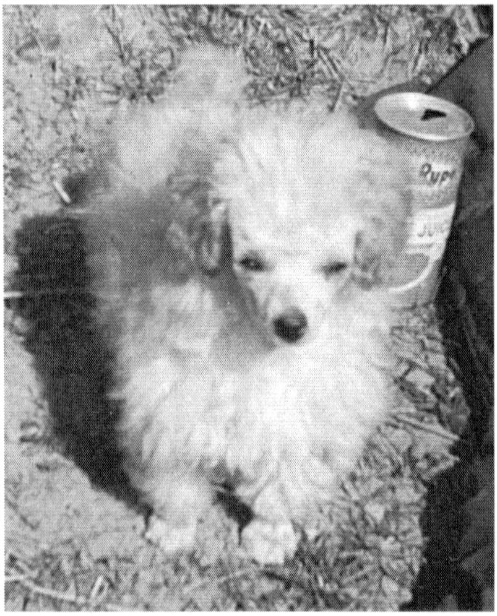

Barika was small, but a fierce and formidable enemy to the rabbits.

dark-brown patches. I named him Casper and made him welcome, thinking I would have no problem with mice invading my space so long as he was in residence. Later I thought there might be some danger for my little poodle pal: Barika was much smaller than a rabbit, and I knew weasels could and did kill rabbits.

This added new drama to my home scene, and for days I was very worried and very careful of where the dog was every moment. The weasel seemed to keep to the pantry area, and I quickly got into the habit of letting him know when I was going to be rummaging through the shelves. The introductory experience of meeting by surprise didn't happen again. It must have been a week or so after Casper's moving in that I witnessed a really amazing sight: the dog and the weasel were playing!

Maybe the weasel was stalking the dog, but it certainly looked harmless. Barika would run around the perimeter of the cabin walls and Casper would follow, not so close as to make me worry, about three feet behind her. Then, at some unseen signal, they would reverse roles and she would follow him. They would do this every now and then for the length of time we all shared living quarters, and I never felt there was any nasty intention by either of them. Other than that interaction, they ignored one another—Casper in the mudroom and Barika either upstairs with me or in the main room of the cabin. My own relationship with the weasel was a distant one: we left one another respectfully alone.

Casper moved out in the spring, to parts unknown, but came back every winter. He and I had just two other close-up encounters in all the time we cohabitated. I had a large plastic garbage can that I used to keep my household water in, refilling it bucket by bucket from the creek. One night I was awakened by the sound of splashing that could only be from the water barrel. It was covered, but something had obviously gotten in.

My flashlight revealed Casper, desperately thrashing in water too low in the barrel for him to climb out. How and why he'd come to be there remained a mystery, but he obviously was in need of rescue; the question was, how? I knew better than to reach in and grab him. It was certain that he would bite, not recognizing my intention to help him, and his teeth would do serious damage. All I could think of was the handle of the broom, which I held out while keeping my hands as far away as possible from the part he would use to pull himself from the water. It worked; the weasel crawled along the handle, wet and red-eyed with anger, but I dropped the broom on the floor as soon as he was clear of the barrel. I went back upstairs and he went back to his room, neither of us having anything more to say or do regarding this event.

A couple of weeks later I was opening a package of ground moose meat when I noticed he was sitting in the doorway between the main room and the mudroom. He was showing a rare interest in me, or rather in what I was doing, and I realized it was the meat calling his attention. Carefully I broke off an egg-sized piece, and crouching, I held it out to him. He took it without the least hesitation, leaving immediately for "his" room with the offering, but I swear he shot me a look of thanks.

After this I would leave him food once in awhile, never again chancing the hand-feeding trick. I figured we'd done our exchange of trust and the act didn't need repeating.

Stumbling on Truth

I was longing for snow, to begin my first winter in my cabin, but although it got colder, the snow held off. However two things happened to distract me, to keep me busy in new and novel ways.

I got a cold—not just any old cold, but the mother of all colds. It began with a runny nose, a perpetually running nose that soon saw my upper lip covered with peeling skin. It then moved to my chest. By this time, alone with it, I was beginning to think it was something more serious, like lung cancer. Nights were sleepless as I coughed up gobs of an elastic green substance, the evidence of my disease. I drank ginger tea for the first while and then moved to hot rum and lemon. At least the latter not only helped me to sleep but also put me in a cheerier frame of mind. I was a mess of scales and snot when Michelle, or Mic, as we called her, came to stay with me.

Mic was my niece. She was in the care of my mother in Watson Lake while my sister and her husband sorted their way through a marital crisis, and Mom needed a break. Mic was three years old. Not only had I not entertained the idea of a child of my own, but I also hadn't ever been particularly interested in children. They were a mystery to me—what they ate, and how to entertain them.

Mic was easy. She slid right into my life as though she'd always been there, and she was a daily delight. She was a kid with lots of energy and a curiosity to go with it. Nothing fazed her; here she was staying with an aunt she didn't know in a place she'd never been and she was not in the least shy or timid, simply interested. I made her a makeshift bed from emptied cases of canned food. In it I put a sleeping bag, which she referred to as her "sleeking bag," and she nestled in quite happily. We soon settled into a routine, Mic and I, and after just a few days I was finding it hard to imagine life without this bright, busy little person around.

Lorri wasn't interested in children, not even this wonder child, and she didn't encourage visits and didn't come over while Mic was with me. She'd had an accident as a young woman and had been told she would be unable to have kids. I believe this was a tragedy for her and Claude; they would have been great parents, and maybe simply not liking children was Lorri's way of dealing with it. I missed her, but not as much as I would have if Mic had not been there to engage and amuse me.

Tee arrived for a few days and was as quickly enchanted. We all three hiked out to a beaver dam and sat on the bank with our warm drinks, watching the beaver do all their last-minute winter chores, Mic quiet and attentive between us.

The snow finally arrived, in spades. There was all the snow anyone could wish for, and Mic and I went out to play in it, me in layers of wool and Mic in her one-piece pink snowsuit. We crawled around the cabin, inventing games and laughing at Barika's antics in her first experience of the white stuff. Indoors, warming up, we drank hot chocolate and danced to Bachman-Turner Overdrive. We made cookies. One day we went to Tatogga, Tee to saw lumber for a greenhouse and me to copy recipes from Jeannie's many cookbooks. The Flemings, too, immediately became devotees of our charming child, with their kids taking her off to read stories and play games.

Just before we were to sit down to supper with the Flemings, some strangers arrived, Americans. They'd hitchhiked from where their truck was stuck in deep snow several miles south on the highway. Leon and Tee decided to play Good Samaritans and go and pull them out.

The guys didn't get back till midnight. Mic was put to bed along with the Fleming kids. Around ten, Jeannie and I were convinced they'd become stuck themselves; we were on our way to look for them in my blue truck when they drove up. Leon's truck bed was loaded with cases of apples—thirty of them. The Americans, having no extra cash, had insisted on some sort of payment, and this was it. We stayed up the rest of the night peeling and coring and freezing this unexpected, deeply appreciated bounty.

The next morning Mic and I played in the snow again before I went in to paint. Tee, returning from the village a couple of hours later, poured himself a cup of tea, sat at the table and asked, "Do you think Mic should come in now?"

Horrified, I realized I had left her outside! After our games, I'd rushed back into the cabin with a picture forming in my mind and demanding to be put on canvas right away—I'd forgotten Mic. I was in a panic till Tee told me to just open the door: there she was, in her pink snowsuit and matching toque, curled up on the step fast asleep, her cheeks rosy and whole demeanour one of peace. Guilt assailed me: I was an unfit aunt, a selfish bitch, an irresponsible woman unworthy of assuming the care of any living creature. Tee let me beat myself up for awhile before pointing out that she was perfectly safe and perfectly warm, and had she wanted to come in she would have banged on the door and hollered, as she'd shown herself entirely capable of doing.

By the time we took her back to Watson Lake, I was bereft. Mic had filled my life in places I hadn't known were empty. A child was out of the question for me in my present relationship. Tee had four grown sons and had had a vasectomy after the birth of the last one. He'd told me of this soon after we'd begun our affair, and quite naturally, the subject of children had not come up.

Now, after Mic's bright presence, I wondered if there ever might come a time that I would want a baby; what would I do?

With Mic and Tee gone, the cabin felt hollow and cold. Lorri and Claude had gone to Terrace to shop and visit. I had a few days of mooning around missing everyone before the rhythm of winter in the bush caught me up and moved me along.

I'd been reading Isaac Asimov and from a short story took the name Elsevere for my cabin. The name pleased me, having a fairy-like quality in the sound but a realistic look to the word. Although it came to be known as the Funny Farm to family and friends, it was always Elsevere to me. I'd bought a lot of books in Vancouver expressly for this winter, and I loved my long lone evenings, Leonard Cohen singing, or Laurie Anderson, the fire crackling in the stove and the wolves howling outside as I lounged on my couch/bed

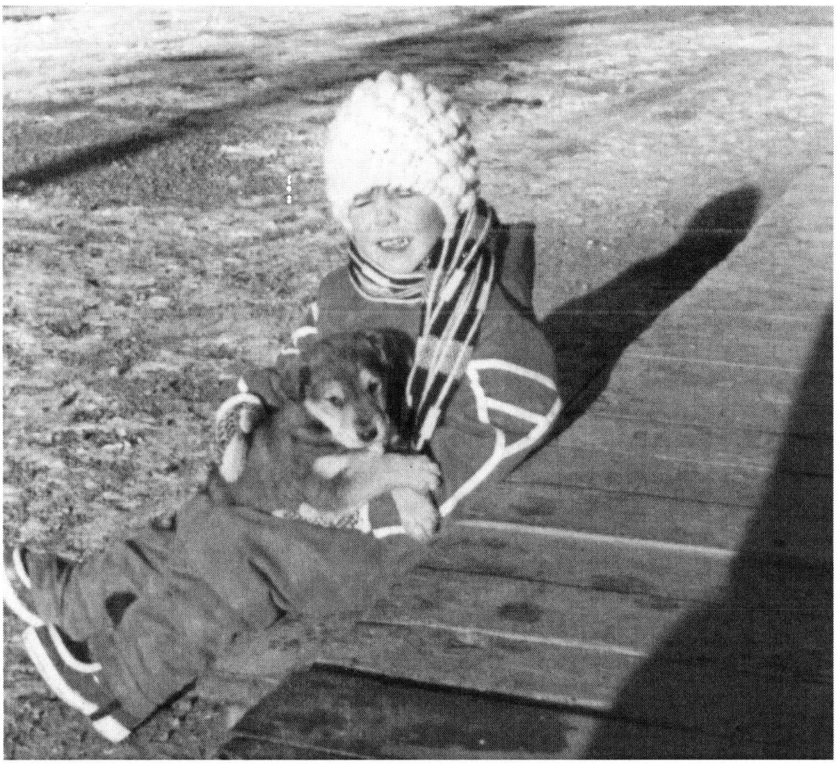

My niece Mic was welcome company for me and the puppies.

and lost myself in other worlds of thoughts and ideas and feelings.

One of the books I'd brought from the city was on yoga and meditation. I began to practise both, sometimes becoming so engrossed that I would forget to put wood in the fire and the cold would bring me out from wherever I'd been. I read the *Tao Te Ching* and books by Krishnamurti. My painting slowed down; I was more interested in reading and meditating during this time, though I would often sketch some of the images and visions I was experiencing while sitting in stillness. I'd begun a journal of these days in the bush, and it always surprised me how many pages I could fill in what would appear to be a quiet life—there always seemed to be something happening or something to ponder.

It grew colder, and the daily chores became something to be done in a hurry. There were ice crystals visible in the air, and brilliant and startling sun dogs circling the pale sun. Each morning I would go out and haul wood from the woodpile to the porch so that I wouldn't have to go far during the night to get fuel for the stove. My water supply ran low, and I began melting snow for all the washing.

Tee had bought me a little chainsaw that I'd named Princess and had learned to use fairly adroitly during the building of the cabin. This was a good thing, as the cold spell ate up my wood at an alarming rate, and it soon became obvious I was going to have to saw up some of the logs we'd hauled to the site to be cut and stacked. This task was hard but rewarding, due not just to the pleasure of being in the pristine and beautiful winter outdoors, but also to the good feeling of my body responding effortlessly to do what was needed.

One night, after spending most of the day cutting and stacking firewood, I lit candles, put on some Mozart and took a full-on proper bath and hair wash. The water was wonderfully soft, the cabin warm and the light kind and gentle. Barika stood watching, fascinated but nervous she might be asked to participate in this ritual and relieved when it became clear she was not going to be invited in. Afterwards I put on perfume and mascara along with my clean clothes and felt a tiny desire for company—for someone to appreciate how nice I looked.

Sometimes in the night I would be awakened by the sound of horse bells and would scamper down the ladder to the mudroom where I would pull on some boots and a thick jacket before going out to scoop pellets from the barrels for the eager horses. They would be black shapes against the snow, their breath making clouds over their heads, their coats shaggy with winter fur. It was a relief to see them and to run my hands over their warm hides, to know they hadn't been hit be a truck or hurt by wolves or bears. Every year saw some losses of this kind to the roaming bands of horses, and I worried a lot about mine: it was their first winter as free-range animals. So far they were fat and seemed glad to be having this sort of freedom, for all its perils. Tiny was greedy; I would have to stand in the snow until all the horses had finished their pellets because Tiny would gobble hers and then try to eat Poon's share. Sometimes they brought friends home for a snack, and I would be feeding one of Lynch's horses, or a horse from the village.

On moonlit nights I would put on my snowshoes and make a trail through the woods, the snow looking blue and the deep hush of the trees pushing against my ears. Once I was followed by wolves, turning to see their loping black forms keeping well behind me, and noticing their attentiveness when I stopped. I wasn't afraid of them; the word was that wolves did not attack humans, and I was willing to believe that. I was careful, though. I didn't go too far from the cabin, and I was very conscious of not wanting to fall down. Their presence certainly added a new element to these nocturnal jaunts.

Daylight snowshoeing was a constant source of wonder: tracks, tracks everywhere, telling story after story. Here an owl swooped down on a mouse, leaving a beautiful pattern of wing feathers in the snow. Here a moose browsed, and here a rabbit was killed—by what? Were those tracks a marten or a mink? I would draw them to show Lynch and find out what made them.

The air was delicious and almost felt like nourishment. The trees, boughs weighted with snow, would sometimes creak against one another, or make a swishing noise as the snow slid from the branches. Ravens surprised and startled me with their amazing variety of sounds, many of which were eerie to hear in this isolated spot. I would be miles from anywhere and suddenly hear the sound of an axe chopping wood, or a chainsaw or even a human voice calling.

Sometimes I would stop and build a fire, using the black, hair-like growth close to the trunks of the trees for my fire starter and the dry little twigs for kindling. I could sit for hours, staring into the flames, sipping tea and losing myself in the surroundings. Some of these times were revelatory—some insight or understanding would arrive like a gift. Other times it felt almost like prayer, or some form of worship, just to sit and melt into the landscape.

I practised cooking and baking, making dishes that sometimes appeared odd but tasted fine and other times appeared fine and tasted odd. I was making all my own bread. My ingredients were of necessity limited, and I often found myself yearning for a proper grocery store. There were only so many things one could make from moose and tinned tomatoes.

Once in awhile I would walk down to the LV and ride with Lynch when he checked his snares. We were so bulky with winter clothes that we would have to stand on bales of hay to get on our horses. These were the days before Gore-Tex and Thinsulate: to stay warm while immobilized on a horse one had to wear layers of wool, goose down and leather. The best discovery I made during the years of living in the bush was silk underwear. Very light and supple, it was the perfect thing to wear against the skin before layering on the rest of the winter clothing.

The ride up the valley was always beautiful, with the snow heavy on the trees and the horses' breath making clouds of frost. That winter the snow was up to the horses' bellies, and the trail we followed had snow on either side that brushed our knees. The little expedition was mostly for pleasure and exercise, I think, as there were few snares and rarely anything in them to cause us to dismount. The first time I went on this little trek with Lynch gave him yet another opportunity to have some fun at my expense.

Returning from the trail, we dismounted and threw the reins over the top rail of the corral, taking the tack off the horses before putting them in the corral and giving them a feed of oats and hay. Flame, his saddle and bridle off, decided to go for a bit of a run on his own and went lunging through the deep snow. Lynch hollered at me: "Sis! Catch him quick! If he runs off the wolves will get him for sure."

Obediently, I set off after Flame. Of course in the deep snow, clumsy and thick with clothes, including leather chaps, I was scarcely able to move let alone run. Lynch let me wallow around after the horse for about ten sweaty minutes before he simply opened the gate of the corral and Flame ran in. As Lynch told me later, when he was able to quit laughing, no horse being fed is going to go anywhere in the winter.

It was early that winter that my dog Benson began to disappear. At first he would be gone for hours, then for an entire day and then for a day and a night. When this began I was frantic with worry, certain that wolves had gotten him. Every winter there were stories of dogs killed by wolves. Sometimes the wolves came right into the village and took the dogs off the chains.

Benson always returned unscathed from these adventures, but with each return he was more distant. Soon he would not come into the cabin, preferring to eat his food on the porch and to sleep in the woodshed. Someone in the village told me they'd seen my dog hunting with a pack of wolves. Someone else said there was no way the wolves would accept a dog. All I knew for sure was my dog was becoming a stranger to me. He was never threatening or scary, he just looked sort of confused when he paid his more and more infrequent visits. Eventually he was inapproachable, though for the rest of the winter he would appear once in awhile, circling the cabin as if he knew there was something there for him but he had lost access to it. By spring he was gone, but for years there were stories about a big white dog with brown patches that was with the wolves. I missed his big warm presence in the cabin and on the trail when I snowshoed.

There was a time when I didn't see another soul for a stretch of eleven days—and it could have been longer. I began to feel as though I were living in another dimension, and it was blissful, full of new and fascinating messages and rousing complex feelings. I was pursuing knowledge and understanding, and there was no end to the journey, just another corner or hill every time I thought I had achieved a destination.

These periods of pure solitude became entirely necessary to me; I was in search of something that I now believe was a connection to the divine. All I knew for certain was the peace, the stillness, that every now and then I seemed accidentally to stumble into. It was an egoless place, and it was perfect.

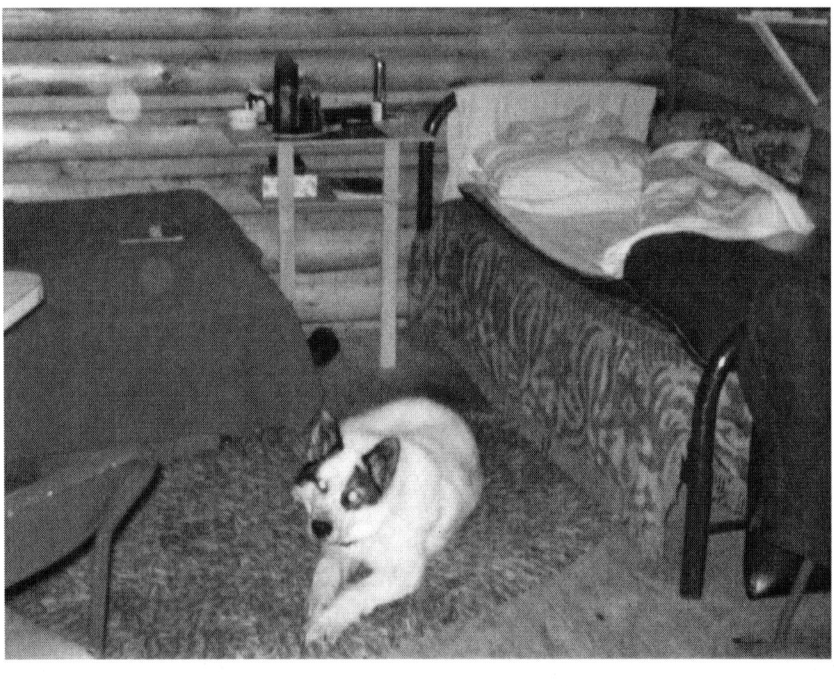

Eventually Benson moved out of my cabin to run with the wolves.

The Wolf Still Howls

The cold spell broke, and the weather became almost warm, with a luscious and caressing wind. The mountains were so etched and clear against the blue sky that my every outdoor activity, even going to the outhouse, was interrupted while I stood and simply stared.

Jeannie Fleming broke my solitude, coming to check in with me and see how I was doing and if I wanted to go to the village to pick up mail and see the movie. When I first heard her vehicle I'd experienced a feeling of dread, but by the time I saw her smiling face I was jumping up and down with excitement. Before we could leave, however, she had to have a cup of tea while I went to my "bank" for some money.

The nearest banks were in Stewart or Watson Lake, and to keep some cash on hand, I had begun to hide money in my books. I tried to choose titles that I thought related to finance, such as *Bread into Roses*, or *Agricultural Science* by B.N. Money, but soon ran out of titles and squirrelled the bills in any book that came to hand. This meant several minutes of reaching down books and shaking them over the couch until I had enough money to go to the village.

Good thing Jeannie had come because my truck wouldn't start. We used her jumper cables to start it, and I elected to drive myself to the village to warm up the truck and recharge the batteries.

The movie was *Born Free*, and Sister Rhonda was there and a lot of the locals, glad to be getting off their lonely homesteads after weeks of isolating cold. We all went to the Blacks' place for coffee after the film and sat around catching up on one another's news. I was eager to hear news of the world: my radio picked up only one station and it played pop music twenty-four hours a day. Robin and Tom Black had sold their store to a couple named Ken and Betty Burris. The Burrises had two daughters in their teens, Ann and Sherry. They were a nice family and looked to be a welcome addition to our little community. Much as I'd enjoyed my socializing, I was happy to get home and be alone again.

The horses had come in while I was away. I caught Tiny and Poon and put them in the corral, planning on doing some riding now that the weather was kinder. Poon was kept in as company for Tiny—horses so hate to be without other horses. I saddled up the next morning to ride over to the LV, with a stop at the Charettes' to visit with Daddy and Jackie and find out when Lorri and Claude were coming home.

There was an old cabin near the Charettes', and thinking I would ride in that way instead of staying on the road, I turned Tiny's head towards the cabin. I may have forgotten how much snow had fallen and how deep the ditch was, but Tiny had not—she flat out refused to leave the plowed road. Remembering Lynch's admonishments about showing your horse who was boss, I insisted, even smacking her across the butt with the reins. Tiny gave a horse shrug, gathered herself and leaped off the road, sinking up to her neck into the ditch full of snow while I sailed over her head to land up to my neck in the snow in front of her. I was embarrassed; I was embarrassed in front of my horse—there was no one else around. She stretched her head out towards me, laid it on the snow, and looking me right in the eye she let out a long sigh. She couldn't have more clearly said, "I told you so."

I crawled and fought my way back to the road, finally rolling onto the packed surface to lie like a beached whale, gasping and blowing. It was hard work to get clear of the stuff, and I wondered if Tiny would be able to do it on her own or if I would have to suffer the additional humiliation of getting Lynch and his mares to pull her out. She let me stew awhile and then thrashed her own way to the road where she stood above me, scarcely winded and utterly full of herself.

Lynch was as usual glad to have company, though Daddy and Jackie were already there, along with some people travelling south on the highway. I drank tea and ate bannock and chatted, finding out that Claude and Lorri would be home in the next few days. It turned out the visitors, Dave and Kathy, knew of me and my painting; they'd bought one of my canvases in Vancouver the previous spring. They were very pleased to meet me and, once they knew I lived here, very eager to see more of my work. I invited them back to my place, leaving Tiny in one of Lynch's corrals while I rode back in their vehicle.

It was a happy encounter for all concerned, not only because they bought two canvases, but also because we all three talked till dark. We talked about Krishnamurti and B.F. Skinner and Cohen. They told me about their trip to India two years earlier. We talked until was too late for them to carry on to Stewart. They slept on my downstairs bed/couch, and the next morning I made them breakfast and we talked some more. We talked in their truck on the way back to the LV, and we talked as we had some of Lynch's coffee in the lodge. Lynch was clearly miffed at us. He didn't know or care what we were discussing, he just knew it wasn't about anything he knew or was interested in. Lynch was never a book man, and he often gave me trouble over having my head in a book all the time.

Dave and Kathy finally left, with promises of staying in touch by letter, followed by a get-together in Vancouver. Standing in the road waving goodbye till I could no longer see their truck, I felt flattened, emptied, with nothing around with which to fill up again.

Even riding home on Tiny, even cleaning up the cabin and bringing in wood didn't change this feeling that I was a fool to be here. I was wasting the valuable time of my youth to live in the bush alone when all the world and its myriad peoples were out there for me to explore. Suddenly I was missing Tee; I was missing talking with him and going places with him. I was missing sex; God! But I was missing sex! How could I have been out here so long without such an elemental need being met, I wondered, as I went about the rituals of preparing for evening. I went to bed that night resolved to go to Watson Lake and then on to Mexico with Tee.

Enough of this mooning around, going nowhere and doing nothing of any importance. I had a lover to love and a career to get busy on. It was time to rejoin the world.

The night after making my big decision to give up on bush life and get back to civilization was the stuff of nightmares.

I was awakened by the sound of howling; it was incredibly loud because it was incredibly close. I leaped out of bed to throw open the little upstairs window and lean out. There, right on the step in front of my door was a huge black wolf. Alone, he was howling—a howl of passion, of yearning, of hunger so deep his heart was breaking. I thought of two things simultaneously: the .30-06 hanging loaded on the wall downstairs and that the door to the cabin didn't lock. There was even a hole drilled in the door where eventually a locking doorknob was going to be. In the meantime, the hole had a knotted piece of yellow nylon rope in it, and that was all. A good nudge from the wolf, and he would be inside my cabin! I was frozen with terror as I shone my flashlight into the face of the wolf. He gazed up at me, his eyes glowing an unearthly green in the light. He licked his jowls and howled some more. He didn't look injured or starving; what did he want? Has he come to tell me Benson is dead? I wondered, as my mind raced with possibilities, none too bizarre to be given consideration.

Another thought struck me: Barika had come into her first heat. I turned to look at her beside me on the bed. She was not whining or distraught, nor seeming to be in any way disturbed by our nocturnal visitor—a visitor who in ordinary circumstances would not hesitate to devour her in one big gulp. Instead her face wore a look of smug satisfaction.

At the same time that I realized the wolf might be in love, I became aware that the whole cabin was shaking, and that in addition to the sound of the wolf's howling, there was another sort of howling: that of wind. And what a wind! It was bending the big spruce trees. I could see their tops tossing, and the cabin was creaking and groaning as the wind shook it. There was the sound of a tree crashing to the ground, and the plastic on the big window downstairs was snapping.

Imagining that the wind, the wolf—or both—could be coming through the door at any second, I shot down the ladder and into the mudroom. It was one of the many times that the high degree of organization of everything was justified; I was able to locate the hammer and a large nail quickly and in almost total darkness. I hammered the spike through the edge of the door and into the frame, effectively nailing the wolf and the wind out and myself in.

I took the rifle upstairs with me, and leaning out the window again, I fired into the yard, thinking a display of my superior killing power would scare the wolf from my door. The wolf didn't move, just continued to howl up at the window. I wasn't prepared to attempt to shoot the creature, and certain he would not be able to get in the cabin now, I returned to bed.

There was to be no sleep for me for the rest of that awful night. The wind threatened to blow the windows in, the wolf howled with the wind, my bed trembled on its legs as the floor moved under it. I ended up in a sleeping bag on the downstairs bed/couch, drinking tea and praying for morning.

By daybreak the wolf was gone, the wind had stopped and Lorri was pounding on my door. Pulling the big nail out was harder than pounding it in, and by the time Lorri tumbled into the cabin, all excited about her trip to Terrace and the shopping she'd done, I was a wreck of nerves and sleeplessness and very, very glad to see her. It took her a few minutes to recognize that her bushwoman guru was not well, but when I told her about my horrendous night her response was not, in my bleary eyes, appropriate: she laughed.

She actually laughed quite a lot, despite my refusal to join in. When she'd gotten herself under control we went out to survey the damage the wind had wrought. Lorri was amazed; they'd heard the wind at their cabin but hadn't felt it at all. Here at Elsevere, several trees had blown down, some close enough to the cabin to be frightening, and the tops had blown off others, snapped like toothpicks. The roof Tee had started on the outbuilding that was to be a greenhouse come spring had blown entirely off, and the plastic on the big picture window of the cabin, for extra insulation from winter cold, was in tatters.

And there, close to the doorstep, was a pile of wolf scat, easily identified by the hair in it. Lorrie was sobered by now and wanted me to come and spend the night with her. Jackie and Daddy had gone to Terrace as soon as she and Claude had returned, and this morning Claude had gone back to the highway camp where he worked driving heavy equipment. Lorri was never desirous of solitude; she hated and resented any time left alone, and was more than glad to have Barika and me for a sleepover.

I agreed to go home with her for the day—we wanted to have a good long visit and catch up on one another's news—but I would not spend the night. I felt sure the wind was over, and the wolf, if he should return, would be frightened off by some firecrackers I'd remembered having brought home from Hyder and stowed in the porch.

We had a lovely day. Lorri had acquired her own little dog, a poodle/Maltese cross she'd named Baby, and while we chatted and examined all Lorri's shopping loot, our dogs happily played together. I stayed for dinner and then went home, tired from the intensely social aspect of this day after my quiet days of being alone.

Just after midnight, the wolf and the wind began again. I threw the firecrackers down onto and around the wolf; he moved politely out of the way and merely watched as they fizzled and went off. He was not at all dismayed by the sparks and the bangs, moving back to his position outside the door as soon as the fireworks were over and recommencing his lonesome song.

I slept downstairs again, or tried to sleep—the wind was relentless. At some point in that endless night I remembered the elders saying my choice of site for the cabin was not a good one. Could this wind be what they meant? It came down the broad valley sounding like a train, gathering speed and intensity until it arrived at my cabin, which it shook like a rat in the teeth of a terrier before continuing on.

I was to learn that no one else's place caught the wind like mine did. I guess everyone else who had built in this country had heeded the elders. The winds arrived mid-winter, blew like hell for a few days and then were gone until a sudden reappearance in early spring. Those days never got any easier for me; wind was and still is my least favourite force of nature. Luckily the spring winds performed without me, while I was on the trapline, but those winter ones were brutal and always meant sleepless nights for me.

The next day saw me and my dog at Lorri's, this time to spend the night. We had a great time; we danced, sang along to Lorri's favourite country-western tunes and drank beer. We were in our beds just after midnight when Baby started barking and Barika's suitor started howling—right outside the window of the cabin. This cabin was small and low, with the ceiling barely high enough for me, taller than my French-Canadian pals, to stand upright. The noise filled every inch of space and made us shiver. Baby would not stop barking, which added to the stress. Lorri's door at least had a lock on it. We pulled a chair in front of it for extra security and spent the rest of the night awake, the howling and the barking making any sleep out of the question.

The next night we all stayed in my cabin. The wind didn't show up that night, but the faithful, lovelorn wolf did. We didn't even try to sleep, but stayed up all night drinking hot rums and singing. The following day we drove to the Eddontenajon Hotel so that I could use the radio phone to call the game warden, Brock Bailey, in Cassiar. He promised that he and his assistant, Chris, would come and deal with the problem that very afternoon. Lorri and I went back to my place and spent the remainder of the day cooking and baking—I'd invited Brock and Chris to have dinner with us before beginning the Wolf Watch.

From the moment of their arrival I could see these two genial young men did not for a moment believe my story. They pretended to; but they didn't have to pretend to love the dinner we'd made. They just happened to have a couple of cases of beer with them, and Chris had brought his guitar. We settled in for an evening of beer and song and pleasant company. I fell asleep at one point, despite Lorri and Chris's singing. I hadn't slept in three nights, and I think I would have fallen asleep even if the wolf had showed up, which of course he did not. The guys ended up sleeping on the couch, and at some time in the wee hours Lorri crawled in with me. No one stirred till mid-morning.

We all had breakfast together. Brock wanted to know about the incense I had burned last night—he'd never heard of such a thing and was very taken with it. No one said anything about the absence of the wolf. Farewells were made and promises to get together again for another hootenanny night. Of course Romeo, as I'd decided to name the wolf, showed up again that very night and again for the following four.

By the time I'd learned to sleep to the sound of his mournful wails, and even to find some humour in the situation, Barika's heat was over and peace was restored.

Before closing this chapter of the story of the wilderness, I put some of Romeo's scat into the small box that had contained the incense and mailed it to Brock with a note: *The wolf still howls*. He told me weeks later that he'd been excited to receive this package, assuming it was indeed some of my incense, and what a shock it was to find wolf poop instead.

By the time things had settled down again from Barika and her wolf's courtship drama and the clearing up of the yard from the wind's visit, I had forgotten all about my resolve to leave this place and was again caught up in the magic and the mystery of the land, the fascination of being here and learning to thrive in a harsh environment.

One moonlit night Benson returned. I happened to look out the window and saw him there, his white fur lit by the shimmering light of the moon, making him appear a creature of fantasy.

I put on boots and a jacket and went to meet him in the yard, careful not to get too close, respectful of his not wanting to be patted or handled in any way. Something about him told me he had come to say goodbye, but he wanted me to see he was well, that he was happy with his new life; it was full of danger, but it was the life he had chosen.

He started to run back and forth in front of me, an invitation to play that I remembered from when he was a puppy. I ran towards him and he feinted at me, his tongue hanging out, and spun away at the last second. I spun too, as best I could in my down jacket and clumsy boots. He went mad with joy, leaping and twisting all around me as I too leaped and twisted. We danced until I was exhausted, flopping down in the snow to marvel at the night, with Benson sitting a little distance away also regarding the scene.

Everything was so clear in this silver-blue light; every shadow, every twig on every tree was visible, familiar but new. I threw out my arms and waggled my fingers, just to see that the humanoid shadow on the snow was mine. High clouds were scudding across the sky; the wind must have gone up there, I thought. I imagined what the earth looked like from that height, and I could see myself in my mind's eye, bulky with clothes, my skin a silver-grey, my eyes huge, my big silent dog sitting near.

I sat staring at the moon for ages, not noticing when Benson slipped away on his ghost paws, and only going indoors when my feet and hands grew numb. Falling asleep on the couch, I was conscious of an enormous happiness filling every corner of my being.

Hollywood Far North

The winter seemed to be endless at this point, and I was wearing thin with the constant hauling of wood, cleaning the wood stove and hauling water. The truck didn't start for a week, until Leon came over and gave it a jump. I'd most likely drained the battery with my tape player.

The horses came in more often for food, and I would give them hay as well as pellets. They were all looking healthy and strong. I'd turned Tiny and Poon back into the wild as soon as the weather got too cold for me to ride.

Jeannie and her girls visited at least once every two weeks, and those evenings were full of foolishness and laughter and were immensely cheering. Lorri came by on her way home from the village to tell me the latest gossip. Someone in the village got shot through the neck by someone else in the village. Albert ditched his truck, but then Albert was always having vehicle disasters of some sort, so that wasn't too interesting. There had been no mail plane for three weeks but the RCMP were able to get a plane in today to pick up their prisoner—the fellow who shot the other fellow.

I began a series of dreams. I say a series because they were related in some way I could not consciously determine. These dreams featured fires, small girls and collie dogs. My father, dead these many years, also showed up in my dreams for awhile. In these images he was represented by photographs I had of him, as though my mind could no longer remember on its own what he looked like.

The first dream was of him in the cockpit of a de Havilland Beaver aircraft. He was the pilot, sitting in the pilot's seat, and Erik Nielsen, long-time Progressive Conservative MP for Yukon and a friend of the family, was beside him in the passenger seat. In this black and white photo, taken when Erik was campaigning, my father is handsome and smiling, but his eyes aren't.

The next photo dream was about one of the times he took my sister and me snowshoeing. We are all at the back of the truck. I am standing ready to go and Dad is kneeling to tie Cindi's snowshoe. This photo was in colour, and in it he is not smiling; he is still handsome, but he looks tired. I woke in tears from the father dreams, and I woke in tears from the fire/girl/collie dreams, but I didn't feel sad. It was baffling. Needing to see Tee, and to have a break, I went to Watson Lake.

Of course I wanted to go back to Iskut almost as soon as I'd unpacked my duffel bag. Watson Lake seemed so busy! There were so many people and they all wanted to talk to me and I didn't have anything to say. Tee seemed a stranger, like someone I'd met but didn't know well. I felt like a wolf in a pen; I needed to keep moving around, taking long walks in the day and again at night. It took days to reacclimatize myself to a daily life with other people in it. Barika, on the other hand, loved it. She was made much of, being tiny and pretty and cute, and she played it up, soon becoming the darling of the family.

Tee was, as always, willing to try to understand, undemanding and kind. His impeccable behaviour made me feel guilty and ashamed. I really had to try for his sake to not be weird, an alien in the world he occupied as comfortably as he did the world of the wilderness. Why couldn't I move between the two with such ease and certainty? Why did it feel as though it had to be either/or? For all my reading, pondering and meditation, I felt further than ever from a state of grace. It was discouraging.

Inevitably, events transpired that were to pull me out of my self-obsessed restlessness.

My mom and my stepfather lost their hotel/motel in a fire. It was a traumatic event for everyone involved, though my mom handled it with a classic British stiff upper lip, worrying more about her husband and the effect on him. My young brother, too, was shocked by the suddenness, the totality of the disaster. The fire was followed by an investigation, and it took months before all the insurance paperwork was sorted and done.

I got another cold, this time convinced it was some horrible lung disease that I wouldn't be able to spell. I quit smoking and went on a cleansing fast of tea and oranges, like in the Leonard Cohen song.

A Hollywood director named Lawrence Schiller was in Watson Lake. He was making a movie for TV called *Hey, I'm Alive*, modelled on the true story of Helen Klaben and Ralph Flores, who survived a mid-winter light-airplane crash in southwest Yukon in 1963. They'd survived forty-nine days before being rescued, and Helen wrote a book about the experience. The movie starred Sally Struthers and Ed Asner, but neither of them came to the Yukon. Stand-ins were hired locally for the filming that would take place just outside of Watson Lake, and the rest of the movie would be shot in Cypress Bowl, outside of Vancouver. Tee and I were at a dinner party when I met Schiller, and he asked me if I would be Struthers's stand-in. The idea was hilarious to me as I was twice her size and dark-haired to her blond. Schiller assured me this was of no consequence, and curious as always, I agreed to do it.

At seven o'clock the next morning I reported to wardrobe at the Belvedere Hotel. My wardrobe consisted of all the clothes that Helen actually wore during her ordeal: a hooded sweatshirt, lots of sweaters and a parka, two pairs of Ralph's baggy pants, socks for mitts and, because she'd had no boots with her on the trip, sweaters tied over with bits of canvas on my feet. We were driven to the airport where we then sat for hours—the Piper Super Cub and the helicopter that had been chartered for the shoot were held down on location because of heavy winds.

Finally, Martin (Asner's stand-in) and I were flown by helicopter to a new location and told to set up a crash camp in fifteen minutes! The snow was up to our hips, and we had to haul all the props up a hill and then try to set up a tent and build a fire—and all the while Larry was shouting over a walkie-talkie "Hurry! Hurry! Hurry!"

Larry and Dick, the head photographer, landed in the helicopter below where we were, and Dick climbed the hill, which appeared to nearly do him in. He told us we were incredible to do all this and then asked, "How can I help, darlings?" He could not; we were done.

When everything was ready to Larry's satisfaction, I had to run back and forth in front of the fire waving a piece of canvas with the downed aircraft's numbers on it, playing to the airborne Super Cub and the hovering helicopter. The first two takes were thrilling; fourteen takes later I was tired and fed up and sweating in all the clumsy clothes. Then I was told I was "fantastic" before getting into the helicopter to be flown to Airplane Lake where the Super Cub flew me back to the Watson Lake airport.

I changed outfits, and Jim Thibideau, a local pilot, and I went up in the Beaver, which had been coloured red and had American aircraft numerals on it. We flew around for some air-to-air shots and then we had to simulate trouble—at one point we were flying just over the treetops. Jim and I enjoyed this, but one of the film guys didn't because he had to lie down in the back of the plane out of the range of the cameras. Jim and I were supposed to be Helen and Ralph, just the two of them. It was nearly seven at night before we were allowed to go home.

The next day, same hour of the morning, I met Helen Klaben herself, and Ralph Flores. They'd been brought together, for the first time since their rescue, for a magazine article and to promote the film. She and I liked one another right away and seemed to have known one another forever, so easy and quick was our talk. She was thrilled to be back and deeply interested in the filming. Ralph was quiet and wasn't interested at all in the process of bringing the story back to life, and was downright awkward at seeing Helen again. He seemed reluctant to be there at all, though he was not unpleasant or rude.

This day was spent almost entirely in the Beaver with Jim. Larry and the cameraman were in the helicopter and not happy with the nice weather. When it turned nasty in the afternoon, they got all excited and had us flying into the snowstorm and lurching around like a great wounded bird. As the weather worsened, Jim became edgy and rebellious, but before he could outright refuse to do any more, the filming was declared over and we landed. There was a gathering of the film crew and all the local people who'd been involved. It was interesting, and fun.

The next day they filmed Jim and me doing more fake crash scenes. Jim really got into it and went for as much authenticity as he safely could. Larry and Dick declared themselves thrilled. We then flew to Whitehorse with two of the crew and masses of equipment. The plane was freezing cold as Dick had the front window open half the time shooting POVs, which I was told means "points of view." At six that evening, Jim and I landed at Watson Lake airport, our movie careers over.

I got paid $150 for the three days, and I would have done it for nothing. It was not only an interesting experience but had also completed the process of diverting me from inwardness, forcing me to be more social, more giving of myself and my time.

▲

The Sourdough Rendezvous is a February celebration of life in the North. Taking place in Whitehorse, it features events such as dog-sled racing, flour packing, axe throwing and chainsawing. At that time there was a Sourdough Queen and Keystone Kops, who ran around catching beardless men and putting them in makeshift jails scattered around the city streets. It has since become more of a family event, but then the Rendezvous was really a catharsis, a gargantuan piss-up, with people dressing up and misbehaving in a manner mostly harmless, noisy and colourful.

The Fleming family arrived in Watson Lake for a couple of days of skiing at the town's excellent downhill ski facility before going on to the Rendezvous. Our place became a madhouse of people, dogs, ski equipment and constant comings and goings. I threw myself into all the activity and enjoyed the chaos.

Days before the family arrived, I'd acquired a harlequin Great Dane. He was a beautiful animal but had been mistreated and was very shy and sad. He wouldn't leave my side since I had taken him on, and being the size he was this presented a few problems. Luckily he was okay with all the new folks suddenly living with us; they were a dog-loving bunch and were careful and sweet with him all the time.

When Tee and I decided to go to Whitehorse for Rendezvous with the Flemings, it was quite a show. Tee, Leon and his son, Brett, would go in Leon's pickup truck, leaving Jeannie, me, the two girls and two dogs to travel in Tee's station wagon. The trip up the highway was smooth and trouble-free, with the fellows passing us early in the journey while we women and children dawdled at the highway lodges and stopped to take photos. When we arrived, the guys had checked into the hotel and were gone to the bar, leaving young Brett in the hotel room, ensconced in front of the TV with a Dairy Queen lunch. Jeannie and I joined our men, and the girls and the dogs joined Brett, all quite happy to be eating fast food and enjoying television.

The next day we all attended the dog races, thrilled with the scene on the river of the dogs yelping and leaping in their traces, eager to be off. We watched the flour-packing contest, and from there, the one-dog pull, where a St. Bernard, Duke, broke his own record and set a new world record by pulling 1,700 pounds! All the events were well-attended by enthusiastic crowds, many wearing Klondike costumes. We had to have coffee in the lobby of our hotel—the café was full.

That night we went to the Showboat, a tavern where the Canucks, a popular local band, played. The crowd was boisterous and fun, with everyone in the place on the dance floor. The girls went to a teen dance, and Brett ate Dairy Queen burgers and watched TV in the hotel room with the dogs. The next day we all drove out to Takhini Hot Springs and basked in the steaming water for three hours. Jeannie and I took the girls to a scary movie, and the fellows stayed in the room to watch the news.

The trip home was fraught; about a third of the way to Watson Lake, the gas pedal on the station wagon became loose. Being centuries-oppressed, ignorant women, we could not figure out why we were unable go more than twenty miles an hour, so with our centuries-oppressed predisposition to resignation, we simply carried on, knowing the trip would be longer. Twelve hours longer, to be exact.

Outside of Cassiar, we were stopped by the police. We were going up a hill at a mere eight miles per hour, and the officer had lots of time to look us over and notice that the 1975 decals were not on our plates. Tee had purchased them but not stuck them on the licence plates or given us the papers to prove he had them. The nice policeman looked inside the car: two tired women, three grubby kids, an enormous Great Dane and a toy poodle looked back at him from a welter of luggage, boxes, bags and ski equipment. Plainly he was sorry he'd stopped us, having no idea just what to do about this little gang of lawbreakers. He finally let us go, asking us to tell Tee to phone and let him know the dates on the papers.

We also managed to run out of gas just after the turnoff from the Alaska Highway onto Highway 37. Ed Asp, a resident of Dease Lake, happened by and luckily had enough gas in a jerry can to get us to Dease Lake, where we persuaded the store owner to open up so we could get gas and some much-needed food.

I drove Jeannie and the kids home and ended up spending the night at Tatogga with them, too tired to drive back to my cabin.

The cabin was a haven after those exciting and eventful couple of weeks, and I was glad to sink into the silence and my winter routine. I found I *needed* my morning meditation the way I used to need my morning coffee and cigarette; I needed to find my stillness, my centre, before getting into my day.

Mancha, the Great Dane, was not a bush dog, but then neither was Barika. The difference was that Barika thought she was big and tough and acted accordingly, whereas Mancha clearly saw himself as small and weak and acted accordingly. He refused to learn the rudimentary rules of the cabin. He never did get the hang of being housebroken; my descent from the loft in the morning was made perilous by the necessary leap from the third rung from the bottom to avoid the pile of feces he would leave there every morning.

I could not move without him beside me, and my jeans developed worn spots at the hip from his head pressing against me. His beautiful coat, with its vivid black and white markings, was in no way designed to keep him warm in a northern winter, but he insisted on coming outdoors with me, his shivering, trembling presence complicating my outside chores. I had to come in every few minutes so that Mancha would not get frostbite.

Nuisance that he was, I loved him. I loved him with a heart-aching love, feeling his history of abuse and neglect, forgiving him for his fear and his timidity, cherishing his awkward devotion. It was as though I knew he was not long for this world and wanted him to have some happy times. A year later a pack of wolves killed him, right out in the yard. That was over thirty years ago and I still can't remember him without tearing up. He was a tragic creature, but I like to think he did have that brief time of being loved and cared for.

Mancha's brutal death, and my stupid helplessness in the face of it (I didn't take the rifle from the wall and shoot at the wolves; I'd thought of it but was afraid of hitting the dog, and it was all over so fast . . .) haunted me for the rest of the winter.

Everyone was sympathetic, though from the beginning most of them had thought I was crazy to take and keep the poor creature. Lorri offered me a cat, and I listlessly agreed to take it. Barika would like the company as she missed Mancha too, and we both needed to stop moping and move on.

Lorri changed her mind when it came to actually giving me the cat; it was obvious to her I would not be up to her standards of cat ownership. But as it turned out, one of the wives at the Bob Quinn highway camp sent me a grey cat named Carse. I was not particularly interested in or fond of felines. I had never lived with one and had never felt a desire to do so, but I recognized that the cat brought by a trucker to my cabin had had no choice, and the least I could do was to house him until I could find him another home. If he was meant to ease the loss of Mancha, I thought, it wasn't going to work.

Carse may not have eased my grief, but he certainly provided a distraction. He was the most curious of cats; there was nothing

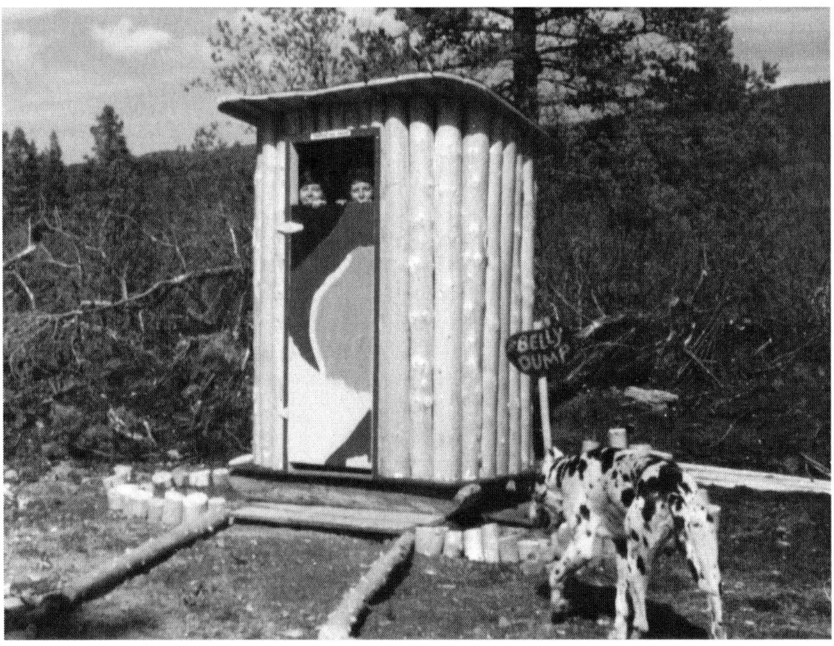

Mancha the Great Dane (right) rarely left my side.

he didn't thoroughly examine, and he was fearless. He proved to be a hunter of some skill, choosing to eat his kills rather than the cat food I provided. He also preferred to be outdoors, coming in only on cold nights when he would choose his place near the stove, oblivious of Barika, who would attempt to get him to play, or Casper, who after the first chittering at him, ignored him.

Carse returned my lack of interest in him; he was polite, but not in the least desirous of a closer relationship. On the rare occasion I had a visitor, the cat would attempt to leave Elsevere by hiding in the guest's vehicle. He was as interested in leaving as I was in his departure.

We did get used to one another eventually, though we were never close. I appreciated his self-sufficiency and he was grateful for the warmth of my wood stove and the reliability of food when his hunt was unsuccessful.

A Full House

It was spring and time to go to the city. I was having a show at the Vancouver East Cultural Centre, and then another in Calgary at a hip little gallery called Subway.

Vancouver was glorious, with perfect weather to show off the mountains and the sea and the burgeoning greens of a coastal spring. Tee had accompanied me. We were in the apartment and things were not great between us. I was having a hard time being part of a couple again after my lone-but-not-lonely winter. I was having a hard time being in a relationship, taking on the responsibilities of a role, remembering to consult before making decisions. Tee had reached a place where he'd decided he wanted this—he wanted us to live together and "be as one;" he loved me. I knew he was a good man and that I was fortunate to have someone like him care for me. I felt the burden of his goodness, how he put up with me without complaint.

I was feeling my way along, going carefully because I could see the hairline cracks and hear some bricks falling and the thin sound of seams ripping. It was all threatening to fall apart, and I wasn't ready for that finality. We agreed we would try to make it work for us, in our own way. There was relief in discussing our issues, and things got brighter from then on.

Larry Schiller and his film crew were still at work on *Hey, I'm*

Alive, and we went up to Cypress Bowl to watch. It was fascinating to see how movies are made and how much is smoke and mirrors. Many of the crew were staying at the Hotel Vancouver, and we were invited for dinner and drinks with them. Ed Asner and Sally Struthers were there, and it was a fun and friendly evening with lots of stories of Hollywood to astound us.

My show went well. Schiller bought paintings, as did some of the crewmembers from Los Angeles and those from Vancouver. All together, I sold enough to make me feel solvent for awhile, and then it was off to Calgary. Tee went back to Watson Lake.

I did everything I was expected to do while in the cities—I saw the people I needed to see and carried on my business with aplomb. All the time I felt as though I wasn't really there, as though I hadn't left the cabin at all but was still there doing my meditation and daily chores. It was not an unpleasant sensation. I hurried back to Iskut and Elsevere as soon as I could, in time to revel in spring.

The horses were shaggy and unkempt with their winter coats dropping off them in clumps. The beaver pond was active again; there were kits swimming around exploring their world. The trees were bursting into that bright lime green of spring leaves. And I was offered a job: several mining companies were coming into the area again this summer and they needed an expediter.

I was happy to do this. It meant some extra income as well as the promise of a busy and exciting summer. I was given a two-way radio and schedules were set up. The deal was, they would tell me via the radio what they needed at their camps. I would search and find the articles and arrange to have the goods flown to them by airplane or helicopter. It meant having to make trips to Terrace and to Stewart, sometimes to Watson Lake, because many of the supplies needed were not available at the co-op store in the village. It was the sort of job that did not keep me busy every minute, giving me time to keep up with my painting and time to enjoy the summer months riding and boating and hiking. It was the perfect job for me.

⮝

Everything went well. The expediting was challenging and fun; I enjoyed having the area beside my driveway turned into a helicopter landing and refuelling place, and I liked the influx of people from outside our area coming and going. My meditation practice suffered a bit; some days were too busy to carve out the time, and somehow the need was not so intense during this time.

I was due for another adventure, or misadventure, as it turned out. Craving a good fresh trout dinner, I decided one quiet day to take my rubber boat to Kinaskan Lake and catch some fish. Kinaskan Lake is a very big lake, and like most very big lakes, there are winds scudding across it most of the time. Such a wind soon took my small craft and sent it bobbing down to the far northern end of the lake, with me helpless to stop it. Trying to control the direction of an almost round rubber boat with oars is sort of like trying to nail Jell-O to a wall—it just doesn't happen.

I was in trouble. The end of the lake was a swamp, infested with mosquitoes, and there was no trail to the road from there. I would be effectively stranded. Of course I had not told anyone where I was going or what I was doing—who was there to tell? Although I'd become familiar enough now with some of the perils of bush living to realize how potentially grave a situation I was in, all I could do was mentally kick myself for once again being so stupid and careless as to create such a mess. Planning on being out on the lake only long enough to catch some fish, I hadn't brought any insect spray with me. I hadn't brought food or water or even cigarettes and a lighter, though mosquitoes and black flies were about to be the most immediate danger I was facing when my boat was finally stopped in the swamp. There were many stories of people and animals being driven to death by these critters, unable to stop moving even long enough to eat or drink, so maddening and painful were the hordes plaguing them.

Hard as I tried, I could not get the boat pointed towards a friendlier shore, the one where I could bushwhack my way the short distance to the road that ran alongside the lake. It would, by this time, be a walk of a few miles to where my truck was parked, but it was infinitely better than where I was headed: the swamp was an impassable distance from the road.

One of the mining exploration companies in the area for the summer had leased Hyland Post, an old camp across the lake from the road, accessible only by helicopter, float plane or boat. The lake was so wide that the camp was not visible from the road; my chances of getting my boat across that vast open space were nil. The wind was in charge. I was going to the swamp, where I was unlikely to be found before dying a slow and agonizing death, and where even my bones would remain, scattered by scavengers.

These grim thoughts were interrupted by the far-off sound of an outboard motor. Scanning the lake (no binoculars—had left them at the cabin, along with every other piece of equipment that might have given me a better chance of survival), I thought I could see a tiny dot on the far side. If it was one of the boats from the mining camp, the likelihood of my tiny craft being seen was minimal, but despite this, I found myself praying.

Having renounced the Christian god when my father died, and having found no other deity, I don't know who or what I was praying to, but soon I could see in my mind a figure, and I knew it was listening to me. Straining my inward eye, I saw her at last: a tall brown woman with long grey-black hair, standing naked in a forest clearing. She had her head cocked towards me, and an enormous smile on her face.

I began to babble and pray and promise, the sweat and tears running down my face, my hands reaching towards her. The woman threw back her head and laughed. She laughed and laughed, a great burst of pure merriment that filled the air with joy. I could not stop myself from joining in, wiping my eyes with the backs of my hands as my tears of fear and desperation fled, banished by the liquid sounds of delight.

That is how Larry found me, sitting in my boat, which was

pushed up into the tall swamp grass, laughing my head off. It took me a few moments to realize I had been saved, and when I did my laughter got even louder, causing Larry to stay a safe distance away and begin to wonder if he should call for help before attempting this rescue.

Seeing his face, I wanted to laugh more, but the thought of sitting in the gathering swarm of mosquitoes for any longer sobered me. "How did you know I was here? I'm so glad you found me! Do you have a rope?" I fired these and more questions at him as he pulled in closer, reassured by these inquiries.

He was the cook, the only person in camp during the day when everyone else was out prospecting. He'd been sitting at the table in the lodge having a coffee break and idly glassing the lake with a pair of binoculars when he'd noticed a tiny yellow dot scooting down the water. It hadn't taken long for him to see the occupant was in trouble, and he'd gone down to the dock, jumped in one of the motor boats and come to the rescue.

He was a young fellow, about my age, and he was now clearly enjoying his role as hero and saviour. I know I ought to have been grateful, and I was, but I also felt silly for having gotten myself into such a predicament, and nothing in his demeanour suggested he saw me as anything other than a goofy girly-girl.

Larry was quieted by the gruffness of my gratitude and my reticence as we crossed the lake to where my truck was, his boat towing mine. I was now acutely aware of how silly my boat was; why, oh why had I not listened to those who knew about these things and gotten myself a canoe? I vowed to give my toy boat to the Adams's two boys—they would have fun with it.

The ride seemed interminable. I was too embarrassed to look at Larry or respond to his friendly questions and his obvious interest in me. Soon the only sounds were those of the motor and the water parting to give us passage. All I wanted was to reach the shore, throw my frivolous rubber toy in the back of the truck and get home.

There was also the vision of the mysterious woman: who was she that some part of me recognized and instantly loved and trusted? Her joyous presence had reassured and calmed me to such a degree that I had laughed—laughed in the face of a serious life-threatening event. I wanted to find her again somehow; I wanted to find the path to her, the access to what she had for me. I felt I had met the teacher I'd been searching for.

"So. I guess you're a feminist," was Larry's remark as he watched me load my boat and fishing gear. I'd been stern about doing it myself, wishing only for him to go away, imagining the story he would tell that night when the crew got back to camp, and how in no time at all the tale of the helpless chick on the lake would become part of local folklore, as indeed it did.

"Yes, I guess I am," I told him, climbing into the truck and starting the engine. "Thanks again for your help." I drove off, feeling not only a fool but also an ungrateful one, leaving him standing in the road.

My sister and Mic arrived, without warning. She had left her husband and wanted to stay with me until fall, when she would go to Vancouver and get a job. Tee had arrived two days before, bringing with him two young American fellows he'd picked up hitchhiking their way to Alaska. He'd persuaded them to come and spend a couple of weeks at Elsevere, cutting firewood and clearing more land around the cabin. Suddenly the cabin went from being a sometimes brief stop for mining crews in transit or local visitors for coffee, to being full all the time.

It was perfectly grand to have Mic back, and my sister, Cindi, was enthusiastic, helpful and a lot of fun despite her domestic worries and the uncertainty she must have been feeling about the future for her and her little girl. The Americans, Bob and Wynn, were quickly nicknamed by Lynch—Slab and Rawhide—names they wore with pride. Lynch was jealous of our good fortune in

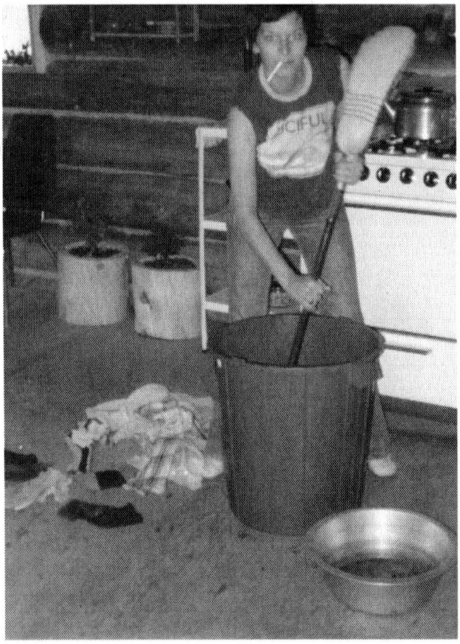

Cindi was great at finding ways to make chores fun and easy. A broom and a garbage pail, and presto we had a washing machine for laundry day.

having these two strapping fellows to help us out; it was always difficult to find anyone to work in this area, especially since none of us could afford to pay anyone decently.

The boys were wildly keen and totally green. They didn't know how to use an axe, let alone a chainsaw, and they got lost quicker and easier than I did, necessitating a search party almost every time they left the property. Tee finally made them carry rolls of flagging tape to mark their way. However, they were willing, and soon were putting themselves to good use, working hard and long in exchange for room and board. The room consisted of a canvas tent, but the board was pretty good. They loved my cooking, eating so much that Tee said we would have been better off just paying them an hourly wage.

Of course this influx of people soon affected my routine, which soon affected my feeling of well-being. I puzzled mightily over this conflict in me. I loved my sister and my niece, and they were easy company; the boys were polite, helpful, appreciative and fun. I could not have had better people around, and I knew it and I enjoyed them. At the same time a part of me always went into deep mourning, grieving my solitude. How to reconcile these vastly different aspects of myself was a consuming issue for me, not just in the Iskut years but for many of the years that followed.

The summer passed thus, busy from morning till night, and often well into the night as we played crib or Scrabble or simply sat around talking. Cindi and I painted and decorated the outhouse, naming it "the belly dump" in honour of the big earth-moving trucks that every summer were part of the efforts to improve Highway 37. The outhouse was a pretty little building, constructed of small peeled logs placed vertically. It had a swinging door that featured a graffiti board, complete with felt pens attached by string. It was ready for any scribblings or sketchings from users, and by the end of the summer it was well covered; it seems the outhouse was a place that inspired creativity in its visitors.

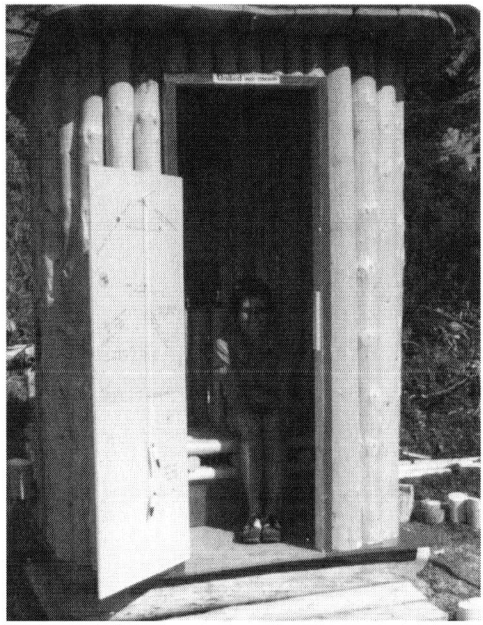

We decorated the outhouse and nicknamed it "the belly dump."

It was my sister who came up with a way to do our laundry. With so many people, it was not really appropriate to take our wash to Tatogga every week to use the Flemings' facilities. Welcoming though Jeannie unfailingly was, they too were having a busy summer with the resort. Cindi took one of our large plastic garbage cans and filled it with heated water and laundry soap before putting in a load of laundry. The agitation of the clothing was provided by her: using a plunger and a vigorous up and down and swirling movement, she did get the laundry perfectly clean, which then dried quickly on the clothesline.

Cindi brought a sense of fun to everything she undertook—nothing was simply a chore. This gift made the month she and Mic spent with us memorable for days and evenings of laughter. I was sorry when they left and felt their absence for weeks afterwards. I was not so jolly to live with when Cindi's bubbling energy was gone; I got tired of feeding people and having them around all the time. I wanted some time just with Tee.

Slab and Rawhide had given up the idea of going to Alaska. They were getting odd jobs with Leon and the Adamses and with Lynch, and they wanted to stay. They decided to build their own cabin, about a quarter of a mile from mine. It would be on the property that Tee and I had staked, but we had no objection. They were good kids and would be company for me in the coming winter.

We could hear the sound of their chopping and sawing and banging in the distance over the next few weeks. They were doing their own cooking, and we saw them rarely; when they did show up I insisted they stay for dinner. They were very intent on their building. When they weren't odd jobbing for someone they spent every daylight hour working on the cabin. We were asked to stay away; they didn't want us to see their place until it was finished. They'd gotten brown and muscular—very different young men from the pale, weedy-looking lads who'd arrived with Tee early in the summer. Finally we were invited to come and see their new home. We walked through the bush on their well-worn path (no driveway) until we came to a little clearing in the middle of which was the oddest-looking structure I had ever seen.

They had put all the butt ends of the logs at the same end! This meant that the logs were separated by several inches at the other end. It looked hilarious, but I knew I mustn't laugh. Tee gravely asked what sort of chinking they were going to use. I could see his lips twitching, though he kept his face straight. Slab and Rawhide knew they'd goofed. They weren't exactly sure how, but they knew their cabin didn't look like any other cabin in the country. As to chinking, they didn't have a clue and showed themselves eager to listen and learn. Finally Tee told them that the logs would have worked better had they trimmed the tapering ends, making the logs a uniform thickness; perhaps they might want to start again—he would help them. I was made to promise not to show or tell anyone about their first attempt, and I didn't (except Lorri—we had a glorious, roll-on-the-ground laugh when I took her there), until this book. They built another cabin, and by the time the snow came, they were fairly snug.

My family from Watson Lake visited, bringing a huge and luxurious fifth wheel trailer, and a great aunt and uncle from England. Typically, Mom had brought all sorts of thoughtful and useful things for me and for the cabin. She often provided me with items I hadn't thought of and later wondered how I had managed without them. They were all charmed by our cabin and appropriately awed by the magnificent setting in which we lived. We could not have had better guests; they were interested in everything, ready to experience anything that was offered and brought a readiness for fun to all we did.

Uncle Chuck hadn't fished before. Tee took him out on Eddontenajon Lake where they caught as many fish as they legally could take and from where Uncle Chuck came home with the brightest sunburn I had ever seen. He was so thrilled with his catch, with the whole day, that if he suffered any pain from his burn, it went without comment from him.

My little brother, Buster, fell off of Tiny, an event that to this day he claims gave him a lasting fear of horses. To hear him describe this experience—"her nostrils were red with blood, foam dripped from her jaws, she reared and galloped off, leaving me crumpled on the ground"—is hilarious to those of us who witnessed his wild ride. Tiny trotted a few steps, he slid off her back and was caught almost immediately by me. I don't think any part of his body other than his feet hit the ground.

Aunt Brenda helped with the cooking, a lit cigarette dangling from her mouth as she stirred and chopped, talking all the while. There was no fear of ashes falling into the food—her generous bosom jutted out far enough to catch them. Her language was colourful, larded with expletives all spoken in an elegant British accent. She was an indefatigable walker; she and my mom and I walked miles every day, all of us talking and laughing the whole time. I didn't worry about bears—not with the racket we made.

It was sad to see them leave. Tee and I felt quite dull for days after they had gone, and the very forest seemed stilled with the silence.

Winter with a Poodle and a Weasel

The summer was over, and everyone who didn't live here had gone. The mining camps had been shut down, the two-way radio returned and the crews dispersed to their homes, their real lives in cities and towns.

Not only did I make money expediting for the mining companies, but also many of the geologists and other people involved in the season's explorations bought paintings from me. I also got the groceries and propane bottles left from the camps, the latter particularly handy now that the cabin boasted a cookstove, lights and a deep-freeze, all run on propane. The freezer was packed with moose, caribou, fish and berries. Slab and Rawhide had cut masses of firewood and stacked it. I'd ordered and received dozens of books, and art supplies. My second winter at Elsevere was going to be a cushy one. There were bales of hay in the greenhouse, barrels of pellets and oats, and a salt block in the yard: the horses too would have a comfortable season of snow.

Slab and Rawhide had gone to work in Terrace for the winter. When the prospectors, the road crews and the few tourists departed, so did the work the boys had been able to get in the area. They promised to be back for Christmas. Tee left for Arizona; he would be back around Christmastime too. Casper, who'd moved out for the summer, took up residence again days after Tee had gone.

My morning meditation resumed, and the easel occupied space in the living room. There was another battery for the truck so that I could play music more often, alternating them, without worrying about draining one and not being able to start the truck.

Lorri would be alone for a good part of the winter too, with Claude working at a highway camp and Daddy and Jackie gone back to Terrace until spring, when Daddy was going to spring trap with Lynch and me. Lorri and I planned times together, snowshoeing and cooking. I was not as social a being as Lorri, a characteristic that was to cause her many moments of impatience with me, though none that jeopardized our friendship.

My plans for the months ahead were largely about painting; I needed to reach further and deeper to accomplish on canvas what I could see in my mind. I'd also planned a dedicated search, through reading and meditation, for that mysterious place I longed for, where the spirit of the earth dwelt. During my vision quest, meditations and unexpected moments in the wild, I had experienced rapture, bliss. I knew it was there, in the wild. Organized religion had not provided me with access to that place. Everywhere I'd looked in those organizations, the spectre of patriarchy and the accompanying greed for power had turned me away.

There I was for another winter, just me, my poodle and my weasel. It was 1975; I was twenty-seven years old.

The days and the weeks went by without me noticing. Lorri reluctantly gave up trying to engage me in anything other than my painting and studying when I was in the flow, which was most of the time that winter.

Barika loved the snow as much as I did, especially the fresh snowfalls when we would go out to leap and run and cavort, regardless of the time, day or night. She came snowshoeing with me, snug in the same bag I carried her in when we went riding. This tiny dog was great company, seeming to understand my every mood; when I wanted to be alone, she amused herself or slept, and when I wanted to play, she was instantly available. A dog was practically a necessity, to my way of thinking, if one was to be alone in the bush. Benson didn't come around at all this winter, and I missed him. I missed Mancha, his heavy head pressing on my hip or in my lap. He'd been a lot of work, poor old fellow, but I missed him just the same. I went out and about just enough to maintain human relationships, going to pick up my mail every couple of weeks, sometimes carrying on to Tatogga for a visit with the ever-welcoming Fleming family.

Occasionally I issued invitations for evenings of homemade pizza and games, and I thoroughly enjoyed those times, as I did my visits with Lorri. I recognized the value of these encounters and took responsibility for my share in them seriously. These people were important to me, not just for survival; their lives, the choices they made and the manner in which they pursued their dreams and dealt with their fears taught me a great deal.

There was no one in the area that I knew of, however, who could or would share my deepest interests at this time, and I yearned for that sort of company. I had grown up in a family and a community where many subjects (religions other than Anglican, politics other than Conservative, music that was not country-western, any of the visual arts) were unheard of. I was accustomed to my passions being solitary ones. Some of the people I'd met in the summer months, those who were on the same quest, had not only provided me with hours of the conversations I craved but had also kept in touch by mail. Those lengthy letters, often accompanied by books, were gifts of a value they probably never realized. Those contacts kept me aware of a world outside the one in which I had chosen to live—a world where there were many people like me, with the same questions, the same thirst to know and understand, the same desire for a spiritual journey.

One cold day I drove to Tatogga for a convivial evening of warmth and good company. Returning late at night, my truck hit a patch of ice a short distance from my driveway. It went off the road entirely and rolled over into a deep ditch that was luckily full of soft snow. When the vehicle had settled, I was up against the door on the passenger side, wondering what had happened, so quickly had the whole event occurred. I had the presence of mind to shut the ignition off before engaging in a frantic search for the bottle of homemade wine Jeannie had given me. The bottle was unbroken. Leaving my handbag on the floor and the keys in the ignition, I fought my way out of the truck, moving snow away with my hands—without letting go of the bottle of wine. It was a long struggle to get to the road, and I was sweating with the effort by the time I was upright and walking to my cabin.

Arriving in the cabin, I opened the stove and put wood in before taking off my outdoor clothing and putting the kettle on for a warming cup of tea. While I waited for the kettle to boil, I sat on the loveseat and held out my hands, watching for the tremor that would mark my reaction to once again being involved in an event laden with drama and dark possibilities. Not a quiver. I was surprised; I was certain somewhere in my body there was evidence, delayed for now, of how shaken up I was at what had happened. That night I kept waking to hold up my hands in the flashlight's beam, checking for even a little shaking.

Nothing happened, leading me to believe I had become, unbeknownst to myself, a brave and capable bushwoman, a woman who was not fazed by a rolled-over ditched truck on a lonely winter night, a woman who could handle anything. It was a fine realization, and I basked in it. Of course, the woman who could handle anything could not get her truck out of the ditch—it took Leon and his four-by-four to do that.

Another resolution I had made regarding this, my first whole winter in the bush, was to get over my squeamishness regarding leghold traps. Lynch told me that if a trapper checked his line often and didn't leave an animal in the trap for days, it was not inhumane. I'd set a line, a short one, with only three traps, that I could snowshoe to from the cabin to check. It was set for marten, meaning the traps were small and light and easy to carry in a backpack.

The first time I checked my line I was disappointed to see the first two traps empty. Coming up on the third and last one, it was clear I had indeed got something: the snow was all tramped around, and I could hear a low growling noise. Feeling some trepidation (no one had said anything about marten growling), I approached the trap, .22 rifle at the ready. There, crouched in the snow, with the falling snow speckling his grey fur, his yellow eyes burning with fury, was Carse the cat. His hind leg was in the trap, and he'd been there overnight. Far from being glad to see me, he hissed and spat; he knew I was responsible for his predicament and clearly held no hope of rescue by me.

In order to get at the trap and release it, I had to hold the cat, and how that was to be achieved I could not imagine. After several attempts that were as frightening to me as they were infuriating to Carse, I took off my jacket and wrapped him in it, leaving the trapped hind leg clear of the fabric. The trap was sprung, but Carse didn't want a ride home—he took off through the snow, dragging the leg behind him. I had not seen a lot of blood, so I assumed the trap had merely held him snugly without breaking the leg or tearing the skin much more than he had done in his struggle to get free of it.

There was nothing more I could do; he would either return to the cabin or not. I gathered up all three traps and went home—never again would I use a leghold trap. I knew that finding a live animal in a trap and then killing it was not something I would ever be able to do. A Conibear, a kill trap, I could deal with, but having now seen an animal in a leghold trap I was horrified at the pain and the stress it caused.

Carse came into the cabin that night, ate hugely of his cat food and went to lie in his accustomed place by the fire, allowing me, finally, to examine his leg. It was solid, like a piece of wood.

The limb had frozen overnight. I figured I would see what it looked like when it had thawed. The next morning it looked no different. I took him to Jean Black, who gave him a shot of penicillin to ward off any chance of infection and told me there was not much else to be done.

The cat became more of a house cat—having a wooden leg no doubt seriously impaired his hunting abilities. He also, oddly, became more affectionate, making me feel even guiltier for what had happened to him. For the rest of the winter we had a new sound in the cabin: as he made his way up and down the ladder steps and across the wooden floors, his solid leg would make a tapping noise. Guests found this disconcerting at first, and I got to feel like an animal-abusing creep every time I had to explain why my cat had what seemed to be a wooden leg.

Early that spring I was watching him run across the yard, when the leg fell right off! Horrified, I went out to pick him up and see what had happened. The leg was lying on the ground, and the stump was almost entirely healed, with a tiny bare spot yet to be covered with fur. He became a perfectly agile three-legged cat, returning to his mostly outdoor life of stalking and hunting. He also renewed his efforts to leave Elsevere, and was finally successful when a family from Dease Lake who were visiting me found him in their truck as they went to leave. They already knew Carse and his story; the kids loved him and he loved them back and they asked it they could have him. They took him home with them that day, and he lived happily ever after.

Christmas! The tree was enormous, and I had a wonderful time making decorations for it. The cabin was filled with the smell of baking as I worked my way through dozens of recipes I'd collected for this occasion. Lynch and his hired man, Gordon, dropped in for some pre-Christmas cheer, and I served them some of my cinnamon buns with their coffee. It was my first-ever attempt at making these buns, and they'd just come out of the oven moments before the men arrived. They looked just like they were supposed to, and smelled pretty good too.

The guys kicked off their toe rubbers in the mudroom, and soon they were ensconced on my wicker loveseat. There they sat, making it look ridiculously feminine and fragile as they took their stetsons from their heads, their weathered, battered faces accentuated by the white line marking the place where the hat brims sat. The smell from their moosehide moccasins began to overpower the cinnamon as I watched to see their reaction to my latest culinary effort. There was silence as they chewed. Gordon, new to the area, tried valiantly to swallow, sipping coffee in an attempt to wash the bun down.

Lynch was not so polite: he set his uneaten bun back on the plate, telling Gordon, "Give it up, hoss; you'll break the two teeth you got left in there."

I was mortified, hurrying to remove the offending baked goods and offer some cookies from the day before, proven edible by me and Barika.

Christmas preparations continued, sans the cinnamon buns—I lacked the courage and the flour to try them again. Barika was bathed in honour of the season, her ears tied on top of her head with a festive red ribbon. Slab and Rawhide arrived, as promised, bringing rum and an enormous turkey. Tee came a couple of days later, looking tanned and fit from his travels in Arizona and California. He brought me a beautiful silver and turquoise bracelet and a guitar. Although I had never even considered learning to play a guitar, I instantly saw myself whiling away the winter evenings playing country-western songs. I went further, imagining myself accompanying Lorri as she sang at parties, with everyone impressed by my ability.

The holiday time was made better by Richard and Susan, two little tykes from the village who Sister Rhonda persuaded us to take for a few days while their parents celebrated on their own. As soon as she was able to reassure me they were both out of diapers and off the bottle, I was all for it. The kids were great, wide-eyed and interested in everything, showing no signs of homesickness or timidity. They were friendly and cuddly; we all got fond of them in the four days they were with us.

The day before Christmas we bundled up the kids and we all went tobogganing. I managed to hit a tree with my foot, bruising it badly and making myself couch-bound for the remainder of the week. Tee and the boys did the whole dinner. It was really good, and we all ate hugely and had naps immediately afterwards.

One evening I was brushing Barika on my lap as we all sat around listening to Christmas music on the radio. I took her ribbon off to comb the long curls on her ears.

"I think your dog's ears came off," Slab said in the slow, calm way he had of speaking, regardless of what he was saying.

Laughing, I looked down to see two crescent moons of

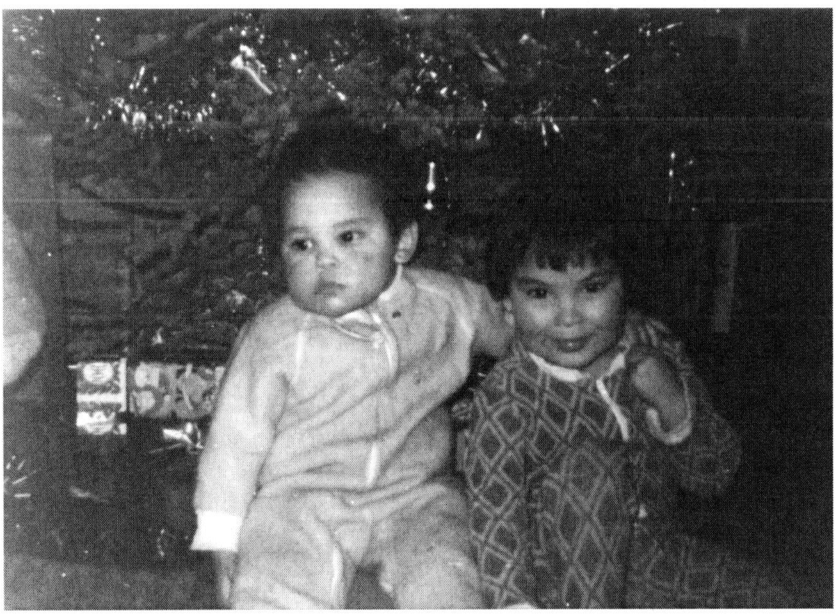

We had surprise guests for Christmas. Richard (left) and Susan (right) from the village came to stay with us for a few days.

stiffened hide with long apricot coloured fur hanging from them caught in the brush. Apparently the ribbon had cut the blood supply to the tips of her ears, and they had indeed come off. She had never exhibited the slightest pain or discomfort from her Christmas decoration, and it hadn't occurred to me that such a thing might happen.

Everyone laughed, but I was horrified. Now I not only had a horse neurotically nervous of any sort of tack and a cat that I had rendered three-legged, I also had managed to disfigure my dog. How, I was to ask myself again and again, could I be so stupid? I didn't deserve to have animals at all, except ones like Casper, who knew to stay away from my dangerous hands.

Tee tried to reassure me that I had not caused Barika any pain, and although she was ruined insofar as she could never be shown, there had never been plans to show her anyway. I could not be comforted. I felt keenly the pain and terror that I had brought to animals in my care, and this was just one more incident of my carelessness. I made Tee and the boys swear they would not tell anyone about this, my latest idiocy; the thought of yet another story about my ignorance making the kitchen table rounds was more than I could bear. They all three solemnly swore to remain silent, their eyes not meeting mine and their lips twitching with amusement.

The boys went back to Terrace the same day the kids went home to the village, leaving me alone with Tee to bring in the New Year. New Year's Day is also my birthday; Tee and the Flemings had planned a surprise party for me before he'd gone south. I was told there was a New Year's party at Tatogga, but I didn't want to go, feeling Tee and I needed some time to ourselves. He was insistent we attend, and I was not gracious in my agreement to go with him. The ride to Tatogga was chilly inside the truck as well as out. It baffled and hurt me that he didn't want some exclusive time with me after months apart.

Arriving at the lodge, we found everyone from miles around was there, some travelling from their remote cabins by snowmobile. All the cabins were full, and the lodge beds too, as many people would be spending the night. It was a wild and raucous party, and I drank lots of whisky and flung myself into the melee, ignoring Tee as much as possible. After midnight, when the New Year had been boisterously welcomed, there was a hush as Jeannie and Tee carried in a gorgeous big cake, complete with the prerequisite number of candles. The big room was filled with the singing of "Happy Birthday" as the cake was set in front of me, my lover and my good friend beaming with pleasure at my surprise.

The combination of feeling awful for having been ignoring Tee and feeling awful for having drunk too much whisky made it impossible for me to blow out my birthday candles. Jeannie quickly and smoothly got her girls to do it for me. There were presents too, and I couldn't open them; I was too overcome by shame and booze. The party went on without me as Tee helped me up the stairs, assuring me, through my blubbered and nearly incoherent apologies to him and everyone else, that he loved me still and that no one would think worse of me for the night's performance.

He did, and they didn't, but I was truly embarrassed by my performance. The episode resulted in two New Year's resolutions: never to drink that much again and never to make assumptions about people's wishes and plans.

Tee and I didn't get a lot of time together on our own. It was holiday time and that meant visiting and being visited. Tee was well-liked, and everyone wanted to see and talk to him. When he left to go to Watson Lake before heading back down south, our relationship was as it had been since the beginning—two people living separate lives with different goals but getting together once in awhile to have awesome sex in a beautiful place and renew vows of love. Although it was working very well for me, I couldn't quite accept that it was okay. It was an uncommon relationship, and I was young, still believing that intimate relationships had to look the same if they were to be called successful.

Once in a tender moment I'd asked Tee why it felt to me as

though he were holding himself back from me. He told me it was because he knew what we had together would not last, and he didn't want to get hurt any more than necessary. I was shocked at this. Although I hadn't used the word "forever" even to myself in terms of our relationship, it was because I didn't use that word in terms of anything. I told him he should trust my feelings for him, all the while knowing he shouldn't because I didn't. It was no wonder he refused me access to his soul: he knew I would come and go as I pleased.

Tee was older than me by twenty years. He was a man who'd experienced the many guises of love, and he was cautious. I was not good relationship material. I didn't live with Tee, and when he was around, I lived *at* him. Despite this surefire recipe for heartache, despite his keeping some distance, he loved me well. I was fortunate to have him in my life at this time, willing to play whatever role I needed. Those roles changed: he was brother, father, lover, pal and trusted companion. Although he played them all splendidly, he was right in knowing I didn't think of what we had together as a lasting thing. I couldn't. Since my father's wholly unexpected death at thirty-nine, I had ceased to believe in "forever," though I was not conscious of that at the time. I lived every moment, rarely making plans of any sort.

Tee was a wise man; he knew me so much better than I knew myself.

Spring Beaver Hunt

This spring beaver hunt was different from my first one in many ways. I had my own riding horse this time. Tiny and I enjoyed one another, though she was an awful tease and a prankster and kept me paying attention. She would never knowingly hurt me; we trusted one another and that trust added a new dimension to my experience of riding. I'd also brought Barika, much to Lynch and Daddy's disgust—they didn't consider her a dog at all, just some sort of animated toy. But she was a brave and game little dog, and she loved being in the bush, participating in everything that was going on. I'd brought my own pack horse, Poon, who had turned out to be a healthy, strong young horse, as Lynch had promised. He was very calm and biddable, having no objection to the pack-saddle and soon finding his place in the pecking order that the horses themselves decided once we were on the trail.

Having my own pack horse meant the tin bathtub came beavering with me, tied to the top of the panniers—again to the bewilderment of the men. Tang had been so traumatized by me and my ignorance when I'd tried to use him to pull logs for the cabin that he got jittery at the very sight of any sort of tack, even a halter. He was going to need hours of patient work if he was ever to become useful. Every time I saw him I felt bad all over again, and so did he.

The ground had thawed, and there was none of the high drama of our first trip. Lynch also chose to go a different route, checking out other areas for the hunt next year. We came across a dam that had been chopped apart by an axe; there were no fresh signs of beaver and the whole place was desolate, with an air of tragedy. Lynch didn't approve of those who shot beaver. He said the chances of actually getting the fur were far less than with a trap because when shot, a beaver would dive into the water where it would live, injured, or die and not be found by the hunter. One of the big old animals we got on this trip had a .22 bullet in his neck, all grown over.

I came on this expedition with a new resolve: I would be in the bush as a trapper, not a voyeur. I would do my share of the work no matter how it made me feel, and I would shut up about it.

At Spruce Island Camp we set up a tent, a big canvas affair. Lynch didn't approve of the newfangled tents with floors that were showing up these days. "A bear comes into your tent," he said, "where are you gonna go? This tent, you just pick up the side and roll out."

We covered the floor of the tent with spruce boughs; it smelled wonderful, all sharp and clean. We would use the old cabin for cooking. As before, Lynch stretched out for a nap, his big belly rising and falling with his snores, his hat over his eyes and his rifle lying alongside his prone body, leaving Daddy and me to organize the camp and put the horses out to graze.

It was Tiny's first experience of hobbles, and she caused us great merriment as she minced around the camp, every now and then looking at me as though to ask, "What have I ever done to you that I deserve this indignity?" She didn't get far from the camp the first night, but by the second she had got the hang of the hopping step necessary for a hobbled horse and was gone with the rest of them. Poon too had issues with the hobbles, but he cottoned on a bit sooner than Tiny—one of the rare instances that that was the case.

I participated in the setting of the traps and the harvesting of the carcasses this trip, and I got much better at the skinning. Skinning a beaver was a long process compared to the quick skinning of marten or rabbits. I would spread a tarp on the ground and sit crossed-legged by the beaver, a posture that naturally made my back sore, but seemed to work best for me. I also stretched my own hides; after sewing up the leg holes, I painstakingly tacked them onto the plywood with a series of closely spaced small nails hammered in as near to the edge of the hide as possible so as to save the fur.

We got a female, somehow, and after carefully skinning the pelt ,I spent a fascinating afternoon examining the inside of a beaver. She was pregnant; there were three tiny perfectly formed kits each in its own thin sack, covered with purple-red veins. The kits were complete but for hair, their skin a pale lilac colour. I

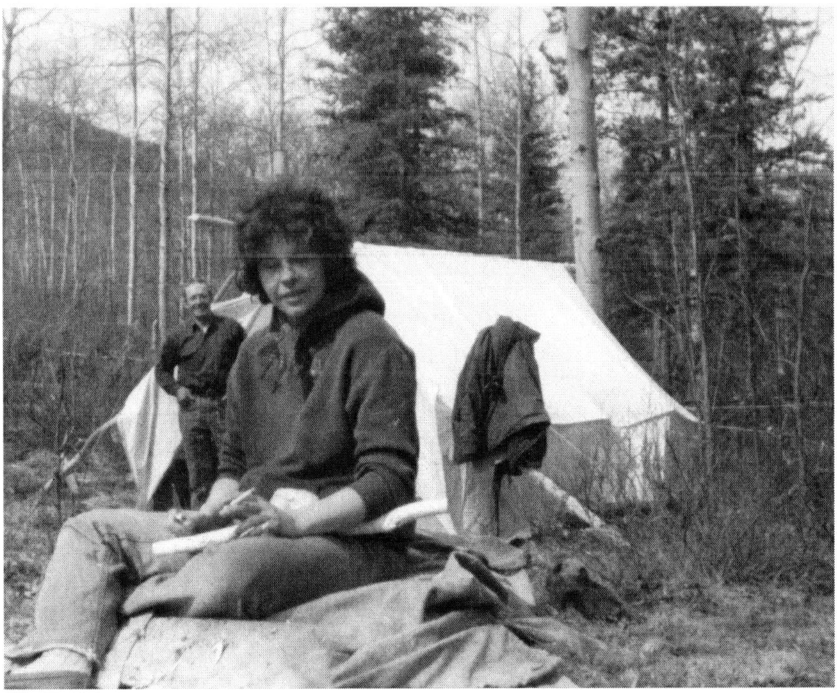

Lynch didn't approve of modern tents, but I preferred the comfort of walls and floors around me, even if they were little protection from bears.

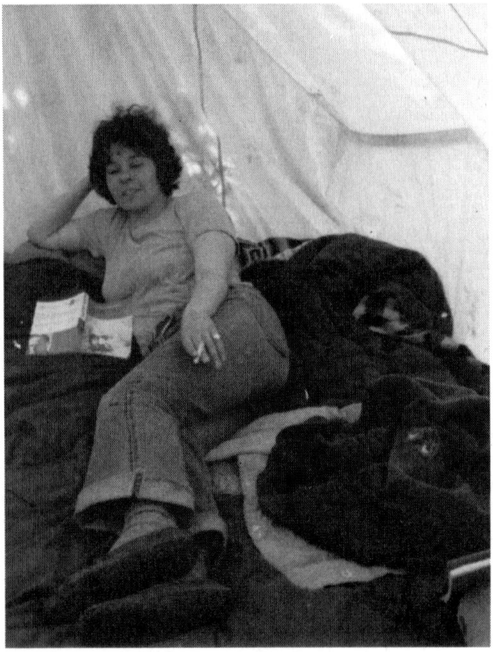

Spruce boughs on the floor of the tent made the bed a little softer.

discovered beaver have two stomachs; one contained bark still intact in shreds and in the other the digestive process was more advanced. Their teeth grow all the way over their heads inside their skulls, accommodating their continual wearing down as they gnaw through tree trunks and strip bark. I couldn't deny I was interested in what my impromptu autopsy revealed and what it taught me, but I also couldn't deny how sad I felt. I offered a silent apology to the land, but it wasn't speaking to me.

I did the cooking; it was my idea as I was interested in eating something other than boiled beaver and rice, though we ate our share of that as well. The menus this time were made more varied by things like canned ham, canned bacon, canned Spam and canned tuna—an improvement, I thought, on squirrel, porcupine and fishy-tasting duck, all of which Lynch had presented on our plates last spring.

For the last couple of years I'd heard stories about the "Jesus mouse," and every time I laughed, thinking the tellers were trying to have some fun at my expense. On this trip, I saw one. There was a small lake about a mile from our swamp-surrounded camp that looked as though there might be fish in it. A feed of fish would be a welcome change from our diet of boiled or roasted beaver meat and fried Spam; I resolved to hike over there and catch dinner. No fish, but there, running on the surface of the water, was a small dark mouse. He not only ran on the water, but he dove underneath the surface as well. When I told the guys about it that night, they both laughed at me and said there was no such thing, it was a joke.

The men, both fellows older than me and old hands at trapping and camp life, worked hard all day, ate the supper I would have ready and then slept around the fire while I cleaned up. They would wake up and have a cup of tea before going to bed. I missed Dwayne, someone to talk to and laugh with, and someone who found all this new and interesting. I got a lot of reading done.

We were out for five days. By the end of the third day, I was ready to leave, and it was not for any reason other than Lynch's snoring and Daddy Charette's teeth. The last time I'd been beavering, I hadn't really noticed Lynch's nighttime exhalations, but this time, in the tent where we all slept, the fabric walls positively reverberated with the noise. Daddy wore dentures—ill-fitting devices that clacked when he ate and clacked when he slept.

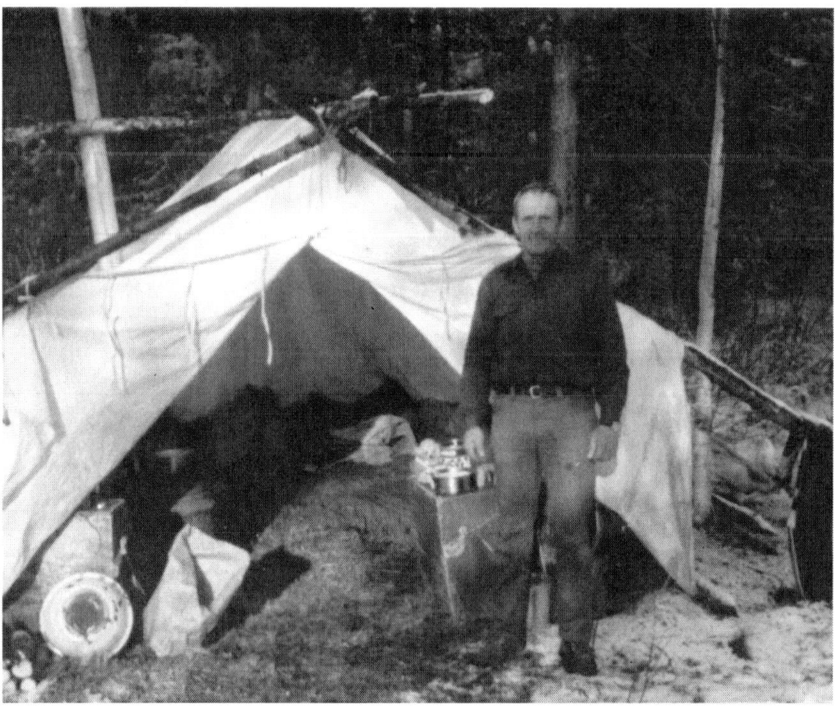

Daddy Charette standing outside the communal sleeping tent.

Between the two sets of sounds, I spent most nights sleepless, falling into a light slumber out of sheer exhaustion just before dawn. I thought of sleeping in the cabin, but it had deteriorated more since the last visit here and the door no longer shut, leaving the space open to a curious bear. We knew there was a bear around; it was feeding from the remains of the beaver that we would put a goodly distance from our camp, and I was certain that if I were to go off anywhere on my own, the bear would come for a visit. I was confined to the tent, where every night for five nights I would lie in my sleeping bag imagining in intricate detail various deaths for my two companions. Luckily, during the day I would forget about their nighttime personas and enjoy being with them, watching and learning.

On the third morning I stayed behind to have a bath, hauling water from the creek to heat on the outside fire. It was a luxurious feeling to lie in the tub in the middle of this pristine wilderness,

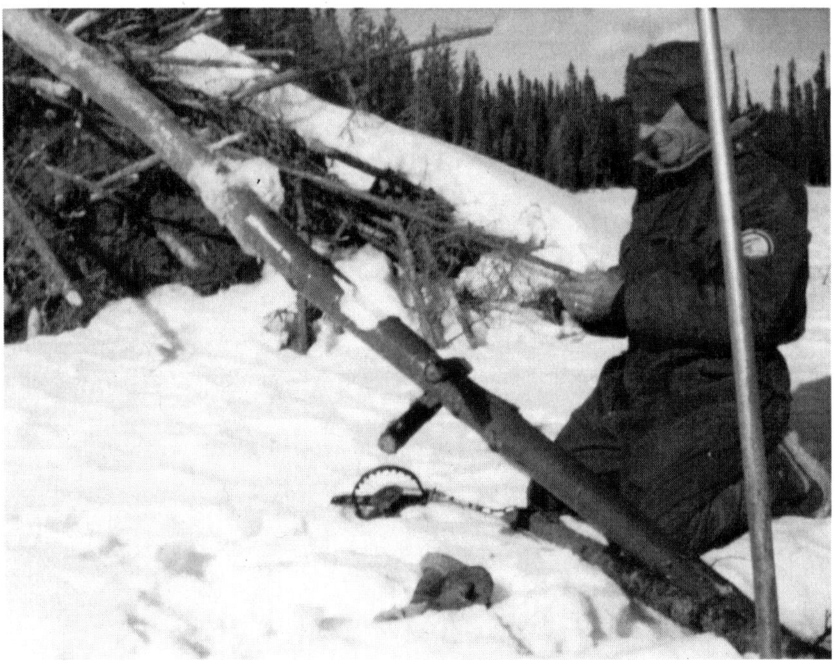

Daddy setting a drowning trap.

though the thoughts of the bear curtailed what could have been a long soak. That night I realized the bath had been a mistake. As long as all of us went without baths the odour of unwashed bodies went unnoticed. In my clean state I was suddenly aware of how the other two smelled, and it was not pleasant. The spruce boughs had lost their freshness after the first night and were no competition for the human odours.

Being in the wilderness with my new approach definitely changed the experience, insofar as achieving a feeling of connectedness in the manner I most loved and desired. The more I learned from my trapping and hunting companions, the more I understood the animals and their place in this grand scheme—in one particular aspect anyway. There was no denying the respect and, yes, the love, the men felt for where they were and for the creatures they sought to kill; it was an ambivalence I recognized but could not understand. Did they understand it, I wondered, or

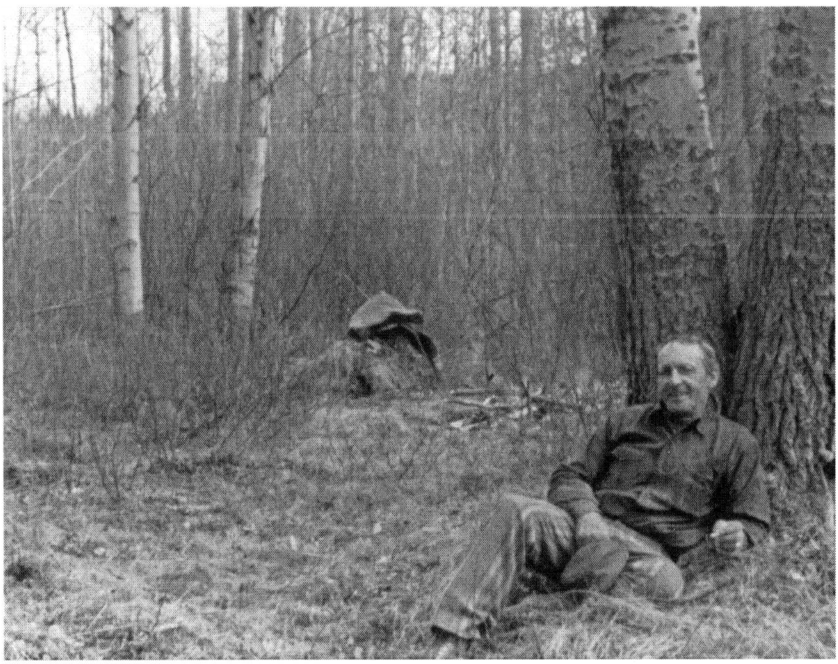

Daddy taking a well-deserved rest.

did they even recognize it? I suspected they didn't give it a moment of consideration and would be genuinely baffled if I asked. I would have done so anyway, but I had a feeling it would alienate them, and I did not want more of a difference between us than already existed. They had brought me into this activity with good grace, and I felt privileged to be here and appreciated their willingness to accommodate my ignorance.

I felt there was a distance between me and the essence, the spirit of the wilderness, when I was there to trap. There was an aspect of what we were doing that felt profane to me somehow. It would not have felt that way, I thought, if we were hunting out of necessity for food and clothing, but to be doing it for income seemed out of sync. Hell, it felt wrong.

The ride home was as easy and pleasurable as the ride out had been. When we did our little gallop for the last stretch before arriving at the LV, I saw some people standing outside the lodge

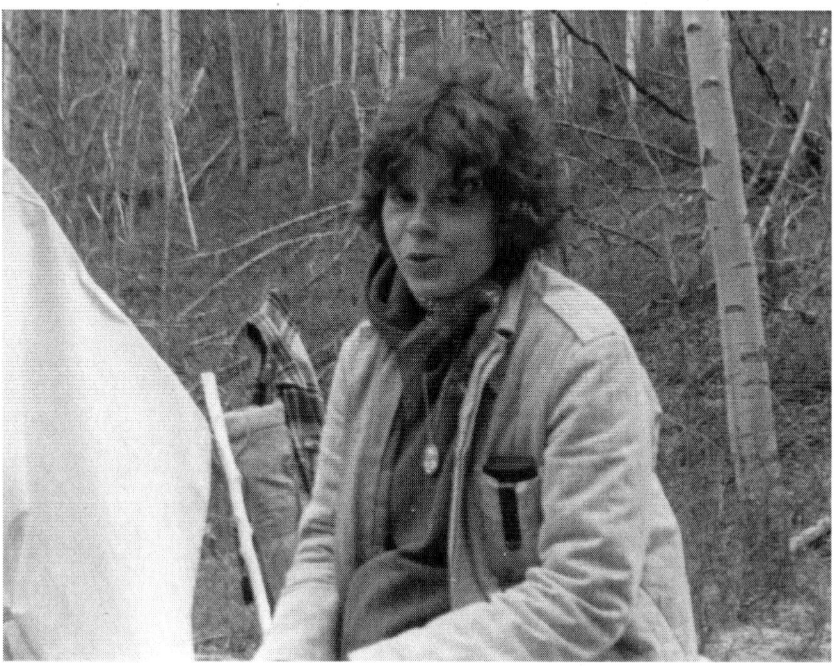

Bannock was not my favourite snack.

watching us come in. I knew we made a fine sight, all rugged and capable and exciting with our chaps and hats and the laden pack horses. It was a fine moment, spoiled only by Tiny and me getting caught up in the middle of the pack horses and ending up milling around in the corral with them while Daddy and Lynch sat on their mounts outside the fence, talking to the tourists and mercifully ignoring my dilemma. As soon as I got my horse and myself out of the melee, leaving my hat to be trampled flat, I set off for home, too embarrassed to stay for coffee and chat.

The next morning when I rode down to collect Poon and the rest of my gear, the visitors were all still there and were very interested in hearing about how I, a young woman, had gotten into beaver trapping. No one mentioned my goofy show in the corral, which at first I thought was kindness but soon learned was ignorance. Once I figured that out, and knew Lynch was away to the village, I relaxed and had a great time telling them all about my experience, thoroughly enjoying their awe at my bravery and prowess.

The mining exploration companies were due to arrive any day now; I had been hired to expedite again this year and was looking forward to the season of old friends returning and new people to meet.

The winter had been a productive one for me, in many ways. My confidence had grown through the time alone—learning how to take care of myself in my primitive surroundings—and my meditations and study had centred me, making me less susceptible to the energies of people around me and more able to maintain my own core. I had found my place of stillness and knowing, and although my moments there had been brief and largely serendipitous, I knew it existed, and I had some inkling of what was offered there.

It was time for some fun, and some work—the kind with a paycheque.

Life with a Two-Way Radio

Expediting was a lot of work, but not all the time. There were hours of free time between scheduled periods when the radio was turned on to take calls and the tasks that resulted. Those hours were well spent: fishing, riding, visiting—all the summer activities that made life in the bush wonderful. The paints, brushes and canvases were put away during those busy summer months of working and playing, but I did keep my yoga practice and my meditation times sacrosanct. Ideally, these kept me from getting stressed when things got difficult and from participating in or initiating behaviours that I knew to be inappropriate to the path I wanted to travel. It was a noble undertaking, but I have to admit I fell off the sacred path far more often than I kept on it.

Mining exploration camps were, surprisingly, hotbeds of insider politics and personality clashes that affected most everyone in them. The pilots seemed to be able to remain neutral, as did the cooks, unless the cook was a partner of one of the geologists, in which case it seemed guaranteed there would be strife. It could and did often get nasty, and it took a great deal of resolve to stay above and out of the swirling mess of hurt feelings and resulting anger that seemed to haunt most camps.

The parties were often a catharsis for all the emotion and could get fairly crazy, but the results were mostly good; once people's feelings were vented, the camp could settle down a bit. I got caught up in it once in awhile—it was hard not to pick a side or defend someone I liked—but I tried to remain conscious of my role, and I believe I did better than I had the year before. I was hard on myself regarding these matters and took little comfort from the fact I was improving, gaining mastery over myself.

The winter had taught me that I needed to keep a large and critical part of myself to myself, and to maintain that part, I needed to be alone—a lot. It was like having a secret life; there was no explaining to anyone that I took my solitude to try to be abstracted from myself. Other times I needed to be a part of something—I'd come to realize that as well, and honour it.

I hosted small gatherings, usually around a game of cards or Monopoly, sometimes just for a visit. The games could get heated, but mostly they were good-natured and fun evenings and didn't involve a lot of booze.

Scrabble was my game. I was good at it—so good that soon no one would play with me. That I was not gracious in victory may have had something to do with it. I was a gloater, crowing over every point I won and tirelessly rehashing every triumph. One of the helicopter pilots that summer was Cliff, a self-described Scrabble champion; it was only a matter of time before he and I sat down to a game. Not surprisingly, it happened that our first game was played in front of an audience. A few people were over that evening just to hang out, and they were eager to watch this match, probably hoping to see me defeated. I was so cocky about my prowess that even my friends would have liked to see me taken down a peg. But it didn't happen that night: I was brilliant, reaching one of my highest scores ever. Cliff tried mightily, and he was a good player, but he was trounced. Of course I strutted and bragged, and when Cliff asked for a rematch the next day I made a great to-do of asking him if he was sure he wanted to suffer another defeat so soon. He did.

He landed his helicopter on the pad near my driveway the

next morning. Having dropped all his crew off to their designated spots for a day of prospecting and dirt bagging, he was free till late afternoon. We played five games, Cliff becoming more and more silent with each game as he lost over and over. The fact that we were alone, without an audience, did not stop me from doing my usual happy dance after each win and talking about how clever I'd been. When Cliff asked for another game the next day, I told him I wasn't sure I wanted to play with him anymore; he wasn't really good enough to give me a good game, I said, mercilessly applying the weapons of psychological warfare.

He was coldly furious, but insisted on another game. I agreed. For the remainder of that season, Cliff flew in as many times as I was available and willing to play Scrabble. He was soon so demoralized—everyone in the country had heard about these games—that I don't think it was possible for him to win regardless of how I played. I never learned anything more about him during those long hours together. I knew only that he was a helicopter pilot with a masochistic streak.

Lorri loved a party, and in the summer there were lots of them. There were the mining camp parties, the highway camp parties and the railroad crew parties. Lorri would have attended every one of them but she didn't like to go alone, and I was not often interested. I preferred small groups and conversation to large groups and loud music. Most of the time, when Lorri and I attended a party it was because she had pestered me relentlessly to go. She was one of the rare people to whom I found it hard to say no; she took advantage of that weakness in me.

Getting dressed for the party was fun. We would meet at Lorri's cabin and I would watch her put on makeup and do her hair, trying to resist letting her make me up and do my hair, but often failing. She also chose what we were to wear, all the time chattering excitedly about who we would see and if the music would be good for dancing.

Lorri was not meant to be living in the bush. She was one of the most delightfully social people I have known, always hospitable, always ready to have fun. Those early years in Iskut were truly tough ones for her and I always admired how, though she complained ceaselessly, at the same time made the best of it, for herself and for others.

We were not at all alike, but we were all we had and we loved each other for exactly who we were. There are few people in my life who have provided me with the hours and hours of innocent fun I had with Lorri. One time we were going to a party at one of the railroad camps, and Lorri was giving me the usual hard time about my habit of finding one person to talk to and then spending the evening doing just that.

"You are no fun," she announced, putting on her mascara. "All you do is sit in a corner and talk. You don't dance; you don't even flirt." At this she looked at me. "Why don't you flirt?"

"I don't know how," I responded with perfect honesty.

"Well, I'm going to teach you," she told me, completing her makeup.

We got in the car, me driving, to go to the party. As soon as we were on the road, she began trying to teach me the fine art of flirting.

It was hilarious. At least it was hilarious to me—she was so earnest, so genuine in her attempt to help me, that I could not stop laughing. When she demonstrated how to bat my lashes, I lost it. I had to pull the car over and put my head on the steering wheel while I howled with laughter. The sight of her, looking up at me with her big blue eyes, and then batting her lashes like some cartoon woman simply did me in. She gave up in disgust and from that moment on I was left to my own devices at parties.

The rubber boat had gone to the Adams boys. I had come to understand that it truly was not a watercraft meant for adult pursuits and had invested in a small canoe. I had many a splendid and solitary time sitting in the boat, fishing or reading a book or simply absorbing the grand freedom of the wilderness.

Greg was back, and he and I resumed our fishing trips to untouched lakes and rivers in the helicopter. We did a trip to Terrace one time when Tee was home and Greg's girlfriend, Maureen, was visiting.

There were a lot of forest fires between Iskut and Terrace. The smoke was so thick as to be impenetrable at one point, and the atmosphere in the Jet Ranger was tense: we all knew enough to know we were in trouble. Eventually Greg spotted the Nass River camp and we put down. Greg had filed a flight plan and was hoping to find some way of contacting Terrace to tell the airport of our delay. There was no one at the camp, just a huge German shepherd dog that was taking its role as guardian of the camp seriously enough that we dared not leave the machine.

We must have sat there for half an hour losing precious daylight while hoping someone would show up, call off the dog and let us use the radio. Greg wasn't supposed to be flying after dark, and a search would be launched if he couldn't get in touch with Terrace. Finally Greg decided the smoke had cleared enough, and we took off, flying into a darkening sky. No one spoke until we landed at the Terrace airport, and our pilot revealed how concerned he'd been by getting out and kissing the ground. He got away with a reprimand from the control tower for being airborne in almost total nighttime blackness, and then the four of us went into town and drank a lot of beer.

In October, with the expediting over, Tee and I drove to Stewart just for fun—no long lists of supplies to shop for, just a relaxing drive on a beautiful route and a visit with Charlie and Jackie and their girls. Although the road was not great, the scenery was stupendous, and we stopped often to enjoy it.

Bear Glacier, beside the highway, was always worth a stop, and this trip was no exception, with the added bonus of arriving in time to see the glacier calving—giant slabs of ice were separating from the mass to float in the brown water below. The sound was like no other, a kind of whishing, with crunching, slithering sounds thrown in. The ice was gleaming white on top, streaked dirty brown on the bottom and a beautiful deep blue in the fissures.

At the Fenners' we met Adam, who was the caretaker for the closed Silbak Premier Mine, and he offered us a tour of the mine site. The mine had been closed since 1967, after being the scene of different levels of activity since 1918. Gold, silver, lead and zinc had been taken from the area in the millions of tons.

The site is situated about sixteen miles out of Stewart at an elevation of 2,500 feet on the west slope of Bear River Ridge, which made for a fabulous drive. We toured the mill, huge and echoing, thick brown dust on every surface. The silence was unnerving; the machinery was clearly meant to make industrial-scale noise.

Adam was an enthusiastic and knowledgeable guide and told us a great deal about the history of this place. Tee was fascinated, but I was less so; I wanted to wander and imagine the people who once lived here, what had brought them to this high and isolated place and where had they gone. The townsite was to me most interesting and poignant. It must have been elegant in its heyday, gracious houses with stone steps and terraces, all built into the side of the mountain. The view was breathtaking; surely the people who once lived here must have been inspired by it every day. I couldn't imagine ever becoming inured to the sheer majesty of this panorama.

The bunkhouse, its roof pushed in by snowslides, was moving as well. To think of all the lonely men who'd occupied this enormous impersonal space, which looked as though no effort had been made to make it homey—it could have been a mental institution, or a jail.

We stopped at Fish Creek on the way back to see the last of the spawning salmon, hundreds and hundreds of them, battered from their long journey, barely moving in the clear shallow water. We spent three days in Stewart and did very little drinking and no carousing at all. It was my first non-carousing time in that town—maybe I was outgrowing the need for wild times.

On the drive home late at night, we suddenly saw, in the headlights, two grizzly bear cubs on the road. One ran off but the other was not so quick, and Tee was only just able to miss it with the truck. The cub, frightened, gave a squeal, and the mother came onto the road to stand on her hind legs in front of the truck. Tee stopped the vehicle, and she roared at us, her eyes flashing kryptonite green in the lights and her brave paws gleaming with long curving claws. It was a mesmerizing, memorable sight, the image and the sound imprinted on my brain for all time, though the whole encounter was over in less than a minute before mama bear herded her kids off the road and into the bush.

Tee stayed at Elsevere for over three months, and it was a time of quiet intimacy such as we had not had till now. We cut wood for the winter woodpile and did the chores necessary to ready the cabin for the season of snow. We took turns cooking, trying to impress one another with our skills in the kitchen. We did a lot of hiking and exploring, taking big lunches and staying out from early morning till dark. Tee couldn't swim, which made me uncomfortable taking him out in the canoe, but we borrowed Claude's motorboat and went fishing.

I rode nearly every day simply because I loved my horse and I loved riding. Tee, less keen, would sometimes accompany me on one of Lynch's horses, but more often these short rides were my time to savour the pleasure of having a willing and able horse companion. Tiny loved a joke, particularly if it was on me. There was a stretch of road on my favourite trail, an old Cat track, and as such it was fairly smooth and straight for about a quarter of a mile, a safe surface for a horse, with no unexpected holes or cracks in which to catch a hoof. Whenever we came to this place, it was understood I would loosen the reins and Tiny could have a run. We both loved this—her mane and my hair streaming out behind us, the exhilaration of the speed and the joy of moving together in harmony.

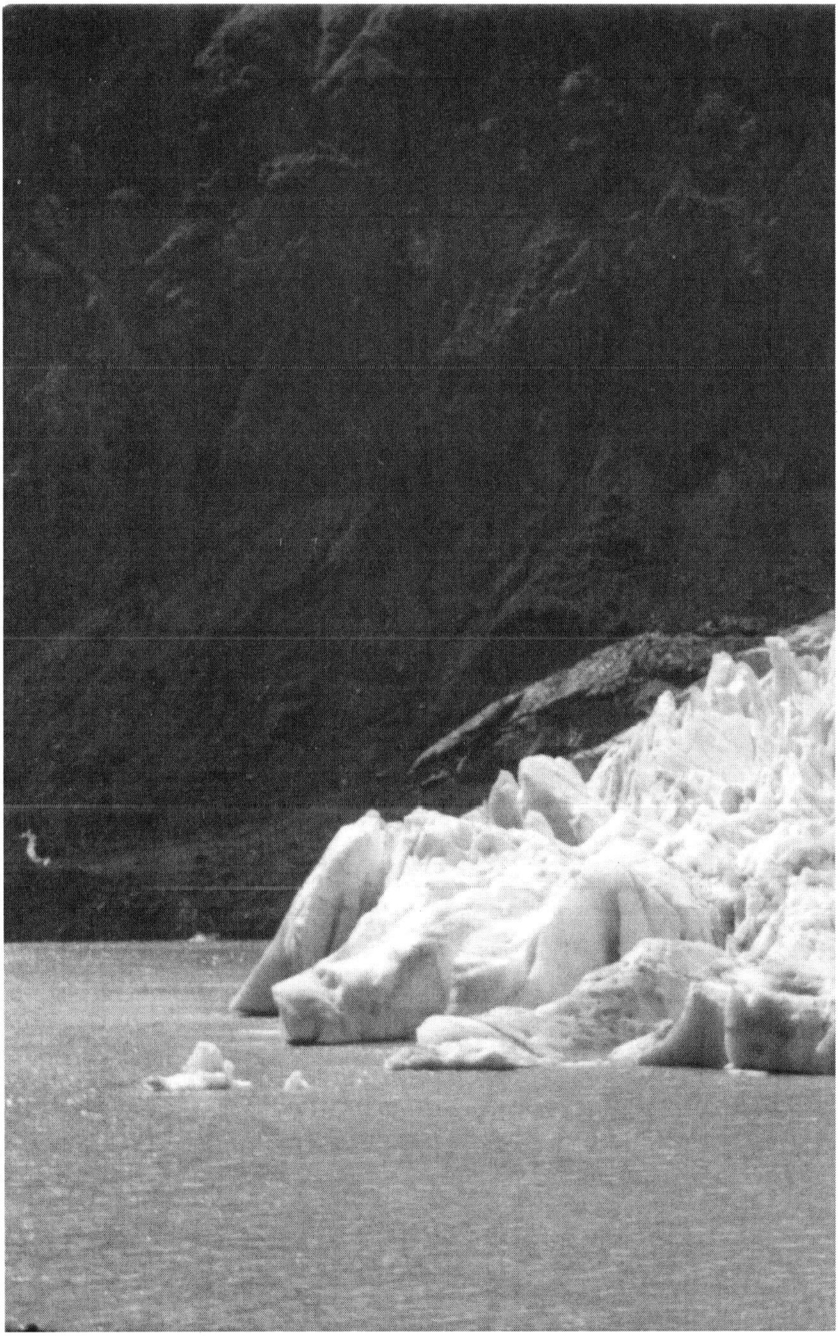

The magnificient Bear Glacier at a rare moment when giant slabs of ice were separating from the mass.

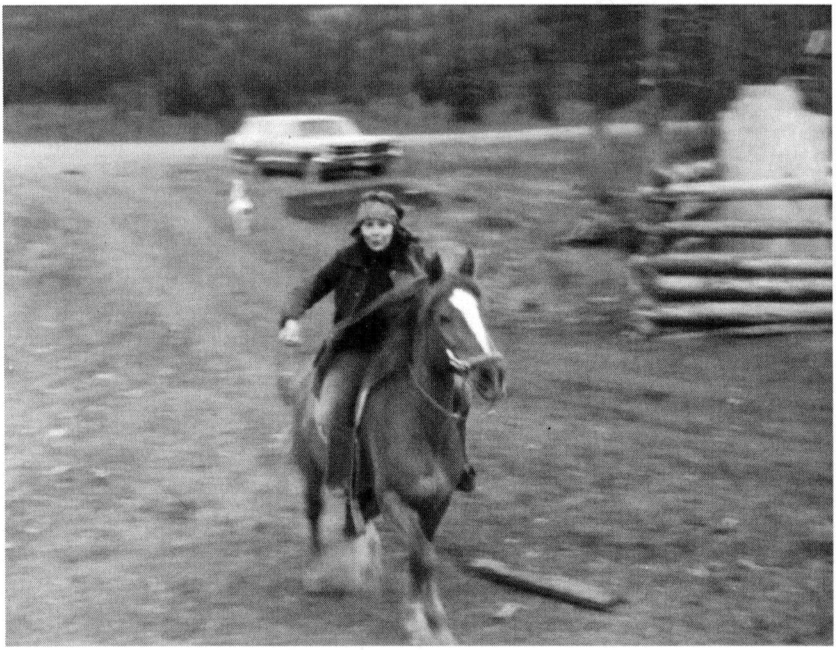

I rode nearly everyday. Tiny, my little sorrel mare, loved to run.

A little creek crossed the path at one spot, just wide enough for Tiny to jump, adding spice to our ride. Every now and then, for no discernible reason, and with great craft, Tiny would choose to stop dead at the creek instead of clearing it in a smooth leap. Naturally this decision on her part, without a sign to me, would result in me flying over her head and landing in the water. I swear she would laugh; the amusement on her horse face was apparent. No matter how I raged and threatened, she never took me seriously and continued to toss me in the creek occasionally, just so I wouldn't take her for granted, I suppose. Tee enjoyed these episodes as much as Tiny did. He didn't dare laugh out loud when I would come stomping into the yard, soaking wet and furious, Tiny walking behind me with a smug look on her face, but there was no hiding the fact he found it funny. So did I, eventually.

I found I could paint while Tee was around. I could lose myself in the work almost as easily as I did when I was alone. This

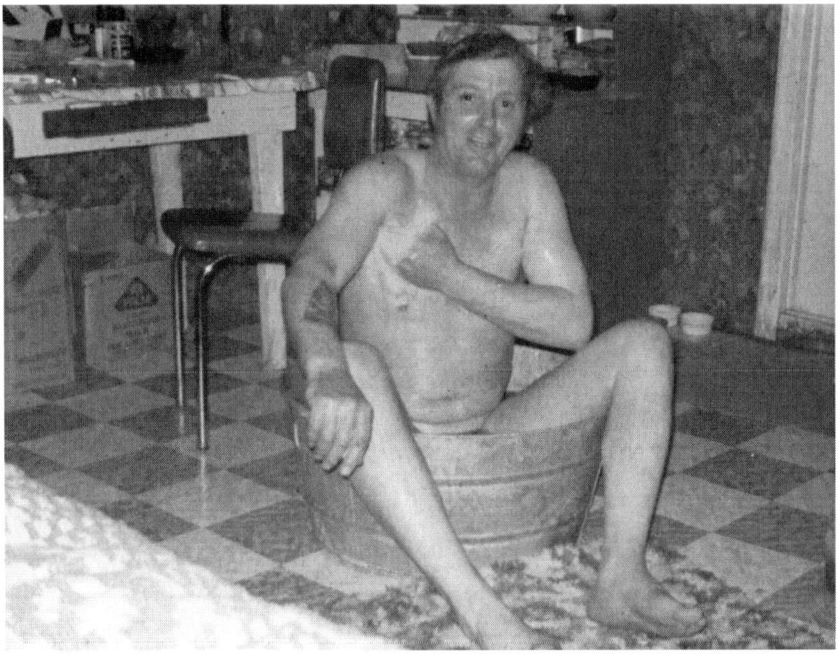

Tee was never shy when it came time to take a bath. The little wash basin was a godsend after a week in the bush.

was significant to me: I had never had any problems being naked around him, or farting or peeing in front of him, or saying anything that came into my head, but I hadn't felt okay painting in his presence until this long period of living together.

Coming into the cabin one afternoon after visiting with Lorri, I found Cat Stevens playing on the tape deck and Tee, oblivious to my presence, dancing. I felt a smile lay itself across my face, and I felt my heart swell with tenderness. He was a taciturn man, and not given to dancing, having a slight limp in one leg from an old injury as well as a nature that did not express itself through the medium of music, poetry or song. To see him moving for the sheer joy of it told me a lot about him that he couldn't or wouldn't tell me. It was a glimpse into a part of his being I'd suspected was there, and I left the room to return noisily so as not to embarrass him at being found out.

My Third Winter in the Bush

Ice fishing was my passion during this, my third winter in the bush. An unnamed little lake north of the LV Ranch was the best place to go. In the summer this shallow weedy lake warmed, and the flesh of the fish was soft, but in the winter the fish was firm and delicious.

Once, snowshoeing with Lynch on that lake, I fell through the ice. He'd told me not to go near the edge, but I wanted to see if the hole I'd fished in the week before was still open enough for me to punch through and drop a line while he checked his snares. The bottom fell from under me, and the next thing I remember is looking up from under the water and seeing Lynch's face and arm. His mouth was moving, but I couldn't hear him and didn't really care as the cold numbed my body and my mind to the point of easeful surrender.

I knew I somehow had to get my snowshoes off if I was to get out of the water; I knew I would die if I didn't, but it was a struggle to want to make the effort. The bindings on my snowshoes were lamp wick and impossible to untie in the best of circumstances. I cut them with my buck knife, a task that seemed to take hours, and Lynch somehow hauled my sodden body from the water. I don't remember much about the next couple of hours. Luckily we were close to the truck, and I got there half-carried by Lynch who never stopped talking and shoving at me until we were in the cab. Then he helped me pull off my frozen outer clothing and wrapped a sleeping bag around me. By this time the heater had warmed the cab, and all I wanted to do was sleep.

I survived the whole adventure without even getting a cold. We were even able to rescue my snowshoes the next day as they had floated to the surface of the big hole in the ice we had made. The oddest thing about this episode was me seeing Lynch's face and arm from under the water. Lynch told me later I didn't go into the lake any deeper than my waist! I was certain I had been submerged; I had the clearest memory of it. But he told me I had been able to lift my legs, one at a time, to the surface of the ice to free my feet from my snowshoes. When I examined my thick wool toque, it was dry, and my parka was indeed wet only to the waist.

It was a scary experience anyway, and Lynch had been worried, I knew. He didn't berate me for not listening to him about where not to go, and he never made this misadventure of mine into a funny story with which to regale people at parties.

Tee had gone to Watson Lake the day before my near drowning, and I was shaken enough by the event to not want to be alone that night. I stayed at the lodge, keeping Lynch from his bed by asking for stories and songs, both of us drinking hot rum toddies till we fell asleep in our chairs by the fire.

Another time, same lake, I rode out with Daddy Charette on a snowmobile for him to check traps and me to ice fish. Somehow on the way across the lake, the rifle must have slid from its scabbard unnoticed by either of us. When we arrived at the first trap, it was a terrible scene. A wolverine was in the trap, and in the one night he'd been there he had managed to dig a deep hole in the snow and frozen earth, making a circle around the tree to which the trap was affixed. He'd also chewed almost through the tree, which was easily at least eight inches in diameter. When Daddy found the rifle was missing, he decided he would cut a pole and club the animal to death rather than retrace our trail and pick up the rifle. I left for my fishing hole, not wanting to witness what was about to occur and wondering if it was really going to be that easy; wolverines may not be large, but they are fierce and incredibly strong.

Before I even got my fishing rod from my pack, I heard a most dreadful commotion—a combination of deep snarls, screaming, the rattle of a chain and the tearing of fabric. Daddy came down my trail to the lake with his parka shredded, the club chewed and his face as pale as the snow. "I'm going back to find the rifle," was all he said as he passed me.

This same lake had a small herd of caribou wintering there, and I would drive to the lake and sit in my truck watching them. Often the weather was good enough to get out of the truck and snowshoe onto the lake. Caribou are curious. The sight of me would make them cautious at first, though they rarely ran away, and I found if I lay down in the snow they would come to within a few feet of me, an odd clicking noise emanating from their ankles, and their breath audible in the crisp air.

Tee was with me for most of this winter, me painting or reading while he read or tinkered. We entertained several times. My cooking was still largely experimental but our guests were good sports and often took the precaution of bringing a casserole or something with them just in case. No one was shy about teasing me about my attempts but it was in good fun—until the night of the gunpowder meat loaf.

I had been given a spice rack, a little wooden affair with little wooden shelves holding little glass bottles, all unlabelled. My spices at this point were non-existent; I used salt, pepper, garlic salt and sometimes in moments of daring, dried dill.

Lynch, going through a box of stuff in one of his sheds one day the previous fall, had come across some gunpowder. He was about to throw it out, but I asked for it (I have no idea why), and he gave it to me in a bag. When I got home, I put the powder into the little glass jars of the unused spice shelf that Tee had nailed to the wall above the stove preparatory to the day I may acquire spices.

On this night, the dinner was an impromptu affair. Several people had dropped in, and we'd ended up playing Monopoly and drinking a lot of beer. The fun was too good to end, so I asked everyone to stay for some dinner. I had some ground moose meat thawed and figured a meat loaf with lots of chopped onions and topped with mashed potatoes would make a good main dish. I assembled the meat loaf, all the while talking, taking my turn with the dice for the game, and drinking more beer. Forgetting the contents of the little bottles, and in a haze of alcohol and good fellowship, I put some from each bottle into the loaf.

When it was time to eat, I refrained, worried that there may not be enough to serve all my guests. The meal was eaten with great appreciation, and everyone settled back into serious Monopoly.

Gunpowder, we were about to learn, has one reliable effect on the digestive system—it cleans it out thoroughly. It wasn't long before my guests were dashing through the snow to the outhouse. The facility accommodated only one person at a time, and soon most of our company was in the yard, some without taking the time to put on boots and jackets.

Tee drove down to wake Lynch up. We needed to know what, if any, would be the long term effects of our friends ingesting gunpowder. Tee was able to drive, as he too, as a good host, had not eaten any of the meat loaf. Had I poisoned everyone? I was sick with worry.

The truck came back and I ran out to meet it, chagrined to find Tee laughing so hard he was barely able to get out of the truck. Lynch says not to worry, he told me, all you've done is worm everyone.

The next day our yard looked like a Jackson Pollock painting, only with more substance, and the story of the gunpowder meat loaf had spread like wildfire.

It was my last dinner party. Not only had my budding confidence been effectively destroyed, but also everyone in the area claimed to be leery of eating anything I had cooked.

▲

> Even in early youth, when the mind is so eager for the new and untried, while it is still a stranger to faltering and fear, we yet like to think that there are certain unalterable realities, somewhere at the bottom of things.
>
> —Willa Cather

Tee left for two weeks after Christmas, and I sank myself into my painting, going hour after hour without stopping for food or drink and feeling as though I was living in another dimension, a place of moving colours and shapes known only to me.

During these times I found not only did I not seem to need to eat or drink, but I also seemed to forgo such things as bathing and changing clothes. My hair was tied atop my head with whatever came to hand when I noticed it falling in my face, and my painting clothes were stiff with acrylic paint from my brushes and palette knives getting wiped in the armpits and across the backside—anywhere at all. The collar of the big shirt had been crudely cut off, as had the sleeves from the wrists to elbows. The shirt featured a button that read *Abortion—A Woman's Right to Choose*, also smeared with paint. The painting went well, and when I wasn't painting and smoking, I was reading and smoking.

The reading was less satisfactory. I was not finding in me what my reading had led me to expect, and I was frustrated and angry, blaming myself for not being educated enough to understand, or simply too stupid to get it. I wanted answers. I wanted those "certain unalterable realities" Cather talked about. I wanted someone to talk to about these things. There was no one to give me a loving, muscular push, or even lift an arm to point. I wanted a teacher. As always, I wanted everything at once.

Tee's absence made me critical of him, of what we had together. I felt he didn't have enough curiosity; he never got excited by anything. He didn't seem to feel enraged or concerned by the happenings in the world—I had to do it for both of us. He didn't talk enough, he didn't care about the things I agonized over. The moment he walked in the door, however, all my negativity regarding him vanished, and a vast relief eased through me. Such is the power of sex; it seemed I had one unalterable reality I could rely on.

Spring arrived and the horses came in, a bit thin, but basically in good shape. We corralled them and spent days readying them for the spring beaver hunt—worming them, trimming their hoofs and brushing the rough winter fur from them to reveal their shining summer hides.

Along with the others, Tiny had to be persuaded to be a working horse again. She liked the wild-horse life and at first wasn't convinced that even the promise of oats was worth the price of her freedom. In a few days though, she'd been reminded of the pleasure of the plate. Out of the corral, she wandered around the

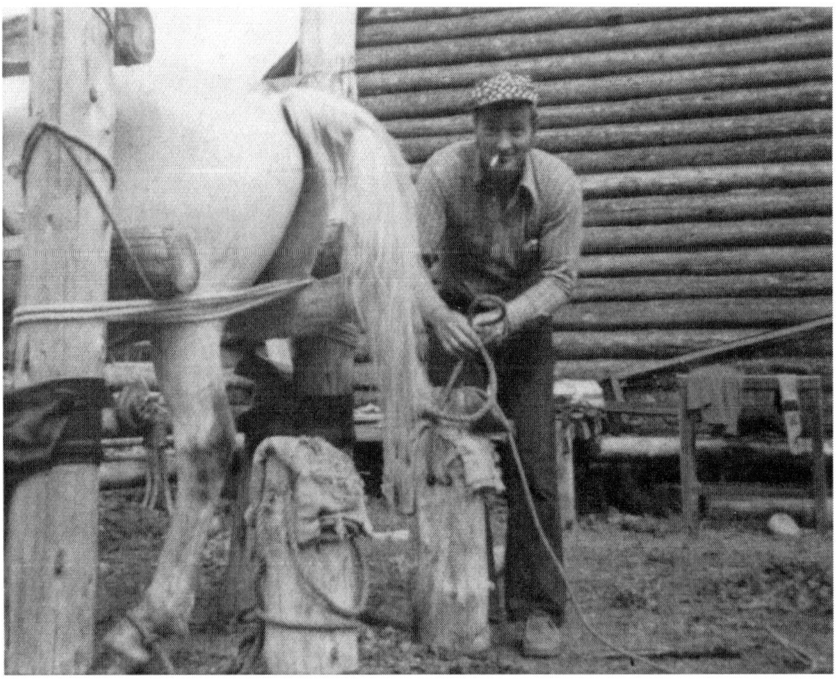

Tee was a handy guy. The horses on the ranch got new shoes every spring and Tee was always willing to help.

yard, loath to leave her herd and the possibility of a carrot or an apple. She would eat anything on offer and often would stick her head right in the open window of the kitchen, hoping for a snack. I gave her a clove of garlic one time, and we laughed to see her walking around for hours after she'd eaten it, twisting her lips and showing her teeth as she tried to decide whether or not she liked this strange new flavour. She was very jealous if I rode another horse, and it seemed this jealously was not confined to steeds.

The Adams family came to visit, bringing their two boys and their long-awaited new bicycles to be ridden around the yard while the adults drank coffee in the cabin. Before going in I had ridden one of the bikes, just to try it out. The boys eventually came in for juice and store-bought cookies, leaving the bikes lying in the yard.

Suddenly, there was the ominous and unmistakable sound of metal crunching. Running to the big picture window, we were stunned to see Tiny stomping on one of the bikes. She managed to do enough damage before we could haul her away that I had to buy a new bike, and the poor boy had to wait another month before it arrived. This display did not stop me from buying another riding horse.

We'd been at the LV when Zane Palmer, a guide and outfitter, had stopped in for coffee on his way south. He had a load of horses and one was for sale, a pinto. When he was ready to leave I went out with him to have a look. This horse, Zane told us, was a marvel of comfort and endurance, besides being well-trained and willing. He was also very pretty, and I was smitten. Deciding I had to have him, I made the deal right away without consulting Lynch as to the merits of the purchase. Zane quickly drove off with my cheque, and I was left holding the halter of my new horse, thinking I would ride him on the beaver hunt and Tee could ride Tiny.

Gatedo, as he was named, turned out to be a grave mistake. Lynch told me straight away I'd been a fool to buy a horse from Zane, "that horse thief," and no good would come of this transaction.

He could not have been more right. Gatedo was a good-looking animal, but he was also what is called incorrigible, incapable of being corrected or reformed. He would risk hurting himself in an effort to hurt his rider, flinging himself backwards, ramming into trees, rolling—whatever would dislodge the hated weight from his back.

I was stubborn about him, insisting I could train him, even as I leaped from his back as he went down to roll the first time I got on him. There was no reliability to his behaviour. He would go for days sometimes being impeccable—obedient, smart and willing. During these times he was a most delightful ride. He had a gait that ate up the miles without being jarring; even Lynch said it was a most desirable quality. But, without warning or any understandable provocation, at some unknowable point, he would go mad, flinging himself every which way, bucking and rearing.

When Tee went into town to pick up supplies for the hunt, I rode Gatedo down to the lake to go fishing. There was no one

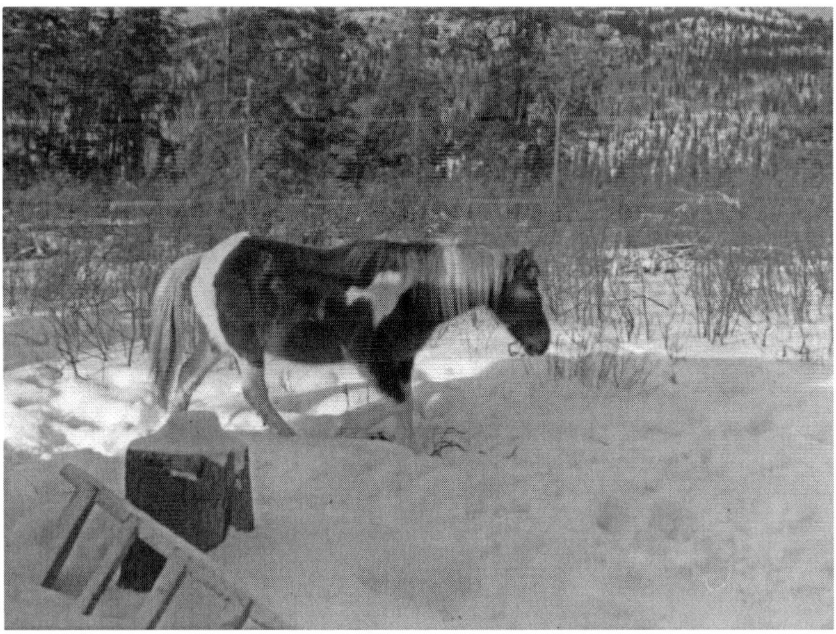

Gatedo was an incorrigible animal and no matter how hard I tried to get the upper hand, he always outsmarted me.

around to tell where I was going or even that I was going. If he had hurt me, my bones would be there yet, so slim were the chances of being found in that thick bush. The horse was in one of his rare good moods that day; he didn't throw one of his really bad tantrums. He did jump around, and he always tried to bang me into a tree, but he refrained from his favourite and most dramatic move, the one where he would fling himself backwards and roll over.

There were several suggestions from various horse-knowledgeable people during the time I had Gatedo, and I tried most all of them. The first one was to get on his back holding a balloon full of water. If he reared or flung his head back to try to hit me in the face (one of his most relied-upon manoeuvres), I was to break the balloon over his head. The theory was he would think it was his own blood and be startled into good behaviour.

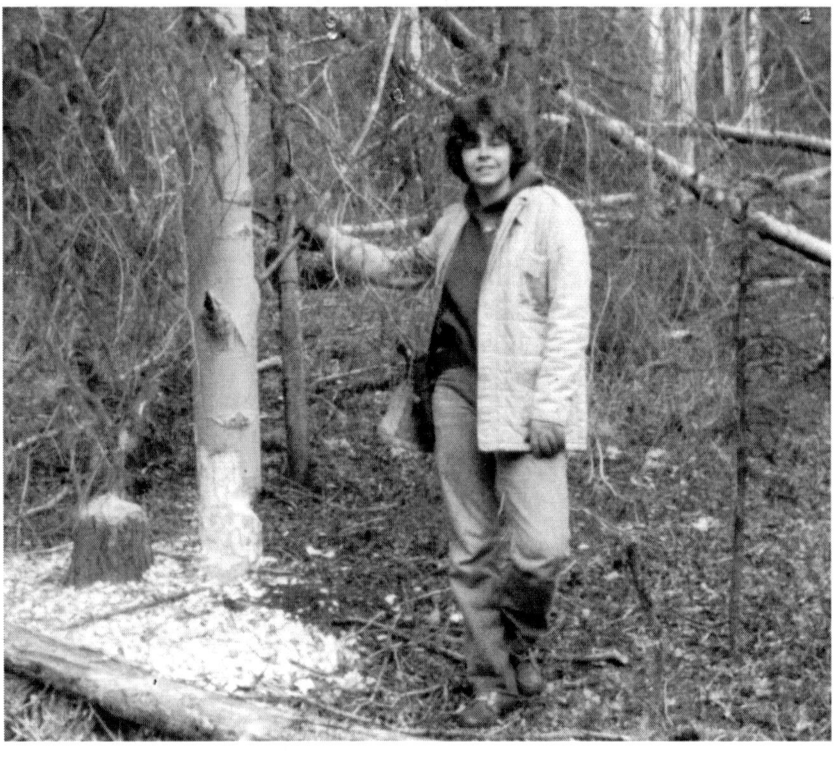

The beavers chewed clean through this poplar.

First off, when one does not have a tap with water running from it, filling a balloon with water is an arduous task. I managed it, however, and duly got on the horse holding tight to my new training tool. Gatedo obligingly reared, and I swung the balloon, aiming for the spot between his ears. The balloon connected just fine, but the force of the movement of the horse's head sent it back at me where it finally did break, drenching and blinding me at the same time. Gatedo won that round.

He won the round where the balloon was replaced by a two-by-four too. I got a little cut on the cheek and a black eye that time, and a sliver in my palm that took Tee an hour to dig out.

I tried a "war bridle" and got rope burns in both palms so severe that I had to wear gloves full of ointment to bed for a week. Eventually I quit trying to change the horse and instead changed myself as a rider, relinquishing any ease or relaxation during the ride to pay rapt attention to every twitch of his ears or quiver in his body. There was no chatting to another rider, or smoking a cigarette, or hooking one leg around the saddle horn to ease an aching back on a long ride. It was tiring, enough to ensure I didn't ride him all the time; I had to be feeling strong and alert whenever I got on his back.

Tiny, jealous as she was of any other horse I rode, did not attempt to harass Gatedo. None of the other horses had anything to do with him; he was tolerated. He knew he needed the herd to survive, so he was with them when they were turned out to range, but there were no friendly nips, no welcoming neighs, no standing nose to tail to cooperatively keep the flies away—that alone ought to have convinced me how really scary he was, but it didn't. I had a blind spot when it came to that horse.

I was learning to shoot Tee's .357 Magnum pistol; it was going with me on this beaver hunt. No more living in fear of bears—I would be armed and dangerous. Lynch had always maintained that a handgun was useless in the bush. One had to be close up to use it, and even then the chances of being able to hit anything accurately enough to be effective were slim and nigh impossible.

The first time he saw me wearing the gun in a holster around my hips he said, "Nice gun, Sis. Next time a bear comes at you, you can shoot yourself." Tee agreed with Lynch, and I figured they were probably right, but wearing the gun made me feel safer.

The spring turned wet and chilly, and I could feel my enthusiasm for the beaver hunt waning as the time for our departure drew nearer. We were to go out for two weeks; Lynch wanted to go into a new area this time, and the ride would be longer and tougher. We would be three riders, nine horses and two dogs.

Beaverin' and the Third Grizzly

There was a cold rain falling the day Lynch, Tee and I left, and it stayed cold and wet throughout the six-hour ride to our first camp, a few miles past Canyon Lake.

It was almost midnight by the time we crawled into our tent, too tired to do more for dinner than eat some cheese and cold bannock. The horses were restless on this first day out, in spite of the long hard ride, and it seemed to take forever to get them fed and hobbled. Gatedo had behaved badly throughout the day and protested so vehemently about the hobbles that I finally turned him loose without them, thinking he was surely too smart to take off into the wilderness by himself. I slept well, Barika cuddled in my sleeping bag with me, Tee at my back in his bag, and the morning dawned cool and clear.

We broke camp. The spot Lynch wanted to set up was another six-hour ride away, but by the time we got underway it was almost noon. I had insisted we all have a hot breakfast, and although Lynch was reluctant at first he was glad of the bacon and eggs when it was served. Immediately after eating he fell asleep beside the fire, leaving Tee to gather up the horses while I cleaned up and packed the panniers.

That day was a longer ride as Rabbit Foot Creek had become Rabbit Foot River, and there was no way we could cross it. I'd started to get into the rhythm of the ride, singing "Pistol Packin' Mama" as I rode at the end of the line of pack horses. Gatedo seemed to have settled down, as had the other horses, and the ride, though long, was warm and pleasant.

Our second camp was beautiful, with water and lots of grass for the horses. Even the ubiquitous mosquitoes were not so thick, making life easier for all of us. Lynch said we would stay here for a few days. There was lots of beaver sign, indicated by fresh-peeled sticks on the house and dam, and fresh chew marks on the stumps of some of the trees that had been felled on the steep bank beside the water. I made chili for dinner. I had been in charge of organizing the food and felt I had done a good job of it; whatever else happened, we would be eating well. When I had unpacked, however, I found I had not been so good about other aspects of living in the bush—there was only one roll of toilet paper, no toothpaste and no hairbrush.

It was heaven to take off my chaps and heavy boots, donning the moccasins I had especially made for camp. They were tanned moosehide, with high canvas tops kept snug around my calves by means of long laces wrapped around them. Everyone in that country involved in bush life wore them; some, like Lynch, wore them year-round, using toe rubbers over them in the winter. The chaps were another necessity, not only for keeping one dry, but also for deflecting the constant whip of willows and branches as one rode through heavy bush, though they were heavy and stiff, impossible to walk in for any distance.

Again, taking care of the horses was the most time-consuming task. They all had to be checked to be certain the packs were not rubbing them into soreness; their feet had to be checked, and then the usual hobbling, belling and feeding was required. Nine horses to tend took a lot of time.

The morning of the third day we woke to fresh snow, though the sun melted it by the time we ate breakfast, and the day stayed

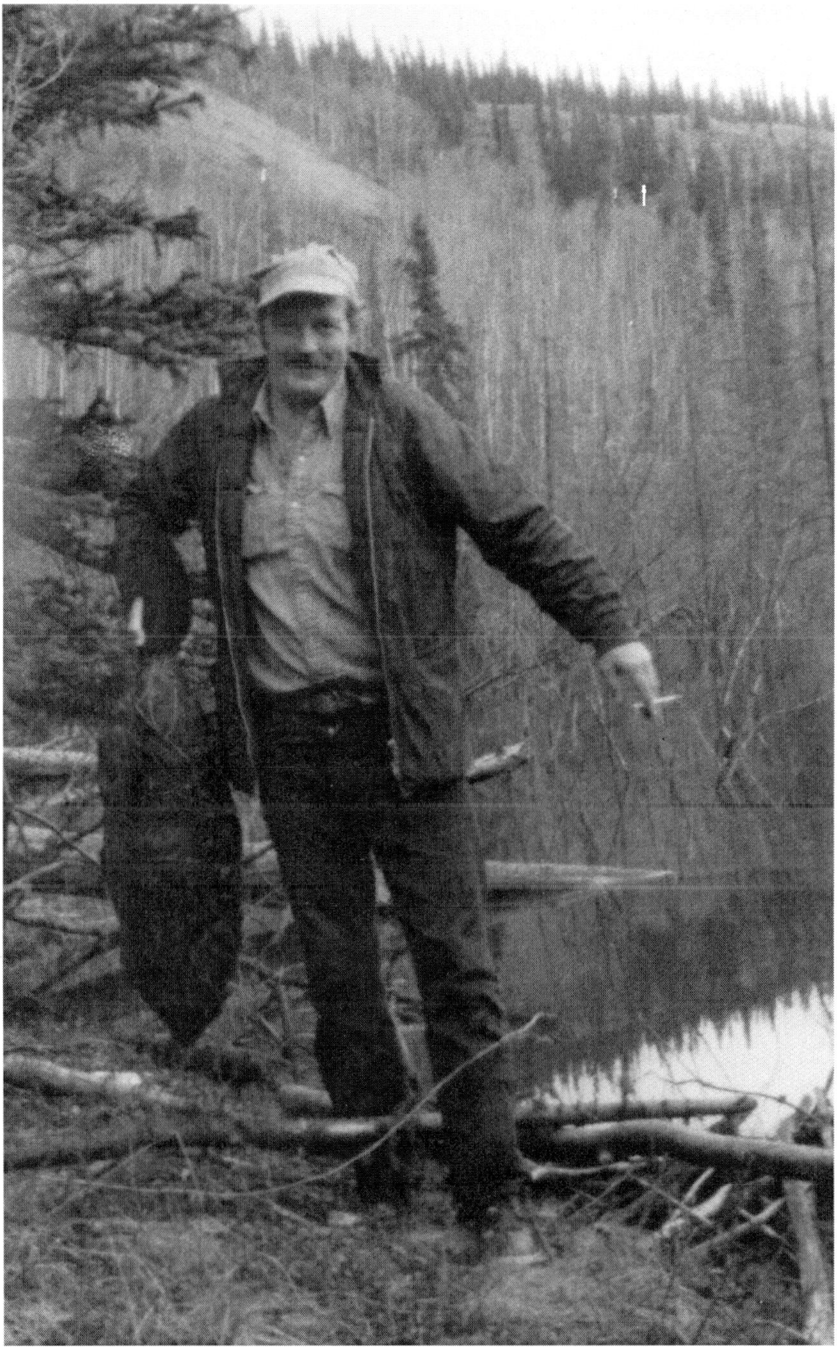

Tee loved life in the bush, but skinning a beaver this size was hard work.

sunny and warm. We had all slept well and were ready to get busy with setting out the traps. Barika and Patsy were left to guard the camp as we set off.

Again I felt the shame at being part of the trap setting and the baiting. I felt the distance it created between me and the spirit of the earth and all it represented. And again I pushed those feelings away and concentrated on doing a good job and enjoying the wilderness—birds sang, loons laughed their inane laugh and the inimitable odours and air of the bush filled my lungs. We set eight traps and found another dam that was bigger while taking a roundabout way back to camp. Bedtime was early that night—ten o'clock.

On day four I burned my thumb on the cast iron skillet while making the breakfast pancakes. It was painful enough that I stayed in camp, making myself useful by organizing the foodstuffs

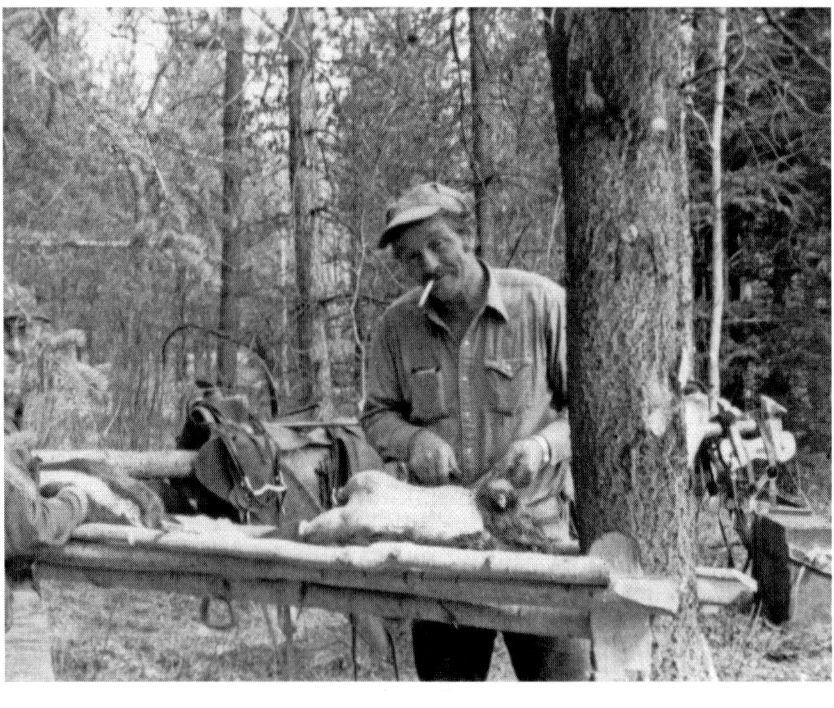

Tee showed off his ingenuity by designing a rack that allowed skinning to be done while standing up. Brilliant!

and airing the sleeping bags on a makeshift clothesline. There was a good climbing tree close to our tent; I did a practice run up it in case a bear visited. I napped in the afternoon, the tent moving gently, as though breathing.

Later I walked out to a meadow to watch the horses grazing in the sun. I read Karl Marx and sketched a bit. By the time the men rode in I had dinner waiting and was eager to hear about their day. They'd trapped four big beaver and they'd seen a black wolf and some bear sign. After dinner they skinned while I cleaned up the "kitchen." Tee cut down two slim trees and nailed them, one on either side, of two trees growing about ten feet apart, thus creating a most brilliant thing—a skinning rack. Lynch was amazed that he had not thought of such a thing in all his years of trapping. It really was obvious, once it was there, and to be able to stand straight to skin was unbelievably easy and comfortable compared

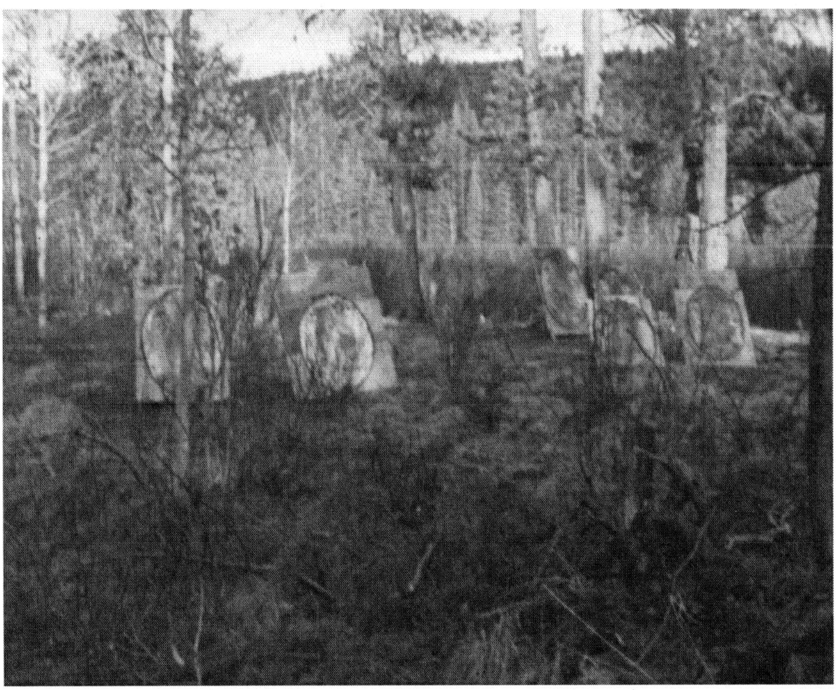

Beaver pelts nailed to boards for drying.

with sitting on a tarp on the ground. I burned my other thumb on the skillet this night, but it was not so bad, just painful.

The camp now looked like a beaverin' camp: hides nailed to boards, hind legs cooking with rice in a big pot on the open fire and a can containing beaver balls—the castor would be used as bait to catch more beaver.

The next morning I went walking with Tee to check traps. Two miles of wading through swamps, climbing up steep banks and clambering over windfalls—too rough for a horse, and damned hard on a human being. We had two beaver to haul back to camp where Lynch was resting, having gotten two beaver as well. We skinned and stretched all afternoon. And so the days went by, hot and dry, a blur of working too hard to pay attention to the beauty all around us. We grew tough and silent; even the mealtimes were quiet, other than a "Pass the salt" or "Saw a bear on the south side of the creek."

Bald eagles ate the carcasses. The sound of the birds exploding into the air when taken by surprise at their feeding was as frightening as anything I had heard in the bush. Interestingly, the first time I heard this strange noise, it never occurred to me to draw my pistol. I still strapped it on every morning, accustomed to the weight hanging on my hip, but no longer with any consciousness of its significance.

By the end of the first week we were all tired and thinner, despite all the food we ate. Lynch declared a day off. We would check the traps and do the necessary chores and tomorrow we would rest. On the holiday Lynch went back to his tent right after breakfast and slept. Tee and I heated water and shared a bath in the big tin tub, showing one another our fresh bruises and scratches and admiring our muscles.

After lunch, restless, we decided to go for a walk. The walk turned into a full-fledged hike, and we didn't get back to camp till nearly nine at night. We were wet to the hips and so tired we could scarcely lift our legs, but we agreed it had been a perfect day.

We'd seen a black bear, two deer, a coyote, the usual bleached bones, a moose rack and more moose sign than Tee said he'd ever seen, though we didn't see a moose. We'd found another active beaver community and sat for an hour watching them go about their beaver business. The kits swam close to us, their tiny ears turning on their heads and their little noses raised to sniff at us. A big old blond beaver swam back and forth, keeping an eye on us. We found beautiful little meadows full of wildflowers and birdsong. It was the sort of day that made me want to stay in the bush forever, not hunting or trapping, just being.

The day after our mini-holiday started with two of the horses not coming in for their pellets—Gatedo and Tang, my troublemakers. Lynch and Tee headed out to check traps, walking and leading pack horses, and I saddled Tiny and went looking for the missing horses. I found them, after an hour of riding, sleeping on the side of a steep hill like a pair of mountain goats—and they were hobbled! I caught them easily enough and led them back to camp. It rained that evening, a hard cold rain, and we had to move all the boards with the pelts nailed on them into the two tents. There was barely room to move, and the smell, while not exactly awful, was pungent enough to make for a restless night.

One of the pack horses had developed a sore on his back. I sprayed it with Bactine, and it was better the next morning but still meant the horse couldn't be used for a couple of days. We ate hugely but continued to lose weight, all of us. Sleep was like falling into a dark silent hole, in spite of the wood stove chuffing, the men snoring, the bells on the horses, the creek swishing nearby and the constant sound of birds. Owls hooted all night long, and sometimes coyotes yapped.

The sun came out at last, and the pelts were moved out to dry. We were going to move camp the next day so the evening was spent organizing, bringing the horses in and readying for a morning departure. Tee annoyed me by repacking the kitchen panniers: it was equivalent to rearranging the furniture in my house and then burglarizing it.

I was getting sick of bannock, making it and eating it, and if I never saw another can of Spam in my life I would be happy. I had a rash under my chin, cuts, bruises and burns too numerous to count and my skin felt as cracked as a desert floor. The flashlight batteries had burned out, my clothes were still damp from yesterday's rain, and moss did not work as well as toilet paper. It was the darkest of times.

Our next camp, on the west end of Canyon Lake, was not nearly so nice—lots of windfalls and buckbrush, and the creek further away from the tents. The mosquitoes came in clouds and were voracious. There was good grass for the horses though, and lots of beaver sign. The lake was lovely. One side was all tumbled huge boulders, very steep, with some big boulders, moss-covered, in the lake near the shore.

At intervals along the trail we came across small spruce trees with knotted tops. Lynch explained that was how the Tahltans used to mark their trails. In the evening as I sat around the fire,

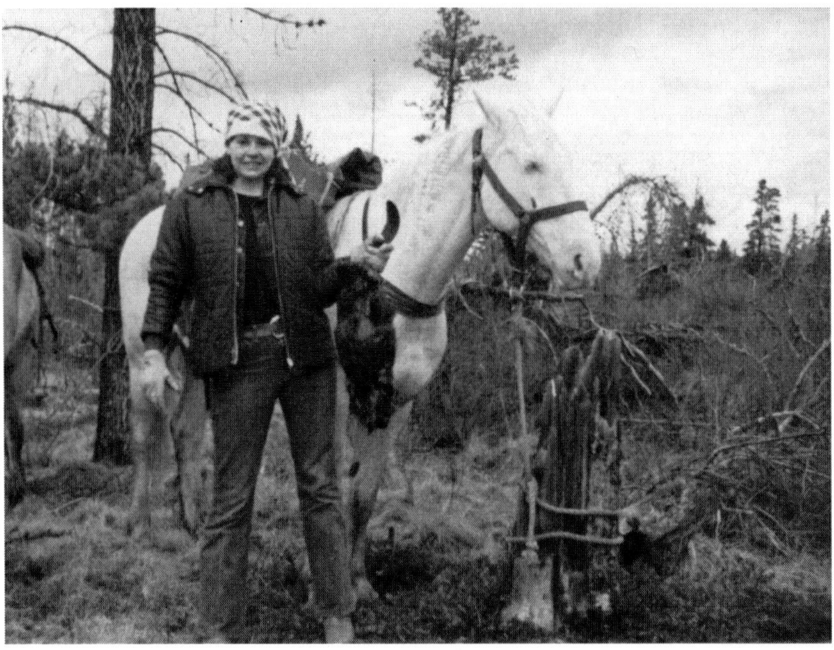

A small catch, but a satisfying one.

I thought about the two traditions: the white men marked their trails by cutting a blaze into the tree; the natives tied this little knot at the top of what at the time had been a young, maybe eye-height tree.

The three of us worked setting up the new camp. We didn't speak; we didn't have to any more because we all knew what to do and who was going to do it. In an hour there was a fire going, tea brewed and the old black cast iron pot of beaver meat and rice was heating our dinner. Barika was a mess. I'd put her in her pack for the ride, forgetting Tee had put a big bar of chocolate in there. It'd melted all over her. She was not unhappy to lick it off as best she could until I could heat some water and clean her.

The work began the next day and we got into the same rhythm, with the bugs adding a new dimension to our efforts. We couldn't stand still for a moment longer than necessary, and sitting was out of the question, except for evenings around the fire. The skinning was horribly uncomfortable and took longer as we had to swipe at mosquitoes every few seconds. There were lots of different sorts of birds at this camp, small mosquito eaters. They weren't shy of us and would sit on the tent poles, beaks bristling with bugs, to stare at us with their bright little eyes. The whisky jacks found us right away, as they generally did, and feasted on scraps of beaver meat and bannock, eating from my hand almost immediately.

We saw a couple of moose and lots of bear sign. By this time I was so immersed in the trapping life that I hardly thought of bears. Couldn't remember the last time I'd chosen a climbing tree, or even jumped at a sound from the bush. The pistol hadn't left the holster in nearly two weeks. The good news was lots of beaver in the traps and weather that stayed sunny and warm. We were down to beaver meat and sardines now. No one complained; food had become merely necessary fuel. Going through the dwindling supplies, I had come across a bottle of rum, forgotten in the bottom of a pannier under a bag of rice.

The discovery led to the first animated evening we'd had in days and days. That night we put rum into our mugs of tea and used the last of the sugar to sweeten it. We built a big smoky fire and sat around it till almost midnight, reminiscing, planning, talking about the horses and finally, singing.

Two more days of beaverin', each evening spent sitting around the fire and drinking rum in our tea, and we were ready to go home. The thought of our simple cabin now seemed unbelievably luxurious, and the dream of a hot bath occupied my mind to the exclusion of all else as we started back.

There had been some discussion about doing the whole trek in one hard day, but Lynch said it'd be too hard on the horses. One more night in the smelly tent in our stinking sleeping bags, one more breakfast of cold bannock and we would be home.

We were on the trail, in our long orderly line, before noon the day we broke camp. Lynch was leading, with Tee and Barika on Tiny off to one side about halfway down the line of horses, and me in the rear. At one point we were quietly "strung out" on the side of a fairly steep grassy hill with heavy bush at the bottom. Lynch and Tee were riding ahead, close enough to be talking to one another, while I was nine horse lengths behind, singing softly to myself and remembering to pay attention to what Gatedo was doing. Out of the corner of my eye I saw a movement up the hill—a large movement. I turned my head in time to see a grizzly bear coming down the hill straight towards me. No one else had seen the bear—even the dogs were oblivious until Gatedo gave a horse holler and took off down the hill towards the bush, the bear right behind us.

I thought I had screamed *Bear!* before the bush swallowed Gatedo and me, but Tee told me later I hadn't made a sound that they could hear. It was a mystery because my throat was raw for days afterwards.

Years later I read something about how abused women and children describe the experience of leaving their bodies when they were being hurt and terrified, and I think that is similar to what happened to me. All I can remember is the sound of the buckbrush snapping and swishing as Gatedo made a new trail, and a second set of sounds as the grizzly followed us. Everything seemed to happen very slowly. I knew my feet had come out of the stirrups, but I had a death grip on that saddle—nothing was going to get me off the horse. I also remember feeling bad for Gatedo because his fear was coming through me, adding to mine. The next thing I remember was the sound of a rifle shot, and then Lynch was there, leaning from his horse and shouting something at me. Gatedo stopped beside Lynch's horse, and then Tee and Tiny were there and everything was calm, except Gatedo and me. Lynch held my horse while Tee pulled me down and into his arms.

I remember seeing blood all over Tee's jacket and wondering if the bear had hurt him. I remember seeing blood on Gatedo and wondering the same thing. I remember I could hear nothing but a roaring in my head with muffled sounds of speech coming from the men as they soothed me and my horse. And oddly, I remember the smell of the bush, and the rank smell of human and animal sweat. (The blood was from the scratches and cuts on the horse and myself, the result of going through heavy underbrush.)

When we came out of the bush, the pack horses were scattered all over the hill, grazing as though nothing had happened. Patsy was sitting on her haunches watching us, her tongue hanging out. Barika, out of her travel bag, was running back and forth, her thin, high yapping penetrating my fog. I looked for the body of the bear but there was nothing to be seen.

Tee found the last of the rum and gave it to me right out of the bottle. My teeth were chattering so badly I couldn't drink or swallow, and the liquor burned my face where the cuts were bleeding. When he let go of me, my legs folded and I lay on the ground, curled up and shaking. I thought I would never get up again, but they told me later I'd recovered quickly, standing up to look at Gatedo's bleeding legs. My first words were "Is he going to be all right?"

Lynch said we were going to camp; it was almost the time we would have been stopping anyway, and there was a good spot about fifteen minutes away. I protested: fifteen minutes was not far enough away from the bear! What if Lynch had wounded it and it would come seeking revenge? Tee told me Lynch had not shot the bear, he'd shot at it, rapidly assessing the situation as one in which the bear could be scared off, and that is what had happened. The bear had not entered the bush to chase Gatedo and me but had gone a fair distance away from us. Tee, at my insistence, rode down to check if the bear was hanging around and reported it was long gone.

We made camp, or rather the men did. They made a fire right away, and I sat beside it with a blanket over me, still shivering and still hearing the steady sound of my blood rushing through my veins. I was badly scratched and my jacket was torn; Gatedo was scratched too, but not as badly as first appeared.

Lynch and Tee relived the episode that night as we sat around the fire with our tea, each telling and retelling their view, adding to the story until it was complete to their mutual satisfaction. I said nothing, and they didn't ask me for my details.

Lynch was mildly surprised that the bear had stayed around when there were all the horses, two dogs and people on the hill. He figured the bear had been somehow unaware of us until we were there, and then he went for the last of the troop, Gatedo and me. Tee wondered why I had not drawn the pistol and fired it; the sound may well have scared the bear off, as Lynch's rifle shot had done.

I didn't answer because I didn't know what to say. It had not occurred to me to pull the gun, any more than it had occurred to me to fire a rifle when Mancha was killed. It seemed I was lacking whatever it was that made people use a gun, even in times of dire need to use one. My silence eventually silenced Tee and Lynch. We were in our tents before full dark, planning an early start in the morning.

There was no sleep for me that long night. I could not be persuaded to get undressed; I crawled into my sleeping bag fully clothed and would not zip it up. I wanted to be able to get out of it fast. The pistol was under my pillow. I couldn't get warm, no matter how many blankets Tee piled on me, and I couldn't quit shaking. All the ordinary background sounds of the woods at night were magnified, and each one made my heart pound as though it were trying to escape from my body; it hurt. Everything hurt—my face and hands from the scratches and my muscles from being tightly clenched.

In my mind, I was okay. I knew the bear was unlikely to come back, but my body would not recognize the message. It was as though my physical being had decided my mental being was a liar. Every fear I'd experienced in the last few years had been stored somewhere in the cells of my body, and now they had gotten together and were rioting in protest. It was a hellish night.

Things were not much better in the morning. The chill wind and rain seemed appropriate to the day. Something in me had undergone a fundamental change; I no longer regarded the bush as a place I was a part of, a place that was part of me. A radical separation had occurred. I was convinced my role as a hunter and a trapper had positioned me outside the magic circle of the wild, and I would not be welcomed there again. I felt as though I had suffered a sudden and catastrophic loss. Sitting in the rain and chewing on some cold bannock while the men tied down the panniers on the horses' backs, I felt alienated from every living thing, including the horses, the dogs, Tee and Lynch.

That was the moment I knew I would be leaving. I didn't know how or when and I probably didn't really know why; I just knew it was time.

Farewell to Iskut

I said nothing to Tee about leaving. I didn't talk about it to anyone, because I had no idea how this departure would look or even when it would take place. It was a knowing buried deep in my gut. There was nothing I had to do but let it happen.

The cabin was cold, as anticipated, but it had warmed up by the time we got all our gear in out of the rain and had seen to our tired horses. Tee and I were too tired to haul and heat water for a bath; we simply fell into bed.

The next morning I stood by the big picture window looking out at the place where I knew Mount Edziza was, though the heavy cloud and rain obscured the view. I had a jug of Tang in my hand, the powdered orange juice of the day. It'd been mixed before we left, but I reckoned it had to still be okay because it'd been kept cold in the mudroom.

I flipped the little round cap from the pouring spout and put it to my lips. After just a couple of swallows, I became aware of something gently nudging my upper lip. Peering into the jug I saw a mouse. It was clearly drowned, floating on its back with its tiny feet and nose dyed bright orange from the juice. It was small enough that I realized I could easily have swallowed it. Calmly, I emptied the jug into the slop bucket under the counter, thinking Casper must have moved out for the summer. He would not have allowed a mouse in the cabin, and certainly not to drown in my Tang. I thought of how a few years ago the idea of a drowned mouse in my drink, let alone having the carcass touch my lips, would have sent me into a frenzy.

Leon Fleming and Slim Jordan came in for coffee, the noise of their arrival awakening Tee. Soon we were all sitting around the table catching up on local news.

In this part of the world, drivers picked up hitchhikers; Highway 37 was too lonely a place to countenance leaving anyone stranded. It had led to a few interesting encounters. Most people thumbing a ride were entirely okay, but once in awhile there would be some individual occupying a different reality than most of us. We all had stories, but Leon, just returned from a trip to Terrace, had the best one I'd heard.

On his way home he'd picked up a fellow just south of Bob Quinn Lake. As soon as the guy was in the passenger seat and they were moving down the road, Leon felt the fellow was a bit "off"—not unusually scruffy considering the circumstances, but odd in his behaviour. First, he'd vehemently refused to allow Leon to put his heavy duffel bag in the back of the truck, choosing instead to hold the unwieldy object on his lap. Then he'd also immediately begun a monologue, the subject being "freaks" and "weirdos" who, in his opinion, should be "dispatched" because they poisoned the world. Leon began to feel uncomfortable, and even a bit tense, feelings suddenly exacerbated when he noticed the bag was leaking some dark viscous fluid. Before he could inquire as to the contents of his passenger's luggage, he noticed some crude lettering on the heavy canvas: *dead lesbians,* it said in black, dripping script. Obeying his next impulse without question, Leon stopped the truck in the middle of the road and, reaching across the man and his bag, opened the door and pushed hard. The man tumbled out of the cab, his oozing bag landing on top of him, and Leon roared away.

"My hair was standing on end," he told us. "I didn't even look in the mirror to see if the guy got up."

He wanted everyone in the area to be warned that this man may be appearing any time, and to be extremely cautious. He'd also sent a message to the RCMP in Stewart and in Terrace in case they knew of the guy and maybe even were looking for him.

Cradling my coffee mug, I wasn't thinking of a crazy man coming down the road carrying his bizarre luggage. I was thinking of how much I would miss Leon, with his wild enthusiasm and boundless energy. I thought of how much I would miss everyone I'd met here in the last five years, these people of courage, endurance and humour. I didn't dare think yet of Tee, or Lorri, the two who would be most mystified and most hurt when I left.

▲

Without being fully conscious of it, or acknowledging it even to myself, the next two weeks were my farewell to Iskut, to Elsevere. Everything I did was with full awareness of the moment, as though I was storing up pictures of my life here, engraving them deep in my mind's eye. I felt extraordinarily calm and serene; I was unusually quiet, and moved slower than was my wont, taking time with every action, savouring every moment. I didn't ride and I didn't go for walks. Whatever I'd felt in the bush had changed, and now I was uneasy about being among the trees and the silence. It wasn't simply the justifiable fear of bears, it was also the feeling of loss.

If Tee noticed anything different about me during this time, he said nothing. Lorri, who did notice, said lots, and it was to put her worry to rest that I eventually told her I would be leaving. She was predictably hurt, a feeling that rapidly translated into anger. She was furious with me for even thinking of going away for good and told me so in no uncertain terms and with no holds barred. I was berated for hurting Tee, reminded how good he was, how much he loved me and how horribly unfair and cruel I was to think of leaving him for no reason. Then she went after me for being a disloyal and uncaring friend. I was her only pal here, she told me; I was abandoning her, and again, for no good reason.

It was useless to attempt to tell her why I was going—I couldn't even adequately tell myself. It had something to do with bears, something to do with a sense, a connection being broken through my own actions. I had been cast out of the circle of wholeness, and my calm was masking a profound feeling of mourning. The only way I could think of, the only way I knew, was to run away from the scene of my betrayal and subsequent loss. It was too painful to stay. This spiritual loss was worse than the idea of losing Tee, or my friends here. None of this would make any sense to Lorri, I knew; it was more likely to infuriate her more.

I didn't pack my belongings; I didn't even sort through stuff. I had no idea where I would go except I knew I would not be going back to Watson Lake. I don't remember even giving any time to wondering where I would go or what I would do when I got there. I was waiting for the time and means of my leaving, certain only that it would come and that I would recognize it.

Meanwhile, I planned a dinner party, an elaborate one, with Lorri and Claude as guests. I had sworn Lorri to silence about my imminent departure, making her promise she would not, through any action or words, reveal my secret. The dinner was a tremendous success in every way. I had never before undertaken a meal so complex as this one, and as much to my amazement as anyone else's, everything was perfect.

There was French onion soup, followed by roast duck with a plum sauce. Accompanying vegetables were roasted potatoes and peas. There was a simple salad of purple onion, lettuce and tomatoes, with an oil and vinegar dressing. The dinner was eaten with a rich red wine, and there was brandy with dessert. The dessert was my *pièce de résistance*: meringues with custard inside, whipped cream on top and the whole drizzled with chocolate sauce.

It wasn't only the food that shone that night—we all did too. The food, the wine and the company combined to create one of those rare and treasured evenings where we all relaxed, revelling in the feelings we had for one another, sharing ourselves openly and trustingly. There was lots of laughter too. The candles lavished their soft, kind light on the scene and made it beautiful.

We reminisced, retelling the stories of our shared experiences. We puzzled again about the evening I was visiting Lorri, both our men away, and a duck fell down the chimney of her wood stove. We described the peculiar noise it made coming down the pipe, and how agog we were to open the stove and find the duck, feathers burned off and skin charred, taking its last breath. How such a thing had occurred remains a mystery. The chimney was a stovepipe from the stove through the roof—how could a duck perch on the edge of something so insubstantial, and how could a web-footed creature perch at all? Was it flying over the cabin and overcome by the fumes from the chimney and then managed to fall into a hole with a diameter scarcely large enough to accommodate its body?

Tee remembered Max, a woman I knew from Montreal, who had come out for a visit one summer and, on her first night under our roof, without warning or any history we knew of, become suicidal. This was one of the summers I was expediting. It was busy and it was fun, with helicopters and crews coming and going, lots of visitors and activities. Max would or could not tell me why she felt she had to kill herself, or why it had to be here, but every morning we were treated to her plans for self-destruction. They ranged from hanging to drowning to slitting her wrists; she could never decide but dwelt with great relish on the methods, seemingly oblivious to my distress or Tee's growing impatience.

One bright morning, after about five days of breakfast drama, Tee brought out his pistol. He carefully and thoroughly showed Max how to load the gun. He then handed it to her, saying only, "Please do it some distance from the house. We've got a meeting this morning with one of the camp party chiefs and don't want to be interrupted or disturbed." Max was what could only be described as gobsmacked. She looked at me, but I got up and began clearing breakfast dishes, conscious that my concern was turning into anger.

"If you decide not to shoot yourself, Max, I would like you

to leave," I told her. "One of the guys is going into Stewart today; I think he's leaving around ten and you can ride with him." She didn't shoot herself, and she did leave.

Claude recalled the winter night a coyote had grabbed Baby, Lorri's adored little dog, outside their cabin, and Lorri had gone flying into the dark in her nightgown, armed with a broom, and made the coyote drop Baby and run for its life.

We ate and drank and talked till midnight.

That was over thirty years ago, and Lorri and I still remember that evening, out of all the times we shared, as a particularly special time.

A semi-trailer took me to Vancouver about a month after we had come home from the beaver hunt.

I was having coffee at the LV when the driver came in for some lunch. There was a group of us visiting, and someone asked Marvin, the driver, if he ever took a passenger. He said he sometimes did, and that was when I knew it was time. I followed him out to his truck and asked if he could give me a ride. He looked surprised; he'd been through here many times and knew all of us. But he agreed that if I could be at the end of my driveway in half an hour, he would pick me up. I went home and told Tee I was leaving as I shook cash from the books on the shelves and threw some clothes in a backpack. Tee didn't ask or argue; he helped me on with the pack and walked me to the end of the driveway where we clung to one another as we waited for Marvin's truck. I had not stopped crying since I'd left the lodge. There was nothing to say except to tell him, as I got into the truck, that I would write. He didn't stand in the road as we drove off. He didn't wave either, just started walking back to the cabin.

The trip to Vancouver took two days; I cried most of the way.

Epilogue

When I'd finished this story, this chapter in my life, I was chagrined by my behaviour in many instances but none more than my treatment of Tee. I knew at the time I was not being kind, or even decent, in leaving him so abruptly, and without explanation. He told me during his visit to see me in Vancouver the following year that he'd always known I would leave; he understood me well and chose to love me regardless. My excuse is my youth, and my own bewilderment. I couldn't have told him why I was leaving a place and a man I loved because I truly didn't know. I do not regret leaving nor do I regret how I left, because in the end we must honour our own path.

Tee and I saw each other again, of course. He visited me in Vancouver and a couple of years later I brought my daughter to Iskut to meet him. The image of him crouching in front of her, his tender attentiveness as he spoke with her, will stay with me always. He died in Vancouver of a brain tumour a few years later. My husband, my daughter and I were living on Salt Spring Island then, and I was able to visit him in the hospital a couple of times before he was gone.

Lorri continues to play a role in my life. She and Claude still live in the Iskut area, in the marvellous house Claude built, as he'd promised he would, and now she complains it is too big and too much to clean—she wishes for her little cabin again. They have all the modern conveniences now; satellite TV and internet, telephones, running water and electricity. Best of all, Highway 37 is now a real road, making a trip to Stewart or Terrace not the undertaking it once was. Lorri started a gift shop many years ago, beginning in one of the small cabins and now occupying a special addition to their big house. The store satisfied Lorri's longing for people, for company, and it was no surprise to me that it became a successful business.

Lynch came to see me when I was living on Salt Spring Island, driving his old truck with the stock box and wearing his big cowboy hat. He had no idea of my address but managed to find me by asking around for "Sis." The island was a small place and Lynch was not a typical visitor. There were enough people who knew of me and my past life that he soon got directions to our little beach house. He stayed for nearly a week, refusing our offer to stay at our place, choosing to camp where the action was, right in the park in downtown Ganges. Camping was not allowed in the park, but Lynch not only did it, but also attracted many visitors. Every time we saw him there he was surrounded by fascinated people, drinking his camp coffee and listening to his wilderness stories. He died several years ago in Fort St. John, leaving a space in my world that will never be filled. The circumstances that created Lynch and the world he lived in no longer exist. I am lucky that I had this time with him and got to see the last of that lifestyle in the bush before technology changed everything.

The Flemings moved back to the States and I have lost touch with them except for the occasional news from Jackie Fenner in Stewart. Leon and Jeannie breed and train hunting dogs now, and where the kids are I don't know.

Charlie and Jackie summer in Stewart and have a home and a business in Hawaii. Moira and Erin, their daughters, both went into the hotel business, one in Stewart and one in Prince Rupert.

Reliving these years during the writing of this book, going through journals and old photos, I was tempted to make a trip to

Iskut especially to check in with anyone I knew who might still be living there. But I finally decided I wanted to leave the book as I left my life there, with all the participants, except those I was closest to, frozen in time.

The events in the book all occurred, but I have sometimes changed the timeline for the sake of flow in the narrative. For instance, Daddy and Jackie arrived in Iskut before Claude and Lorri.

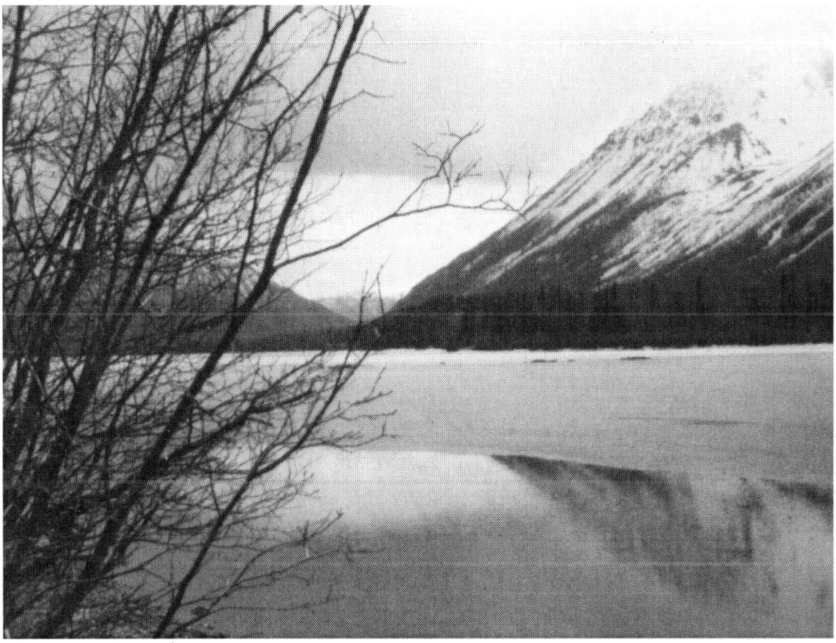

Iskut Lake.